WOLF IN SHEEP'S CLOTHING

GREAT LAKES BOOKS

Philip P. Mason, Editor
Walter P. Reuther Library, Wayne State University

Dr. Charles K. Hyde, Associate Editor
Department of History, Wayne State University

WOLF IN SHEEP'S CLOTHING

THE SEARCH FOR A
CHILD KILLER

Tommy McIntyre

WAYNE STATE UNIVERSITY PRESS DETROIT 1988

Library of Congress Cataloging-in-Publication Data

McIntyre, Tommy, 1936–
  Wolf in sheep's clothing : the search for a child killer / Tommy McIntyre.
    p.   cm.—(Great Lakes books)
  ISBN 0–8143–1966–1 (alk. paper). ISBN 0–8143–1989–0 (pbk : alk. paper)
    1. Serial murders—Michigan—Oakland County—Case studies.
  2. Child molesting—Michigan—Oakland County—Case studies.
  3. Teenagers—Michigan—Oakland County—Crimes against—Case studies.   4. Criminal investigation—Michigan—Oakland County—Case studies.   I. Title.   II. Series.
  HV6533.M5M37   1988
  364.1′523′097743—dc19   88–5738
                                                              CIP

To the
Oakland County Child Killer Task Force
and police officers across the nation

—WANTED—

CITIZEN COOPERATION URGENTLY NEEDED

SEVERAL ABDUCTION-MURDERS HAVE TAKEN PLACE IN SOUTH OAKLAND COUNTY INVOLVING YOUNGSTERS. THIS CRIMINAL APPARENTLY PRESENTS A VERY CONVINCING STORY TO THE CHILD. BE AWARE, AND ALERT YOUR CHILD THAT THIS PERSON COULD BE POSING IN SUCH TRUSTWORTHY POSITIONS AS A POLICE OFFICER, A DOCTOR, A CLERGYMAN OR EVEN AS A FRIEND OF A FAMILY MEMBER.

THE ABOVE COMPOSITE DRAWING OF THE SUSPECTED ABDUCTOR-MURDERER IS AN UPDATE BASED ON THE LATEST INFORMATION RECEIVED BY THE OAKLAND COUNTY TASK FORCE. THE VICTIMS HAVE BEEN KEPT FOR THE FOLLOWING PERIODS OF TIME:

- MARCH 16, 1977 to MARCH 22, 1977
- JANUARY 2, 1977 to JANUARY 21, 1977
- DECEMBER 22, 1976 to DECEMBER 26, 1976
- FEBRUARY 15, 1976 to FEBRUARY 19, 1976

THE ABDUCTOR(S) WAS LAST SEEN STANDING NEAR A BLUE AMC GREMLIN AUTOMOBILE PARKED BEHIND CHATHAM'S SUPERMARKET LOCATED ON MAPLE ROAD IN BIRMINGHAM, MICHIGAN ON MARCH 16, 1977 AT THE TIME OF TIMOTHY KING'S DISAPPEARANCE. THE SUSPECT'S IDENTITY IS UNKNOWN.

THE FOLLOWING PROFILE INFORMATION HAS BEEN DEVELOPED BY THE TASK FORCE:

- HE IS A WHITE MALE; 25-30 YEARS OF AGE; 5'8" TO 5'10"; 150 TO 170 POUNDS WITH AN ATHLETIC BUILD.
- HE MAY BE LIVING OR ASSOCIATING CLOSELY WITH ANOTHER PERSON.
- HE IS AQUAINTED WITH OAKLAND COUNTY AND MAY WORK, LIVE OR SOCIALIZE IN THE AREA.
- HE HAS AN EMPLOYMENT SITUATION WHICH ALLOWS HIM FREEDOM OF MOVEMENT.
- HE MAY RESIDE IN AN AREA WHICH PROVIDES HIM AN OPPORTUNITY TO KEEP SOMEONE WITHOUT CREATING SUSPICION IN THE NEIGHBORHOOD OR COMMUNITY.
- HE MAY HAVE ALTERED HIS PHYSICAL APPEARANCE (E.G., CHANGE IN HAIRSTYLE, GLASSES, ETC.)

If you have any information on the above crimes, please call the Oakland County Task Force at 644-0400, The Detroit News Secret Witness (P.O. Box 1333, Detroit, MI 48231), or your local police, nearest state police or sheriff's office. Reward payable upon arrest and conviction.

$100,000 Reward

JUNE 1, 1978

Preface

Despite the heinous nature of his crimes, the Oakland County child killer has always held a certain fascination for me. The story of this killer who stalked the streets of south Oakland County, Michigan, looking for his young victims is so intriguing and perplexing. In all my years of reporting crime, no one case has captured my imagination more.

In the fall of 1984, retiring Michigan State Police Captain Robert H. Robertson, the coordinator of the investigation, asked me if I would be interested in writing a book on the case. While covering the case as a broadcast reporter for radio station WWJ in Detroit, I developed a deep respect for and close friendship with Robertson. So without hesitation, I agreed. My only condition was that I be allowed access to all records and documents pertaining to the investigation, and that Robertson remain readily accessible as my technical adviser and collaborator. In this role, Robertson would edit each chapter as it was completed for accuracy of fact and police procedure. We also decided we did not want merely a chronological listing of events or a simple report. We wanted a story about people.

My profession has kept me in periodic contact with many of the key figures in the investigation, but it had been years since I had covered the story. Several months of painstaking research — reading through hundreds of documents and conducting some fifty hours of tape-recorded interviews — were necessary before I could confidently sit down at the typewriter. All names are real except those of suspects and certain locations. The similarity of any of the fictional names to those of real persons or places is purely coincidental and not intended. For purposes of story flow, literary license has been used judiciously.

I must thank too many people to list them here. They know who they are. However, I will mention two in addition to Robertson. They are Michigan State Police Detective Sergeant Joe Krease and Southfield Public

Safety Director Rollin G. Tobin. I am forever in their debt for their courtesy, cooperation, and unflagging support.

While the Michigan State Police does not officially sanction projects like this, that premier law enforcement agency has my deepest appreciation for the many courtesies it extended to me. None of my countless requests of them were denied.

I must also express my respect and admiration for the scores of dedicated, professional police officers and other law enforcement officials who so graciously gave of their time and energy so that I might write this story. Theirs was the hardest job, done so many years ago.

Prologue

Mark Stebbins, Jill Robinson, Kristine Mihelich, and Timothy King had at least two things in common — they were all too young to die, and they were killed by the same person. The killer was almost certainly a man, despite early theories on the bizarre slayings, promulgated by the nearly insatiable media, that a woman was involved, at least as an accomplice.

The deaths of these four youngsters, who all lived in an affluent Michigan county twenty miles north of Detroit, resulted in one of the most massive manhunts and investigations in the annals of modern-day crime, a worldwide search for the person known only as "The Oakland County Child Killer." To put the four related crimes in their proper perspective, we must begin exactly one month before twelve-year-old Mark Stebbins of Ferndale, Michigan disappeared.

On January 15, 1976, at approximately 8:30 in the evening, sixteen-year-old Cynthia Rae Cadieux was seen alive for the last time. Cynthia, a tall, pretty, and well-developed teenager, lived in Roseville, Michigan, a middle-class, blue-collar community of tract homes and light industry scattered north and east of Detroit along Gratiot Avenue, a main artery leading into the core of the megalopolis. On one of those damp, penetrating, Michigan winter evenings, the blue-eyed brunette left the home of a girlfriend for the short walk home to her waiting mother and stepfather. Five and one-half hours later, shortly after one o'clock in the morning, a passing motorist spotted Cynthia's nude, battered body on Franklin Road, in a wealthy part of Oakland County about three miles north and fifteen miles west of where she began her walk. Her skull had been crushed by a blunt instrument, and she had been brutally raped and sodomized.

The community was shattered with grief, but before it could recover, horror struck again. About fifteen miles due west of Roseville and twenty-five miles north of Detroit lies the posh little enclave of Birmingham. Boasting one of the highest median family incomes in the entire nation, Birmingham is a picture-postcard community of old and new money, with homes measured in thousands of square feet on streets shaded by giant elms, crimson maples, and century-old oaks. On Saturdays, Maple Road, the main street east and west through Birmingham, looks like a Mercedes-Benz showroom.

At fourteen, Sheila Srock showed the chunkiness many young women display as they tough their way through puberty. She lived with her older brother and his wife in Birmingham, was an average student, and had neither more nor fewer problems than most other youngsters at that awkward age, except both her parents were dead. At 8:20 the evening of January 19, 1976, she would join them.

As Sheila baby-sat in an upstairs bedroom on Villa Street, she was surprised by an intruder who had just finished breaking and entering three other houses in the neighborhood. But this time he decided to leave his signature on the vulnerable teenager. He stripped, raped, and sodomized her, then killed her with a volley of shots from a small caliber, semiautomatic pistol. The burglar-turned-killer collected what valuables he could carry, including a .38 caliber handgun, calmly ambled outside, brazenly mingled for a few minutes with the small crowd drawn by the shots, then slipped into a white 1967 Cadillac parked on the street and purred away.

What he did not know was that while he brutalized and murdered Sheila, a neighbor had watched in horrified disbelief from a roof where he was shovelling snow.

Murder in multiples, or series, tends to have a cumulative impact on the psyche of a community. An isolated murder rarely, if ever, has great impact on the community as a whole. It is devastating on immediate family and friends, but when we hear of a murder "shocking the whole community," the shock is usually short-lived. The citizenry soon sheds the cloak of grief, picks up the pieces, and resumes business as usual. But Sheila had died only four days after Cynthia Rae. When there is no time to recover, shock and grief quickly become rage, and there was more shock and grief to come.

Mark Douglas Stebbins was a strawberry blond with thoughtful blue eyes, a rather quiet boy, somewhat of a "loner" and a good student. Mark lived in Ferndale, not far from Birmingham, but a community light-years away on the socioeconomic scale. In Ferndale the Mercedes of Birmingham give way to used Fords, Chevys, and Pontiacs.

Mark, who was twelve, had left the American Legion Hall in Ferndale about 1:30 in the afternoon of February 15, exactly thirty days after Cynthia Cadieux was slain. Leaving his mother at the American Legion building, he began walking home to watch a movie on television.

Four days later, Mark Boetigheimer, a Southfield, Michigan, businessman, left his office on Ten Mile Road shortly before noon to walk to the drugstore at the New Orleans Shopping Mall. As he trudged through the crisp, cold February air, he glanced toward the northeast corner of the parking lot and saw what he took to be a sprawled mannequin of some sort, dressed in blue.

An autopsy would soon reveal that Mark had died of asphyxia, caused by smothering. The postmortem would also reveal that the anal orifice was widely distended with obvious but superficial lacerations. The body also bore other physical evidence: discoloration of the wrists and ankles that could have been caused by rope burns and two, crusted lacerations on the left rear of the scalp. The youngster was fully clothed in the same blue parka, jeans, red sweatshirt, and black rubber boots he was wearing the last time his mother saw him alive, as he left the American Legion Hall.

At around 9:30 that same morning, February 19, before Boetigheimer took his walk, an occupant of the building where Boetigheimer's office was located had walked his Schnauzer along the edge of the parking lot. He told police that had the body been there, he was certain the animal's keen sense of smell would have picked it up. Not all police officers have this much faith in the olfactory powers of dogs, so the probative value of the incident is in some dispute. For investigative purposes, however, let us say that Stebbins was dropped sometime after 9:30, but before noon, in broad daylight in a parking lot in a shopping center at a time when all the stores might not be open, but there would have been at least some activity. Did the killer not only expect but want the body to be discovered? And even more inexplicably, did the killer want to be discovered? These questions continued to torment investigators as spring came and went without further signs of the killer.

Royal Oak, Michigan, is another blue-collar suburb, which begins immediately north of Ferndale along the north-south artery called the "Woodward Corridor." One of its inhabitants was Jane Louise Allen, who was fourteen years old, but looked older. She had a boyfriend in Auburn Heights, some ten miles away, and being fourteen and "in love," Jane decided to do a crazy thing. She hitchhiked, because it was the only way she could see him. It was Saturday, August 7.

On the following Tuesday, 250 miles to the south, Jane Allen was found floating in the river near Miamisburg, Ohio, hands bound behind her back with the shreds of a white T-shirt. Decomposition of the body made it impossible to tell whether the youngster had been sexually molested. The Ohio Coroner's Office suggested Jane was dead before being pitched into the river and that she might have died of carbon monoxide poisoning.

Notwithstanding street rumors in Miamisburg that Jane had been seen consorting with members of a Dayton motorcycle gang, the most plausible theory is still that she was picked up by a motorist, who simply killed her and dumped the body in the Miami River.

Oakland County had lost four children since the beginning of the year, and three and one-half months still remained of 1976.

It was three days before Christmas. Bright, headstrong Jill Robinson was twelve years old, going on twenty-four. She and her mother, Karol, had been quarreling over some household chores. Like any mother, Karol was at times driven to distraction by her youngster and, like any mother, probably said a lot of things she really didn't mean during the heat of the argument, one of which reportedly was, "Get out until you can become part of the family." And Jill, like any normal twelve-year-old, with more pride than brains, packed her whole world into a blue denim backpack and hit the street.

The day after Christmas, near Troy, Michigan, along the snowy shoulder of busy Interstate 75, lay Jill Robinson, backpack and all, with the left side of her face and head blown off by by a twelve-gauge shotgun. The grisly discovery was made by a passing motorist at approximately eight forty-five A.M. Could the killer help but know that by placing the girl's body alongside a busy interstate he assured that she would soon be found?

The pathologist's report said that Jill died from shock and hemorrhage due to a shotgun blast to the head. But at least one detective who was to spend hundreds of hours on the Robinson case and who inspected the scene of the crime, still challenges that conclusion. Insignificant perhaps, because in the final analysis, by whatever means, the child was dead. But what if Jill was already dead, perhaps from suffocation, and then for some inexplicable, bizarre reason, the killer decided to use the gun. Might then the cause of death, the very public drop site, and perhaps even the presumed time of the body drop link at least the Stebbins and the Robinson murders? Might the killer have inadvertently, or by some grand and mysterious design have begun to weave a convoluted web of gamesmanship, giving police just a bit here and a bit there?

Dr. Robert Sillery, chief pathologist for the Oakland County Medical Examiner's Office, also determined that there were no signs of sexual molestation. Jill's hymen was intact, and a lightly stained tampon was found in the vagina. The tampon had come from a box that Jill herself had purchased.

Detectives were able to retrieve shotgun pellets from the ground where Jill was placed. No shell casings were found, and ballistics science is still hard pressed to identify the make and model of a shotgun from the size or pattern of the shot. Was the killer a ballistics expert, too? Did he know that a rifle or handgun leaves tell-tale bore markings on the spent bullet that can positively match the bullet and the gun?

One other note about the Robinson slaying: about noon the day after her body was found, her bicycle was discovered behind a small store on North Main Street in Royal Oak, not far from where she lived. To this day, it is not known exactly how it got there. Did she take it when she left home, or was it placed there later? And by whom?

At six o'clock on the evening of January 2, 1977, the telephone rang at the front desk in the Berkley Police Station. (Berkley is a short distance from Royal Oak, west of Woodward and north of Twelve Mile Road.) It was Mrs. Deborah Ascroft. Her ten-year-old daughter, Kristine Mihelich, had gone to the Seven-Eleven store at Twelve Mile and Oakshire at three o'clock and had not returned home. At the store, a clerk was able to tell police she'd sold a movie magazine to a girl answering Kristine's description around three.

By noon the next day, all of Detroit's media, still riding the crests of the waves produced by the Stebbins murder and particularly the recent Robinson killing, were sating the public with information about the missing Berkley girl. Scores of tips came into the Berkley Police Station as a result of the media blitz, but none was of any value.

Nineteen days later, about ten miles west of Royal Oak, U.S. Postal Service letter carrier Jerome Wozny was delivering mail on Bruce Lane, a dead-end street in Franklin Village, an extremely quaint, affluent little hamlet, nestled among undulating, heavily wooded hills.

Wozny, as he urged his mail truck down Bruce Lane, glimpsed a "blue something" in the snow by the side of the road. Backing up, he discovered the body of Kristine Mihelich. Fairly leaping back into his truck, he spun it around and almost in a trance sped directly to the Franklin Village Police Department, only a few minutes away.

1

It began on the phone.

Robertson had been waiting for this particular telephone call for almost three weeks. But of all places, a bowling alley in Ann Arbor, Michigan, where the chiefs were holding their meetings this month. Sometimes, thought Robertson as he rose from his chair in the banquet room, it seemed there was some kind of law about not having a chiefs' meeting without being interrupted at least once. But he was thankful for the interruption this time; he was just flirting with that gray area between staying awake and falling asleep when he caught the manager's signal.

"I think it's headquarters," said the manager in confidential tones, trying to sound as official as he could. "You better take it in my office."

"Thanks, Al," said Robertson as he followed the other into a small cluttered office. Al, who was trying desperately not to appear flapped, briskly removed a pair of bowling shoes from the corner of the desk.

"Here, let's punch it up for you." He stabbed the flashing button on the phone. He thrust the instrument in the Lieutenant's direction, spun on his heel, and headed for the door. Robertson cradled the phone, "Hello, Robertson here." It was Bays from Second District Headquarters in Northville. He listened a moment. "Okay, I was afraid it was something like that. Jesus. Okay, thirteen just west of Telegraph on Bruce. Is that B-R-U-C-E Lane? Okay, on my way. Thanks."

The ninety-minute drive to Franklin from Ann Arbor on a bitter cold Friday afternoon in January gave a person time to think. Open highway, hardly any traffic, radio bleating out country and western music, the Lieutenant's favorite.

Michigan is beautiful in the dead of winter, and Robertson surveyed the rolling terrain tucked under a heavy blanket of white snow as he tried for the umpteenth time to sort out the events of the past twelve months. He'd just enjoy the drive, listen to a little "pickin' and strummin'," and try to make things fit. Because if he didn't soon, a lot of other kids were going to die.

He pulled up at the end of a long line of vehicles just off Thirteen Mile Road and began the block-and-a-half trek to Bruce Lane hunched under his topcoat, muscles taut against the cold. A couple of marked cars — one looked like Southfield, the other probably Franklin — guarded the mouth of Bruce Lane nose to nose.

A growing crowd of citizens was being held back by the police guards, who shot Robertson a glare as he approached the barricade.

"Hang on, mister. Far as you go. Who're you?"

"Robertson, State Police, Lieutenant." Robertson reached inside his suit coat pocket and produced his wallet and badge. He could almost feel the rookie's relief as the other apologized.

"Oh. Okay. Sorry, Lieutenant. They told me don't let nobody go down there 'less they show you something real shiny. Go ahead, sir. And thanks, Lieutenant."

Smiling, Robertson flipped his badge and wallet back where they belonged, and tried to recognize faces in the crowd of twenty or thirty in front of the police lines. He wasn't looking for anybody in particular, just checking to see if he recognized any reporters. He'd seen the Channel 2 truck, and figured they had to be here somewhere. They had swooped down on the Stebbins and Robinson murders, but he guessed they were just doing their jobs. Besides, if this thing turned out as he figured it would, he was going to need their help. Unlike most law enforcement officers, Robertson rarely had problems with the media.

Pulling his collar up once again against the drilling wind, he began trudging the three hundred feet or so down Bruce Lane to see Kristine. So far, Joe Krease was conspicious by his absence. The Lieutenant glanced at his watch as he drew near the ambulance parked on the left shoulder of the road, partially blocking the view of the body. It was one forty-five. Where the devil is he, Robertson wondered. He should have had the call by now. Krease wasn't aware of it yet, but he was going to be in charge of the biggest manhunt and homicide investigation in the annals of crime in Michigan.

"Hey, Robbie, wanna be on television?" Robertson's peripheral vision caught six feet, five and one-half inches and 250 pounds of former Detroit police commissioner and current Oakland County Sheriff Johannes Spreen. County law enforcement officers say that when Spreen walks, it registers on the Richter scale.

"Hello, Sheriff. What do you mean, television?"

"It's feeding time for the media and somebody's gotta give them something," grinned Spreen. "And I sure ain't got nothin' to do with this thing. I'm just here to see if anybody needs a hand. You know me, always willing to lend a hand." It sounded like sarcasm. The grin disappeared.

"Appreciate the help, John, but I don't have time for television now. Got to see how far we're into this thing. Seen any of my people?"

The half-dozen men huddled near the ambulance turned to acknowledge Robertson's presence. He picked two out right away, Wayne Waldron and Roger Rivard.

"The son of a bitch could've picked a warmer day," groused Rivard.

"Yeah, I know. Let's get in the car and get warm, and you guys can fill me in."

The three state policemen walked to an unmarked car near the ambulance. "All right, you two. What have we got?" asked Robertson, removing his gloves and blowing on his hands. "Any of the lab people showed up yet?"

"Waiting on them now, Lieutenant," replied Waldron. "You see her?"

"Not really, just something in the snow as I walked up. Didn't want to get too close till the lab is through with her. It is Kristine, isn't it?"

"I haven't been that close, either," said Rivard as he tried the heater fan, "but from what I did see — she's covered with snow — it looks like what she was supposed to be wearing. You know, Lieutenant, looks like the son of a bitch piled snow around her after he put her down, almost like he was tucking her in. Guy must really be some kind of psycho, and he doesn't sound very smart, either. Puts her right alongside the road, houses down at the end of the street. He's gotta know people gonna be going up and down and somebody's gonna spot her. Jesus."

"Maybe that's what he wanted, Rog," suggested Waldron.

"Yeah, maybe," said Robertson. "You say it looks like he piled snow on her, Roger? It did snow last evening."

"No, you can see where somebody's cupped their hands, well, you know, like you scoop up sand on the beach to build a sand castle."

"Any marks on her?" asked Robbie.

"Hard to tell," said Waldron. "Nobody's really gotten close enough. Nothing obvious, though, no blood or anything like that. There's a set of tracks where he carried her in, but the guy who found her may have messed those up when he walked in to take a look. You can see where he turned the car around — he backed up and left some marks, probably bumper or something, in the snowbank, and we've been guarding them as best we can. But no telling how much traffic passed by here before we got the call."

"Who found her?" asked Robertson, as he cranked the passenger window down an inch, then unbuttoned his topcoat. At least the car heater was working.

"Mailman," answered Rivard. "He was headed down the road in his mail truck, and he sees this thing in the snow just off the road. Being one of those guys who collects all kinds of useless stuff, he probably thinks it's something he can stash away in his basement, so he heads back to take a look. You wanna' talk to him?"

"Naw, I guess not. How long did you talk with him?"

"Maybe a half-hour, forty-five minutes," said Rivard. "He'll be available if we need him. It's startin' to get to him, what he saw."

"What time the lab people supposed to get here?" asked Robertson, changing the subject.

"Any minute," said Waldron. "They're going to fly the photogs up here in the chopper for some aerials. The other crew's already left Madison Heights."

"All right," said Robbie, rebuttoning his coat. "Guess we better go find the Franklin Police Chief and see how he feels about this thing." Robertson knew the Franklin Police Chief would need help.

"We're in it pretty deep now, aren't we?" questioned Waldron. "I mean, aren't we supposed to activate the task force as soon as we find Kristine?"

"Yeah," replied Robertson, reaching for the door handle, "But I'd rather do it with Franklin's blessing, just in case there's ever any problem. Besides, I don't want any problems with Spreen. Be a lot cleaner if the Chief 'invites' us in, if you catch my drift. Then it's real official."

Leaving Waldron to wait for the team from the lab, Robertson and Rivard walked back to Robertson's car, finding a crowd swollen by the arrival of more police, reporters, and curious bystanders. The sky had turned from a deep blue punctuated with puffs of scudding, white clouds to a grim shade of grey, accented with darker clouds, bulbous and bruise-colored. The wind kept its low-register howl and cut like a razor, crystalizing the snow, which snapped underfoot like shattered Christmas tree ornaments.

Spreen was standing amidst a small group of onlookers just a few yards inside the police lines, still held intact by the nervous Franklin cop. Robertson recognized one of the men as Undersheriff John Nichols, another former Detroit Police Commissioner, a good one, Robertson recalled, who had banished himself to the suburbs after paying his dues in Detroit. Nichols was a cop's cop, thought Robertson, and he wondered how Nichols liked working for Spreen, one former police commissioner working for another.

Neither Spreen nor Nichols spoke to the two state policemen, but Spreen acknowledged their presence with something between a wave and a salute, which Robertson returned with a cocky military snap salute. Nichols watched from under his lids as the state policemen cut around the little group. Robbie noticed Spreen lean down to the smaller man's ear and say something as his eyes followed the state police, but they were out of earshot. "Just as well," he thought.

"What the hell's his problem?" grumbled Rivard, who'd also noticed the Sheriff whispering.

"Aw, it's just his way," said Robbie. "He's probably teed off because he thinks it oughta be his show. He's not happy unless he's bellyaching about something. You know how he is." At his car, the Lieutenant fumbled for his keys, while Rivard cut around the front and, using his right hand on the hood to steady himself, took one giant step to clear the banked snow and sank to his knees in the snow-covered ditch.

"Dammit!" he spat. That was the last word Robertson heard him say during the ten-minute drive to the Franklin Village Police Department.

2

Franklin Village in the winter looks like a Currier and Ives print. Industrialists, merchants, physicians, and attorneys dwell in manorly residences set well back from blacktop roads that snake through the forested hills. Every fall, outsiders flock to the turn-of-the-century cider mill, guided by the mingled aroma of burning leaves and tangy crushed apples. When winter visits Franklin Village, you expect to find a mare drawing a wooden sleigh at the very next turn of the road, and sometimes you do.

Robertson, less than familiar with the area, came in from the south on Franklin Road. He eased the car down a rather precipitous slope to the village, which nestled quietly at the bottom of a valley, protected from the outside world.

Not surprisingly, Franklin Village has no police station as such. Robertson guided the car into one of several parking slots just off Franklin Road, and he and Rivard picked their way up three ice-clad steps to a windowless hickory door, into which were deeply burned the words "Franklin Village Public Library." Kicking snow from their shoes on the huge mat inside the entry, they opened another heavy wooden door to enter the library itself.

The two state policemen walked over expensive, autumn gold carpeting to a desk at the far end of the high-ceilinged room, which was lit by four grand chandeliers hanging by heavy, medieval-looking chains. An attractive middle-aged woman, with exquisitely greying, black hair, pulled severely back and tied with a yellow ribbon, sat behind the massive desk just in front of the window. Robertson cleared his throat for attention, as Rivard picked up a copy of *The Final Verdict*, by Adela Rogers St. Johns, from the corner of the desk, allowing its Franklin Public Library card to flutter to the floor. The woman, closing the ledger she'd been fiddling with, glared over wire-frame, designer glasses at Rivard, stooping to retrieve the library card. As he popped up and quickly stuffed the card back where it belonged, she turned her attention to Robertson.

"Yes, may I help either of you?" she asked, giving Rivard an impatient glance.

"We'd like to see Chief Wilson, please," replied Robertson. "State Police. I'm Lieutenant Robertson, this is Detective Sergeant Rivard."

"Oh yes," she smiled, revealing a set of perfect white teeth. "Chief Wilson said he'd be expecting someone from the State Police. He's in his office. Here, I'll take you back." She rose, gesturing to a door flanked by bookshelves in the rear wall. She floated across the room, drawing Robertson and Rivard in her wake.

Chief Frank Wilson got up from a captain's chair behind a rough-hewn but obviously expensive antique desk with an old-fashioned upright telephone on it. A matching table held two police scanners and a police radio. The room itself, with its barnwood paneling, thick carpeting, brass lamps, and earth-tone drapes, reminded Robertson more of a study than a police station.

Wilson was much older than the two men he greeted, mostly bald except for a rim of closely trimmed grey-brown hair circling a tanned scalp. The rolled-up sleeves of his well-starched uniform revealed muscular forearms that undoubtedly meant a good amateur game of tennis in the summer and racketball in the winter.

"Good to see you, Robbie," boomed Wilson, extending a right hand the size of a catcher's mitt and flashing a genuine smile.

"Hello, Frank. You're looking in pretty good shape for a guy your age," smiled Robertson. "See you still got a pretty fair grip on life," he winced as Wilson squeezed his hand. "Great place you got here," Robertson continued, looking around.

"Yeah, well, you know. Might as well be comfortable. Actually, this is temporary till they figure where they're gonna put us. Helen, that's the gal who brought you in, she's the librarian and this is really her office."

"Oh," said Robbie. "Frank, meet Detective Sergeant Roger Rivard. Roger, Chief Frank Wilson."

"Hi again, Sergeant," said Wilson, offering his catcher's mitt to Rivard. "The Sergeant and I met briefly this morning on Bruce Lane. Have a chair. I guess I know why you're both here." Wilson reached into a polished oak humidor and produced a Te-Amo Presidente that reminded Robertson of a riot baton. He produced a small, curved pair of scissors from his pants pocket, delicately removed the Presidente from its cellophane wrapper, and deftly clipped the end.

"Don't worry, I'm not going to light it," said Wilson. "I figure that if I follow doctor's orders, with the money I save on the martinis I can afford a box of these a month. They're about three bucks apiece.

"All right, let's get down to business. You been at the scene, Robbie. You've seen what we got. First time we ever had anything like this. You know, most of our stuff is house-watching while the people spend Christmas in the Caymans." Rising to turn down the squelch on the two-way across the room, Wilson added, "As you've probably guessed, we're in way over our heads. I simply haven't got the manpower or the resources to put this guy where he belongs. Roger here and I talked a little bit up there this morning, and I mentioned to him I hoped you guys might give us a hand. Fact is, I'd like you to take the whole thing over. I'll give you any help I can."

"Well, Frank," said Robertson, "I'm thinking the same thing. We didn't want to go poking around too much, though, without your okay. The way we're set up, we figured we'd activate the task force the minute we found a body and got the okay from you." Robbie started to rise. "Matter of fact, I'm probably going to ask you for some help right now. It'd be good if you can keep your car up there until we can send a couple of ours over there because I want the place watched all night. And I'd appreciate it if you could kind of keep track of the mailman. We might want to talk with him again."

"Fine with me," said Wilson. "Hope we did alright keeping everybody back. Sorry about the guy in the Lincoln."

Robertson sat back down. "What guy in what Lincoln?" he asked, turning to Rivard first.

"Sorry, Lieutenant, I forgot to mention it. Some guy in a black Lincoln got there just after I did, pulled some I.D. on the Franklin cop at the barricade, and drove down to where we were. Said he was the council president, or village president, or something like that, and he wanted to see what was going on, and then he wants to let the media come down and take pictures. Kalbfleish gets to him before I do and tells him he doesn't care if he's the president of the United States, he's not going to bring the media or anybody else down there, and furthermore, he'd better get right back into his Lincoln and kindly get the hell back behind the police line."

"That's about the way of it, Lieutenant," interjected Wilson. "I had a little discussion with the council president right after that. He's an okay guy, Robbie, but, you know, we got some people living out here that think they're pretty big shooters. I guess if a guy is used to having people rise

when he walks through the office, he figures it ought to be like that everywhere. But these people are really good people. This is a damn fine little
community."

"I suppose so, Frank, long as he didn't mess anything up," said Robertson, a little tentatively. "Anyway," he continued, walking to the coat-
tree, "Just wanted to make sure we got your okay. I want to be there when
the crime lab goes through, and hopefully, Joe'll be there. Good seeing you
again, Frank. Thanks for all your cooperation."

Robertson and Rivard cut straight to the front entrance, glancing at
the lady with the yellow ribbon in her hair, who smiled. They smiled back
and headed out the door to try to find the man who killed Kristine Mihelich.

3

Sharkey, fists driven deeply into the pockets of his fur-hooded State Police parka, stared blankly down at what, only a few hours before, had been officially recorded as an abduction. "How ridiculous," thought Sharkey, "that people who look at dead people always say they look like they're sleeping. Christ! Dead people have a certain look about them tells you right away they're dead. Color, you can always tell by the color." He could feel himself slipping into a white rage, and his mind raced. Adults are one thing, but children are another. He fumed, thinking of the man who had laid this beautiful child at his feet. Kristine didn't look like she was sleeping. She looked like she was dead. He thought of his own daughter.

Without turning, Sharkey very carefully stepped backward into his own footprints and worked himself away from where he had stood by Kristine to the hard-packed roadway, where he turned and walked past the ambulance to the brown car parked alongside. Several men were leaning against the fender. One of them, Waldron, stepped away from the other two men, advanced, and met the man from the crime lab halfway.

"Recognize the face," Waldron said, tentatively extending a hand.

"Dick Sharkey, crime lab."

"Wayne Waldron. We've been expecting you. Robertson and Rivard went down to Franklin to talk with the Chief. Should be back any minute, they've been gone about an hour. Anything we can do?"

"Well, no," said Sharkey in a voice several octaves below middle C. "I guess you've done it pretty well just by keeping everybody out. Chopper's on its way for some aerials before any of us go walking around and screw things up. Mind if I use your radio?"

Inside the car, Waldron cranked the engine as Sharkey slipped the mike off the dash clip and asked Waldron what his call was.

"Adam three," answered Waldron as the motor jumped to fast idle.

The dot in the grim northeast sky grew as Robertson and Rivard pulled off Thirteen Mile behind a line of parked cars that had lengthened considerably. By the time the state policemen had walked the block or so to Bruce Lane, the dot resembled an insect, and soon the familiar clatter of the blades chopping their way through the subzero air started to build. The chopper began dropping precipitously from its twelve hundred-foot flight pattern to a working altitude of perhaps two hundred feet as it approached and began a slow, clockwise reconnaissance.

By now a television crew had turned its camera skyward to catch the chopper coming in, and a TV newsman was jostling through the crowd toward the approaching policemen.

"Shit, that's Wade from Channel 7, isn't it?"

"Don't worry about it, Roger," said Robertson. "He's got a job to do just like we have, and besides, I'll handle him. He's all right." The veteran reporter, crew in tow with mini-cam levelled at the two detectives, met them as they came up to the entrance to Bruce Lane. Extending his hand as he pulled up abruptly in front of them, Wade said, "Hi, Lieutenant. It is Kristine, isn't it?" His other hand thrust a microphone in Robertson's face.

"Don't know, Vince. I expect we'll have a positive I.D. shortly. Listen, you know I'll give you all I can, but give us some space. I don't think the lab people are through yet. I'm not even sure they're here."

"That's your chopper up there, isn't it?" interrupted the journalist as he glanced at the hovering aircraft. The question was rhetorical.

"Looks like it," replied Robbie. The chopper had suspended itself in mid-air two hundred feet almost directly over the dead girl.

"Your crime lab people in it?" Another rhetorical question.

"I expect so," replied Robertson, raising his voice over the whipping sound of the blades. Rivard started to say something to Wade but caught himself. "Listen, Vince," Robertson continued, "Let me go on down there and see what's going on. I'll tell you this much, though, and you can put it on the record: the state police are running the investigation, and that's all I'm going to tell you period. Off the record, well, you covered the other two." A reference to the Stebbins and the Robinson slayings would open the door for Wade to do with it what he would.

"Same guy?" persisted Wade.

"At this point, Vince, your guess is as good as ours," answered the Lieutenant. "C'mon, give us a break and we'll work with you. We're probably going to need each other before this thing is over."

"I know, Lieutenant, but I'm also going to have to have something for the six o'clock," said Wade, who knew he'd gotten all the information he was going to get. He and the crew began elbowing their way back to the police line. One of the top police and investigative reporters in Detroit television, Wade was good enough to know that sometimes you had to take a "no" now, to get a "yes" later. He had nurtured mutual respect between himself and Robertson on the Stebbins and Robinson cases and didn't want to blow it by pressing his luck. Not that Wade was out to win any popularity contests: matter of fact, he figured if he didn't infuriate someone at least once a week, he wasn't doing his job. But Wade kind of liked Robertson, and he wasn't about to screw up. He knew if he didn't play by Robertson's rules, he'd never get within a country mile of the investigation.

"When was the last time you couldn't come up with something for the six o'clock, Vince," Robertson muttered as he and Rivard turned and headed down Bruce Lane.

Detective Sergeant Joseph Krease had been with the State Police for some fourteen years, had worked a number of homicides, and was considered a first-rate investigator. He was a proud man, but gentle and soft-spoken, and if you couldn't get along with Joe Krease, you'd probably have a tough time getting along with anybody. Like spring steel, he would bend, but he wouldn't break, and the few who mistook his flexibility for indecision or weakness soon realized their mistake. He was the kind of man you hope your daughter will marry.

Robertson knew Krease well and had great confidence in his integrity and in his proficiency as a police officer. This was the man he wanted to run the day-to-day operations of the special homicide task force. As Robertson walked down Bruce Lane with Rivard, he spotted Krease among the detectives clustered around the ambulance, a tallish man with glasses and receding dark hair, wearing a tan topcoat over a business suit, engaged in conversation with Dick Sharkey.

Robertson spoke first. "Hello, Joe. Looks like another one."

"Hi, Lieutenant," replied Krease, turning away from Sharkey. He and Robertson knew each other pretty well, but Krease always called him Lieutenant, even in private. Sometimes Robertson wished he would be a little less formal, but at the same time he liked the other's allegiance to decorum.

"Yeah, looks like. Dick's filled me in, and I also talked with Wayne. We're just waiting for the helicopter to finish with the aerials, then Dick's going to take his people in for a closer look."

"All right," said Robertson, putting his arm on Krease's shoulder and guiding him away from the others. "Roger, I'm going to sit a spell with Joe. We'll use your car."

Robertson and Krease got into the Fury next to the ambulance. Robbie flipped the key and hit the heater fan.

"Joe, I don't have to tell you what's going on, but let me share some thoughts, anyway. We've got a real problem." He adjusted the heater. "We haven't got a positive I.D. yet, but you and I both know it's Kristine. Second, we both know it looks like the same guy is doing it. I mean, it all fits too well, the age, the abduction, keeping the kid for days, taking care of them, then taking them out. If we don't nail him real quick, there's not a kid in Oakland County that's safe."

There was a knock at the window on the driver's side. "Yeah, Roger. What's up?"

"Lieutenant, there's another chopper real low coming in over the trees from the northwest. Somebody said it's Spreen's, and Sharkey's getting crazy 'cause he says he's too low and is gonna blow snow over everything."

Robertson opened the door and stood half out of the vehicle, looking at the approaching chopper beating its way toward the body drop, about a hundred feet over the trees. "You asshole," Sharkey screamed over the roar. And then to the Lieutenant: "He's too close to our chopper, and he's way too low. He's gonna screw up everything." The lab expert began waving wildly at the pilot.

Whether the pilot saw him or just suddenly realized what he was doing, the helicopter suddenly vaulted upward about three hundred feet and settled into an orbit well outside the State Police chopper.

"Stupid bastard," spit Sharkey as he walked away.

Robertson sat back down in the car, and closed the door. "Well, I guess he didn't really do any damage. I don't think he'll bother us anymore," he said to Krease. "Still, you'd think he'd know better. Now we're going to have to listen to Spreen bellyache about how we chased him off. Or I should say, we'll read about how we chased him off in the newspapers. Anyway, Joe, we've got ourselves a serial killer and we've got to do something about it."

Krease nodded agreement. "Where do we go from here?"

"Well, I just talked with old Frank Wilson down at Franklin, and he wants us to take over, so I guess we've officially taken over. Just like we figured we would as soon as Kristine turned up. The special task force. I'm going to want you to do it, be responsible for the day-to-day operations, street investigations, and stuff like that. Administration, too. You've got a history with this kind of thing, and I think you're the man for the job. Also, I know you're not going to rubber stamp everything I say: we're going to need a lot of different ideas, and sometimes I'm just going to sit back and play the devil's advocate with you. I've got my hands full at District—I've still got to keep things running smoothly in the whole southeastern part of the state. What I'd really like to see is this thing kind of run itself through a spirit of cooperation, with you just there to sort of guide it along, and put it back on track if it jumps off."

Krease wasn't one to string together any more words than he had to. He simply said, "Okay, Lieutenant. Appreciate the vote of confidence."

Robertson wasn't going to press him for any quick answers. Krease didn't press well, and besides, Robertson admired the detective's way of not shooting from the hip as so many of the newer Hollywood cops did. Not that shooting from the hip wasn't an alternative, sometimes. Joe could do that, too, if he had to. But Robertson still liked good, methodical, old-fashioned police work. If anybody could trip the killer up, it would be Krease.

Robertson turned the engine off and got out of the car. "Tell you what," he said to Krease over the roof of the car. "Think I'll look Spreen up, and tell him we're running the show, so everybody'll know where they stand. Why don't you stick around here and see if the lab is ready to move in on Kristine."

"Well, Lieutenant, the helicopters should be about done with the aerials, now, and if it's all the same, I think I'll get a house-to-house going. Give Dick a little time."

"Whatever you say, Joe. It's your investigation. Besides," said the Lieutenant, "I think that's a good idea."

The helicopters, both of them, were still making slow circles in the sky, but they'd both risen another couple hundred feet. A quick discussion with Sharkey confirmed that the State Police chopper had finished its picture-taking and was just giving the terrain a quick once-over before heading back to the lab. Sharkey told Krease that in fact he would need some time to poke around in the snow and take a closer look at the body before too many cops tramped around the drop site.

"Give me a holler when you're ready. I'd like to take a quick look myself," said Joe. "Meanwhile, I think I'll have some of our people see if the neighbors saw anything." He walked the dozen or so yards to where Lieutenant Pat Sullivan, chief of detectives for the Ferndale Police Department, stood talking with one of his men. Sullivan looked like a stereotypical, hard-bitten, city police detective. He was a big man, well over

230 pounds and a touch over six feet, heavy-jowled with a voice to match and thinning, dark hair. He was good enough at his profession that he rarely had to prove that he was as tough as he looked. You had to be good if you were a cop in blue-collar, red-neck Ferndale. A lot of the dirt that was swept down Woodward Avenue from downtown Detroit collected just north of Eight Mile Road, where Ferndale began. Detroit's mayor, Coleman Young, had said himself that if people were going to commit crimes, they should "do it to hell the other side of Eight Mile Road." Young put considerable effort into running junkies, hookers, muggers, and rapists out of town and into the suburbs. So a Ferndale cop had to be good or be dead.

"You look like you're cold, Sergeant," noted Sullivan, who apparently wasn't. "Hell, this is a heatwave."

"Hello, Lieutenant," answered Krease with a polite smile. "Glad you're here." Krease thought he'd better get right down to business while they still had a couple of hours of daylight left. "Anybody talked to the neighbors, yet?"

"Don't think so. Haven't been here that long, myself. Just waitin' for the lab to finish up."

"Yeah," said Krease. "Sharkey's ready."

"You guys running the show?" interrupted the big man. Sullivan had been involved in the task force concept from the very beginning, when Mark Stebbins was abducted, and was aware of the plan to have the State Police get officially involved when Kristine was found.

"Yes. The Lieutenant spoke with Frank Wilson, and we're the lead agency," Krease answered.

"Maybe we oughta . . ." Sullivan began.

". . . Start talking to some of the people who live around here," finished Krease. If Krease was running the show, he was running the show, and if anybody was going to do any interrupting, it would be him. "You're right, Lieutenant," he went on. "Like to have you handle that, if you would. Got enough people?"

"Just me and my partner," answered Sullivan, "plus the first eight or ten guys I see standin' around with nothin' to do. We oughta be able to take care of it."

"That ought to be more than enough. We have to touch base with everybody on this street, then probably fan out in case somebody who lives a couple of streets over saw something funny," directed Krease.

Sullivan didn't have any trouble finding detectives. There were a half-dozen different jurisdictions on the scene, all of them keyed up and well informed. Most of the detectives who'd been working the child killer case from the beginning had families of their own, and many had sons and daughters the same ages as the victims. When questioned later, all would say that they couldn't help but see their own children lying in the parking lot, or alongside I-75, or in the ditch by Bruce Lane. A dozen angry detectives fanned out in all directions.

Bruce Lane ended in a blacktopped turn-a-round surrounded by a half-dozen sprawling ranch and trilevel homes. The area around the homes was splashed with trees, and high, thick brush ran the third of a mile of Bruce Lane, separated from it on both sides by fifteen feet of waist-high weeds. Across Thirteen Mile were splendid, two-hundred-thousand-dollar homes. It was into this rarified atmosphere within a one-mile radius of Kristine's body that Lieutenant Patrick Sullivan took his little band of street-wise detectives, with all the usual questions: "Did you see anything unusual this morning between, say, 8:00 A.M. and 12:00 noon?" "Did you see anyone walking along the street?" "Would you have noticed if you had?" "Are there a lot of deliveries made in this area?" "Any strange cars around here this morning?" "Any kind of unusual activity at all today?"

It was late afternoon, and it was already in the news that Kristine Mihelich, or at least a young girl matching her description, had been found. The media were hinting strongly that the youngster was the Oakland County child killer's third victim.

Not surprisingly, the people in those houses had some questions of their own. Generally speaking, police are pretty close-mouthed when working an investigation, especially on a house-to-house canvass. But because the people being interrogated were so cooperative, the police too were especially cooperative. "Yes, the body of a young girl has been found on Bruce Lane." "Yes, it could be that of Kristine Mihelich," and, most definitely, "Yes, we are looking for the killer." But when all the questions on both sides had been asked and answered, the residents of Franklin Village had learned more than the police had.

4

Catlike, Sharkey circled the lifeless body of the young girl, careful to stay half-a-dozen feet from where she lay. Her killer had not been so careful, and had left his footprints in the deep snow. Unfortunately Wozny, the mailman, hadn't been careful either, and had stepped right into the killer's tracks. But, of course, Wozny hadn't known that the object of his curiosity was the body of a young girl and that the footprints he was stepping on were those of the man who murdered her.

It looked as if the killer had simply lifted Kristine out of a chair, one arm under her back and the other under her knees, and had laid her down so she faced east. From this, Krease would later deduce that the man they were looking for was probably right-handed, for whatever that was worth, probably nothing. The hood of her parka partially obscured her face. Had her killer arranged it, the way a parent might pull a child's hood around its face to protect against the biting wind? Examination would later reveal that Kristine's clothing, including her underthings, was fresh and clean, showing no signs of having been worn continually during the nineteen days of her captivity. But Deborah Ascroft, her mother, didn't think Kristine had dressed herself. Kristine always wore her pants outside her boots and her blouse tied in the back. Lying there in the snow, her pants were tucked inside her boots, and her blouse was tied in front. Her mother was to come to the conclusion that Kristine had been dressed by someone else — perhaps after she was dead.

"Footprints aren't going to do us much good, Sergeant," Sharkey said to Krease, who was standing by the front of the ambulance, watching. Sharkey reached into his coat pocket and pulled out a one hundred-foot tape. "The mailman screwed them up. Damn!" he snorted, "Of all the luck. But look at this." He motioned for Krease to come closer. "Look how the snow is kind of packed around her body," Sharkey said, kneeling and pointing with the hand that held the tape. Krease stood about three feet from the body and squinted through his glasses. "You can even see where he scooped it over her with his hands," Sharkey went on, "like he's trying to cover her, and then he's kind of patted it down." Dick delicately tried to brush some of the snow from the dead child's face. "My guess is she hasn't been here all that long," he added, touching her folded hands. They were cold but not frozen. "I mean, I don't think he put her here last night. Probably some time this morning. It's just a guess. The postmortem will tell us." Sharkey stood up and slowly backed away from the body. Turning to Krease, he said, "Guy was pretty careful, sure didn't leave us much. Really clean. Bastard." Then to the ambulance attendants leaning against the front fender: "You guys got a body bag?"

An attendant who had appeared bored by the whole ordeal suddenly hopped to like he'd been pinched and scooted to the rear of the van, producing a folded, black, zippered, and quite substantial plastic bag. "Good," Sharkey said. "Just hang onto it for a couple of minutes. Joe, do we know who made all these tracks, here?" He pointed to indentations all around the body, six or eight feet from it. "Somebody said it was the Franklin police chief."

"Yeah," replied Krease, who'd already started to move onto the road. "Wilson said he circled her once soon as he got here."

"Yeah, okay. Just wanted to make sure," said Sharkey, following Krease onto Bruce Lane.

"Joe, let's take a look at the tire tracks. Maybe we'll get lucky."

The detectives walked about twenty-five feet south to where the killer had turned around. They stood staring at two neatly spaced, reasonably well-defined tire tracks in the banked snow. It looked as though the child killer, if indeed, those were his tire tracks, had gone down this far before realizing that the street dead-ended and had decided to turn around and dump the body where it wouldn't be quite so obvious, in case someone in one of the houses happened to be looking out the window. He had backed the car into the snowbank on the shoulder as he turned, then knicked the opposite snowbank with the front bumper as he completed the 180-degree turn. Not being stupid, he also had wanted to be headed toward the only exit if he were suddenly discovered.

"Hey, Charlie," Sharkey hollered at his photographer, who was still shooting the dead body from every conceivable angle. "Get over here with the camera when you're done there." The photographer, laden down with a heavy brown Domke camera bag, a Nikon slung from one shoulder and another in his ungloved hands, puffed his way to where Sharkey and Krease were squatting. "Get me something real good, Charlie," said Sharkey rising. "Looks like the guy backed in here, then shaved the crest of that

snowbank over there with his front bumper. These look pretty good."
Sharkey and Krease stood back and let Charlie live up to his reputation.

Robertson met the two policemen back by the ambulance.

"You talked with Spreen yet, Lieutenant?" asked Krease as the three
of them crossed the ditch and stood looking down at the body.

"Yeah, told him straight that we were going to be running the show."

"Any heat?" asked Sharkey.

"Naw. Oh, I suppose he would've been happier if I'd asked him to
take over, but he'll get over it. Said he'll give us anything we need."

"Like a little peace and quiet?" quipped Sharkey, not expecting any
response. "You want to get a closer look, Lieutenant?" he continued, changing the subject.

"Not really, I guess," said Robertson. "I've seen all I need to. Tell you
what I would like, though."

"What's that, Lieutenant?"

"The man who put her there." Robertson turned and walked away.

What light remained was fading into darkness. Robertson glanced
at his watch. "Getting on toward five o'clock, Joe," he said as the ambulance people started to position themselves to pick Kristine up and put
her in the body bag. "We'd better get everything together and talk about
this thing. Jerry Tobias says we can use the township offices." Raising his
voice a little, so Sharkey, who was standing by Kristine, could hear him,
he asked, "Dick, you about finished?"

"Pretty close, Lieutenant," replied Dick, "just want to stick around
until they take her out." "Be real careful with her," he said to the attendants. "Don't tear anything. We'll want to go over every stitch of her clothes,
and try not to touch the bare skin."

Robertson and Krease began walking toward Thirteen Mile Road.

"You want to get your people rounded up, Joe? We got a lot to talk
about, but I'd like to keep tonight's session as brief as possible. It's late,
and we want a fresh start early tomorrow morning."

5

Rush hour — once in the morning and then again in the afternoon, in case you missed it the first time. Traffic flowed like a clogged drain, and what should have been a fifteen-minute drive to the township offices, dragged into forty minutes. Robertson, however, had long since mastered the ancient disciplines of patience and tolerance, and instead of letting the vehicular quagmire make him crazy, was instead able to use the extra time to figure out just what he was going to say, and how he was going to say it. If he ever did get there.

He mulled over some other things during that time, too. The case had some built-in administrative problems from the very beginning, and most weren't man-made, although man didn't help. The problems arose from geography and jurisdiction. Mark Stebbins was abducted in Ferndale, and his body was found in Southfield. Jill Robinson was abducted in Royal Oak, and her body was found in Troy. And Kristine Michelich was abducted in Berkley, and her body was found in Franklin. Three children from three different jurisdictions, whose bodies were found in three other jurisdictions. Throw in the sheriff and the Michigan State Police, and you've got the ingredients for some real political infighting, not to mention enough logistical problems for a real law-enforcement headache. Robertson put his left hand up to massage his temple. He could feel it coming on already.

The policeman pulled at last into the well-cleared parking lot of the Beverly Hills Police and Fire Department and Southfield Township offices. The lot was practically empty, save for two black and white Beverly Hills patrol cars, pulled in snug to the rear of the low, white, weathered-brick building, and a white van with rusted quarter-panels in a far corner. Robertson nosed the police car between the black-and-whites, killed the engine, and carefully picked his way over a couple of icy spots to the rear entrance.

Inside he shook hands with a young policeman who said, "You must be Lieutenant Robertson. Tobias said you might be needing a place to meet." He steered Robertson across the slate floor of the main lobby to the city council auditorium.

"Yeah, thanks. This ought to do just fine," said Robertson. At one end of the room was a crescent-shaped council desk, behind which were seven heavy, black-leather swivel-chairs. The gallery was furnished with substantial, burgundy-upholstered theater-type chairs in neat rows. Wall hangings of spun yarn adorned the oak-paneled walls.

Robertson hung up his coat and settled in the mayor's chair. Detectives from a half-dozen jurisdictions began filing through the double doors — Southfield, Franklin, Royal Oak, Berkley, Spreen's people, Eddie Sosnick from the Prosecutor's Office, even a team from Detroit's celebrated "Squad Seven" homicide unit. The high-back swivel-chairs filled up quickly. Robertson was flanked by Krease on his left and Simmons, from Southfield, on his right. Ranking officers from several other departments filled the other council chairs, and about a third of the gallery was occupied by the rest.

Robertson cleared his throat and began speaking to the group of veteran homicide detectives.

"We're not going to keep you here all night, but we've got a couple of things to go over. First of all, I guess most of you here already knew that the State Police would be coordinating the investigation after we found the body, and you'll all remember that even then we were pretty darn sure we'd find a body." Simmons nodded agreement, and Robertson continued. "For lack of something better, I guess we can just call ourselves the Special Homicide Task Force, something like that. Basically, I think what we've got is Southfield, Royal Oak, Ferndale, Troy, and now Berkley, and of course us, the State Police. Detective Sergeant Joe Krease, here, a fine investigator and a good command officer, will be in charge of running the day-to-day investigation. I'm going to be pretty tied up at District — I haven't seen the top of my desk in six months — but Joe and I will be in close touch, probably on a daily basis. Joe, why don't you kind of give us a rundown on what happened today, and where you want to go from here."

The rookie who had shown Robertson in had appeared with four huge white bags from McDonald's. Krease carefully pried the lid off a large coffee, took a slug of it, and began. "I'm not going to go over too much of what happened before today. It's all down on paper, and we'll all be spending time going over the abduction reports for Stebbins and Robinson as we get further into this thing. So let's just focus on Kristine."

Another sip of coffee. "Just to refresh everybody—Kristine disappeared on January second, about three o'clock. Today's the twenty-first, so he kept her for nineteen days. Far as we know now, nobody saw anything. She was going up to the Seven-Eleven store. Clerk there says she thinks she sold a movie magazine to a youngster, a girl, about three o'clock in the afternoon, so we can assume she was okay at least till three, if the clerk is right. But after that nobody remembers seeing her. Now where she was between three o'clock the afternoon of the second and the morning of the twenty-first, today, and more importantly, who had her, we don't know."

Krease fumbled in his suitcoat pocket, produced a tattered notebook, and flipped it open. "Then," he continued, "shortly before noon today, a letter carrier," he hesitated, trying to decipher his notes, "a Jerome Wozny finds her alongside the ditch on Bruce Lane. Again, nobody sees anything. And our own lab doesn't find anything around the body, at least, nothing jumps out at them during the walkthrough. The guy has got to know that somebody's going to find her real quick. I figure he wants us, or somebody, to find her. Anyway, maybe the lab will get lucky after they have a chance to go over the thing, but no marks on her, so apparently he didn't beat her to death. Looks like she might have been suffocated, maybe with his hand, or a pillow, or something. Postmortem should tell us more. By the way, we've got to have somebody up there for the post. Roger," said Krease, looking to his left and up over his glasses. "Roger, maybe you could take somebody and go up there tomorrow, just to make sure we get what we want. Might talk to Sharkey, or Charlotte Day."

Krease took another throatful of coffee and picked at the fries in front of him. "I'm going to suggest something that all of us in this room probably already know, that there're an awful lot of similarities to the Stebbins and Robinson killings. And I'm going to go out even farther on the limb and suggest that we're looking for one person who killed all three of them." A couple of the detectives looked at each other, and nodded. There was some murmuring.

"I'll tell you, one of the biggest problems I'm having with this thing is it sure looks like the killer wants us to find them. I mean, Mihelich and Robinson along the road, Stebbins in a shopping mall. He could have put those kids where it'd take us days, or weeks, or even months to find them. If we ever did."

Krease pawed at the french fries again. "Now, the one thing I'm holding out some hope for is the tire tracks. Dick Sharkey, our lab expert, says they look pretty clean, but even if they are, it's going to be like looking for a needle in a haystack. But I'll just bet you that the two tracks in the snowbank were made by the killer's car when he backed into it to turn around. He probably didn't realize that Bruce Lane was a dead end, but figured it out before he got to the end of the road, down by the houses. We're going to have to ask for a lot of help from 'the Big Three' and maybe AMC, and let's hope we don't have to start chasing down the foreign jobs, too. We're going to have a couple of our units from the Pontiac post baby-sit Bruce Lane all night so we can keep track of everybody who comes and goes." Krease squinted out over the crowd of policemen, and finally spotted the huge man on the center aisle about halfway back. "Lieutenant Sullivan, you come up with anything on the house-to-house?"

Sullivan, without even trying to raise his bulk from the seat he'd wedged himself into, replied, "Nothing yet, Sergeant. We're gonna have to go back out there first thing tomorrow and finish up."

"Good," continued Krease. "So, we'll have the neighborhood search, and Sergeant Rivard will head on up to the M.E.'s office. I'd like us all to meet again tomorrow morning, and hopefully, we can begin to really do some groundwork. I guess that's about all I have for right now, Lieutenant." He mumbled a barely audible "Thank you very much" to the assembled detectives.

"Thanks, Joe," said Robertson. "Anybody got any questions?" There were none. After arranging to meet tomorrow at the Southfield Police Department, Robertson pushed himself up from the deep leather chair, and the first official meeting of the Oakland County Child Killer Task Force was history.

Robertson made a quick phone call to his wife Dee to tell her he was on his way home and that while he'd eaten, after a fashion, he'd still like to take her out for a quick bite, seeing as she probably hadn't eaten and it was getting late. He was still hungry enough to pick away at something. Maybe an omelet.

Robertson cranked the starter. The battery labored but finally caught. He'd stop at District early tomorrow and sign out another car while they put a quick charge on his battery. Why did it always seem colder when it was dark out? Probably because it was.

At least the traffic had thinned out. He'd have to call his boss, Captain Walt Anderson, and State Police Operations in East Lansing to make sure the director knew about the body, since the governor would probably be calling.

Robertson thought about how big this thing had grown.

6

The Southfield Police Department was located in the bowels of the Civic Center, a modern brick, chrome, and glass complex that sits on a wide expanse of manicured lawn just off Evergreen Road. It was barely a generation ago that the chief of police, Milton Sackett, and the chief of detectives, Eddie Rittenhour, were the entire department. Now, it was a state-of-the-art metropolitan police agency of some 150 highly trained men and women, with a crime lab and a skilled intelligence unit.

The bedrock of the intelligence unit was Lieutenant R. Jerry Simmons. Simmons described himself as tough when he had to be, but was always quick to tell you that he still receives Christmas cards from some of the criminals he put away. Simmons was somewhat slight, but carried with him two impressive trade marks. One was a nickel-plated .45 caliber automatic pistol, in lieu of the standard issue .357 revolver. The other was a cut-down, double-barreled twelve-gauge shotgun, with a sling, the envy of every other detective on the force, which he generally kept only as far away as the trunk of his car.

Simmons had been one of the first officers on the scene when Mark Stebbins was found. Simmons was also the officer who officially requested that each police chief in south Oakland County make available a team of detectives to form the nucleus of a special homicide task force as soon as they found Kristine's body.

Krease and Robertson pulled their cars into the Civic Center parking lot at about 8:20 the morning of January 22, 1977. Huddled in their topcoats against the biting cold, the two detectives trudged up the salted concrete steps to the double-glass doors. Simmons met them inside, standing to one side of the front desk, behind which sat a pretty, blond woman, with short-cropped hair, wearing three stripes on her sleeve. The woman looked up, but did not smile.

"Morning, Gentlemen," said Simmons, who was wide-eyed. "Everybody's waiting for us up in the Detective Bureau." The three policemen mounted the single flight of stairs to the Detective Bureau. "I think I got a better place for us than the DB," Simmons went on.

Krease nodded approval. "We're going to have to have some place kind of permanent. Maybe some place where we can work with a computer. I got some ideas along those lines."

The trio entered the door marked "Detective Bureau, Captain Edward Rittenhour."

The dozen or so standard civil service desks and chairs were all occupied. A half-dozen more detectives had dragged in folding chairs from somewhere, and one or two more detectives had perched on desk corners.

Robertson and Krease added their coats to the already filled coat hooks against the rear wall, and made their way back to the desk nearest the door. Robertson sat behind it. Krease lobbed his beat-up Samsonite attaché case on top of the desk, fumbled with the catches, pawed through the contents, and extricated a form.

"Good morning, everybody," Krease began. "Before you head up to the crime scene, let's go over one or two things. Let's see if we can't make some of the paperwork a little easier on all of us. We came up with this form right after the Collins case. It's pretty much self-explanatory. It allows us to standardize and collate the information a lot easier than if everybody turns in their information on whatever happens to be handy. You might not think there's enough space to write down everything, but remember, only write down those things that are important. Take a lesson from the media. Say as much as you can, in as few words as possible. It'll be easier on you, and a heck of a lot easier on whoever reads your report, like me. Hopefully, we can put all this stuff in the computer. Each tip sheet will be assigned a tip number, too, so we can retrieve it after it's been buried away. Any questions?"

No questions, but some shuffling of feet, and the murmur of grumbling filled the room. Krease slipped the form back into the attaché case.

"Yeah, I know," said Krease. "You'll get used to it."

"Okay then, what we want to do is saturate the neighborhood again. Work in teams if you can, alone if you can't. Hit everything within a mile or so of the drop site. We're looking for any, and I repeat, any unusual activity. Maybe somebody noticed a truck, somebody walking, or say a really old, rusted-out junker of a car cruising through Bloomfield Hills, amongst half-million dollar homes. Neighborhoods are not only made up of people, but they are like people. Each has its own personality, its own character. Look for what's out of character. And let's make sure we hit the houses on Bruce Lane, the same ones we did yesterday. They've had time to sleep on it, and maybe somebody you talked to yesterday forgot something with all the commotion. Let's check and double check. Any thoughts anybody wants to share?"

Since there apparently were none, Krease turned to Robertson. "You got anything, Lieutenant?"

"Couple of quick things. First, Mihelich has been all over radio and television and the papers. The media is covering this thing like a cheap suit. We want to keep the investigation as low profile as possible. Just good police procedure. The media is sure as hell going to try and use us, it's their job. I don't mind so much if they use us as long as we can do a little using ourselves. I think we're going to be able to use the media to our advantage — they might just be able to help us find the guy we're looking for. So I'm going to be straight with them, but we also want to be able to control what they know, and how they know it. I don't know if the press can make our job any easier, but I do know they can make it a lot harder if we start trying to jack each other around. At any rate, I'm going to ask Brooks Patterson to handle all the media. At least that way there'll only be one person they can go to to get information. Besides, when we tell Brooks he's handling the media, he'll think he died and went to heaven. If Brooks ever dies, it'll only be because he's figured out a way to be reincarnated as a TV anchorman . . . "

Robertson let the laughter subside before going on. "We're going to take a look at Southfield's intelligence office over at Northland for a permanent meeting place. So, if we're not here by the time you get back in later this afternoon, we'll probably be setting up over there. You can check in with dispatch by radio, they'll know where we are."

One of the worst-kept secrets in law enforcement was the location of the Southfield Police Department intelligence unit. It nested in what was affectionately known as "the bunker," a cold, grey, concrete fortress that was part of the underground shipping and receiving area of the giant Northland shopping complex. Under solemn, grey skies at 8:30 Sunday morning, Krease left his car, leaned into a stiff, chafing wind, and began carefully slip-sliding his way the twenty yards to where the treacherous, icy, concrete ramp led downward to the black maw of the loading dock.

Down below, a steel door marked "Shipping and Receiving Office" opened before he got there.

"Morning, Sergeant."

"Good morning, Lieutenant," replied Krease to Simmons. "How'd you know I was here?"

"We have ways. That's why we're intelligence," Simmons said. "Actually, I was just headed topside to see if I couldn't catch you before you parked. No reason you couldn't have brought the car down here — there's room for half-a-dozen of them."

"Fine. I got some stuff I brought with me from District this morning. You know, files, yellow pads, office supplies, even brought my own typewriter."

The two walked across a large loading stage and through another steel door marked "Employees Only," then down a grey, block hallway. After several turns they came to still another heavy steel door. Krease had counted three surveillance cameras so far. Simmons keyed the door, and they entered.

The room was perhaps twenty-five feet square. At one end five steps led up to a raised stage with three grey metal desks. On two of them sat police radio equipment of every description, and the third had a small plaque that identified it as Simmons's. A control console sat off to the side, its three video screens serving the surveillance cameras. The three walls enclosing the stage area were covered with huge, roll-up maps, showing every nook and cranny of Wayne, Oakland, and Macomb counties, with insert maps of each city and town in the tri-county area. Seven more desks were spaced evenly throughout the rest of the room.

"We going to disrupt your guys much?" asked Krease.

"Don't think so. Most of the time, they're out on the street, and that's just where I want them. The place should be practically empty most of the time. Way I figure, if this place is full of cops every day, I'm not doing my job."

Krease screwed up his face. "What the devil's that?" He sniffed the air like a dog. "That smell?"

Simmons snickered. "There's a Coney Island just the other side of the wall. It isn't the executive suite, exactly, but we sure do a lot of police work out of here," he said, somewhat apologetically.

"Looks just fine to me."

And the two men began moving the Oakland County Child Killer Task Force into its new home.

7

Krease inched his way along the Lodge Freeway in his unmarked Plymouth Fury, one of thousands of pairs of taillights forming a blinking red line all the way into Detroit eighteen miles away. Everything was falling into place as far as the mechanics of the investigation were concerned. He couldn't ask for more cooperation from the local chiefs, or from the dozens of detectives he'd put in the field. And of course, the community had responded overwhelmingly, almost too overwhelmingly, and a lot of his detectives had even volunteered their off-duty hours to the manhunt. By now, there wasn't a uniform or plainclothesman in the state of Michigan who wasn't aware of what had happened in Oakland County, and the case was the subject of an electronic dialogue between law enforcement agencies from coast-to-coast. The Federal Bureau of Investigation had also pledged its vast resources of manpower and equipment, for there was certainly the possibility that the abductor had traveled across state lines.

But one thing was still bothering Krease as he killed the Fury between two yellow diagonals at Northland. It was the nothing he was getting from the street. Three kids snatched right off the street, held for days, then dumped right out in the open. God knows, the community at large was anything but quiet — every place you went, bars, restaurants, schools, gas stations, people were talking about the Oakland County child killer. But of useful information, there was none, and that just didn't make sense.

"Morning, Rog," said Krease, toeing off his boots, as Rivard tried to place a white, styrofoam cup full of steaming coffee on his desk and mouthed an unintelligible curse as his white shirt cuff changed to the color of mud brown where the coffee landed.

"Morning, Sergeant," muttered Rivard, dabbing futilely at the cuff with a quickly snatched piece of blank State Police tip sheet.

"Everybody out, or not in yet?" inquired Krease as he cleared the short-barreled .38 from his hip and put it in the lower right drawer of his desk. He knew he probably wouldn't be going out today, at least not before lunch, and it gets heavy after all these years. Besides, the darn thing was always knocking into something and he always managed to hook it on the arm of his desk chair when he got up.

"They're in, but they're out," Rivard answered. He sipped at his coffee, scalded his tongue, and grumbled the name of the Lord in vain. "We've got two teams on the street already. Itami and Piche from Berkley are out. Itami called about quarter to eight and said him and Piche want to go back to a house they drew a blank on the other day. Came in on a tip—woman thinks her ex-husband is the guy we're looking for, but she wasn't home the first time they were there."

"Yeah," said Krease, glancing at his watch. It was three minutes to eight.

"Sullivan and Cattel are going to do the Woodward strip. Pat called just before you walked in. They're supposed to talk with the owner of one of them fag bars over there. Said they're gonna roust him and the guy he sleeps with out of bed. Somebody tipped them Tuesday. Pat says he left the sheet in your tray. Sullivan don't think much about the tip, but then, you never know. At any rate, he says they'll be in as soon as they have a talk with the two queens."

By half past eight, four two-man teams had popped in and right out again, after picking up their high-priority tips.

The lady in Berkley told Itami she was sure her ex-husband was the one they were after, because he drank a lot, threatened to beat up her boyfriend, and had slapped their twelve-year-old kid three days before. But the kid said he thought the boyfriend was the killer, and anyway his dad had been vacationing in Nassau for the last two weeks. This was quickly verified by both the hotel desk clerk in Nassau and the father's boss at Bendix.

Krease was not particularly happy with this kind of lost motion. He had to figure out a better way. Everything that came in, and they were getting better than fifty tips a day, had to be checked, of course. With three kids dead, they couldn't afford to let anything fall through the cracks. But there had to be some way to insure greater efficiency with the same fixed amounts of time, manpower, and resources. He'd been thinking about it ever since that first day when the TV reports generated something like two hundred phone calls. Most of those had gotten lost simply because there was no method of keeping any of them. Everybody had been caught short-handed.

Krease sat at his desk, sipped his coffee, and punched Robertson's private number into his phone.

Two rings. "Robertson."

"Lieutenant, this is Krease."

"Morning, Joe." Robertson sounded a little down.

"Lieutenant, any chance you can have lunch out this way? Got a couple of things I want to run by you."

"Project: Victimization" consisted of a legal-size sheet of white bond paper, the result of countless telephone conversations with the chiefs of detectives of the various local departments and especially with Detective Sergeant Philip Hogan at the Michigan State Police Data Center in Lansing. The sheet of paper would contain both victim and suspect information in a form that could be fed into Hogan's computer.

It was simple. The officer, upon investigating a possible child abduction, would put his police department name at the top, followed by the department's complaint number. The first third of the page provided data as to type of incident, ranging from "suspicious person" to "rape" and "sodomy," each preceded by a digit for Hogan's machine. Blanks were also provided for the date, time, and place of the reported incident, the victim's physical characteristics, and even blanks for a body drop, if it ever came to that, as, of course, it already had. The bottom two-thirds of the sheet had space for "suspect information," "method of operation," and "vehicle type."

"What do you think, Lieutenant?" inquired Krease, as he attacked the special at Olga's restaurant in the mall.

"I like it, Joe. You touched base with Hogan on this?"

"Yeah, I have. He seems to think it'll work. I sent him a sample form so he could hone some of the rough edges. He's going to run a sample program this weekend, just to make sure, but he doesn't see any problems. I suppose the biggest problem might be just getting everybody to take the time to sit down and fill it out properly."

"What about your people—you talk about it yet?" asked Robbie. He took out his silver Cross pen, the one Dee had given him just because it happened to be Saturday, a long time ago, and began following the victimization form, line by line, blank by blank.

"Not really, except maybe Roger a little. Wanted to run it by you first, and to make sure Hogan can work with it."

"How soon can Hogan go with it?" Robertson asked.

"If the computer likes it, we'll start Monday," said Krease, blotting a bit of Olga's special sauce from the corner of his mouth.

"Good enough. By the way, have we got the post results yet on Kristine?" as he signaled the waitress for the bill.

"Roger was headed up there about eleven o'clock, but he won't be back much before 4:00 or 4:30. Had a tip he wanted to check himself up in the Pontiac area."

"Oh, okay. If there's anything on it that really jumps out at you, why don't you give me a call this weekend. Otherwise, I suppose it can wait till next week. Let me put this on my expense account."

"Thanks, Lieutenant."

The two detectives made their way through the noontime crowd in the mall. Robertson headed back to Northville District, and Krease disappeared into the bunker.

The temperature hovered in the low teens.

Dr. Jerry Tobias was a professor of Education and Human Services at the University of Detroit. He was also a cop who had earned his spurs on the street and not only gave birth to but was Southfield Township's Youth Bureau. Tobias's familiarity with young people and his expertise in the field of adolescent behavior made him invaluable to Krease, who hoped that just maybe Tobias would have a perspective that the rest of them didn't have. If Joe could only know what made each of those three kids go off, apparently willingly, with a total stranger, he'd be a lot closer to solving the crimes. Or had it been a stranger? He would certainly have to consider that possibility, too. All indications were that Mark, Jill, and Kristine were lured into a car. Krease was itching to know what the lure was.

"All right," announced Tobias to the dozen or so detectives assembled in the "bunker." "Let's stop thinking like cops — and start thinking like kids. Everybody here was one, once. Let's just assume — and this can only be an assumption — that these three kids were all told repeatedly, by their parents, and their teachers, or whatever, that they shouldn't get too chummy with strangers. And from their school records, we know that we're not dealing with a bunch of dummies, here. And let's say," continued Tobias, rising from the edge of Krease's desk, "let's say that this guy didn't use any of the standard crap about the litter of kittens, or the parents being in an accident. And let's complicate matters even more by guessing he doesn't force them into the car, primarily because we haven't got anybody yet who saw him do it, or heard anything that sounded like a kid making noise like you'd expect. Let's say," Tobias went on, stepping to a chalkboard just to the rear of the desk, "that the kid knew better than to get enticed over to a strange car by a strange man, or men, or," Jerry stared at the ceiling, "maybe even a man and a woman. But maybe our man isn't a stranger in the true sense of the word." Tobias let that sink in for a couple of beats. "What if our man is dressed in some kind of garb or uniform that's pretty much universally accepted as being a friend." He let that sink in, too.

"You mean like a cop," blurted out a lieutenant from Detroit. It wasn't so much a question as a statement.

"Or a priest, or a fireman," Tobias picked it up and continued, "or a doctor with a white coat. Any of the above will do, the kinds of people we keep telling our children to turn to in a jam, even if they don't know their names. We start drumming this kind of stuff into their little heads soon as they're old enough to understand. Christ, he'd be like the Pied Piper. Or how about this? We're really reaching now, but suppose this guy's an athlete or just looks like one of the Detroit Tigers, or the Lions, or the Wings. Our look-alike calls a kid over to his car, and the kid says, 'Geez, that's Joe Potatoes, star running back for the Detroit Lions. Better go over and see what he wants.' I'm not suggesting we start dragging every top athlete in town in here for questioning, but it's something to think about, however ridiculous it might sound. I guess all I'm saying is let's try and get into the kids' heads. Pretend you're twelve or thirteen years old again, you're walking along the street, and some stranger pulls up in a car, or doesn't have a car, but just stops you on the street, and he starts a conversation. Now your parents have warned you about strangers." Tobias hesitated. "What kind of magic does the guy have to work to convince you that even though he's a stranger, he's okay?"

Tobias picked up a piece of broken yellow chalk. "The other thing we've got to do is try to get into the guy's head. What makes him tick?" He moved to the corner of the chalkboard. Somebody coughed. "I'm not going to list all the things we think we know about this guy now, just a couple of the more significant things that might give us a clue to what we're dealing with. First of all, the thing that hits me right between the eyes is that he's keeping these children for days. Mark for four days. Jill for three and one-half days, over Christmas, no less. And this is the one that blows me away, Kristine for nineteen days. If your next door neighbor, who is single (and we're going to have to start making a lot of assumptions here that may be way off base) suddenly brings home some strange kid for two weeks, you're not going to notice? Especially if we're talking about the same person bringing home three different children.

"And what about the kid? Coroner didn't find any unusual marks on Stebbins or Jill. Well," Jerry corrected himself, "I guess Mark had some very faint marks on his wrist and ankle, but that could just be tight socks or cuffs. No overwhelming evidence to indicate that he might've been tied up, anyway. I'm going to guess that none of the three children was tied and could've escaped, and this is where it really gets weird, if they wanted to. Was this guy watching them every minute? He had to sleep sometime. Yeah, Glen?" Watson from the Oakland County Sheriff's Department had started to speak, then put his finger to the corner of his mouth as if suddenly he wasn't quite sure if he was ready.

"I was just thinking. If this guy's got all this time to spend with the kids after he takes them, then maybe he's unemployed. Maybe he's even got a little place way out—some of the property out the north end of the county is pretty remote, and the houses are few and far between. But with the freeway he's only fifteen or twenty minutes from any one of the places the bodies were dropped. A guy could bring a dozen kids home to some of the places I've seen on patrol and nobody'd know for a month."

Tobias nodded. "Sure, the killer might be unemployed, or he might have a job that allows him great freedom of movement. In other words, he doesn't have to punch a clock, or account to a boss or supervisor every day."

Tobias addressed the chalkboard, hand raised, with the chalk between the thumb and first finger. "So what kinds of jobs allow a lot of unsupervised movement?" Silence. "Okay, let's say a priest."

"Aw, c'mon," somebody blurted out. "Priests don't go around killing kids."

"Where's that written," somebody else muttered. Tobias rubbed the word "priest" off with the heel of his hand and replaced it with "clergy." "And how about a salesman?" He wrote the word on the board.

"Why don't you write down 'unemployed' there, too, Jerry," added Krease.

In the next twenty minutes the board filled up with another eight or ten occupations, including policeman, reporter, executive, any profession that might allow freedom of movement.

Tobias put the chalk back in its tray and once again took his perch on the corner of Joe's desk.

"Another really significant thing. The postmortems on Mark and Jill appear to tell us that neither of them was mistreated while they were alive. No signs of malnutrition or dehydration. Stebbins had a couple of small cuts on his scalp, but they were old. Doc says he died from suffocation. I'm guessing Kristine was suffocated, like Mark. The shotgun he used on Jill really bothers me, because it destroys the pattern."

"What about sex, Jerry?" somebody from Detroit asked. "Didn't he jam something. . . . "

Tobias was still thinking about the shotgun. "Yeah, I'm coming to that. Well, he left Jill alone. At least there's no obvious signs of sex, though the key word is 'obvious,' because you've got to remember that there are all kinds of things short of penetration that wouldn't leave traces, but I guess we have to go along with the M.E. and figure she wasn't sexually molested. But," continued the juvenile officer, returning to the comment, "as you so delicately put it, Chet, he did do some 'jamming,' but with what, is anybody's guess." He opened the manila folder he'd placed on the desk earlier. "It says the 'anal orifice was widely distended over and above the expected normal, membrane torn, obviously upon insertion.'"

"So, we've got ourselves a homosexual?" Chet grunted.

"Maybe, maybe not," retorted Tobias, putting the medical examiner's report on Mark Stebbins back into its folder. "I just don't want to paint us into that corner too quickly. Personally, I'm not ready to put that label on him, till I talk with somebody who knows a lot more about sexual preferences than I do. However, I think I'm on pretty safe ground in saying we've got ourselves a certified, 100 percent pedophile. Joe Krease says he's going to give the M.E. a call and ask him if he won't meet with us and go over Kristine's report, so that'll be a good chance for questions. Not only hers, but Mark's and Jill's, too." Tobias looked to the rear of the room for a nod of agreement from Krease. "I might suggest that you guys take notes so you don't forget anything. At this point in time, everything's important."

Krease, who was leaning against the back wall, with his arms folded across his chest, interrupted. "Dick Sharkey and Charlotte Day will be here too. They've put everything else on the back burner to try and get our stuff done, so in addition to the postmortem results, maybe they'll have something for us, too."

"Could this guy be black?" someone asked.

"Most likely not," said Tobias, who began pacing back and forth across the stage. "I suppose somebody's gathered some sort of data on just how many black men assault white children, and how many white men assault black children. I haven't seen any figures about cross-racial child molestations, but we know it's happened. Still, nothing tells me we're looking for a black man. All three kids were white and from predominantly white neighborhoods, particularly Berkley and Royal Oak. And anybody who's bent on taking a kid right off the street in broad daylight has got to know that he's taking a real big chance, and he's going to want to minimize the risk. A black man who even thinks about grabbing somebody in a predominantly white neighborhood isn't exactly minimizing the risk. The guy's going to stick out like a sore thumb."

"But, Jerry, he's obviously sick," interrupted a Detroit cop, "and probably isn't thinking clearly, anyway. All he knows is there's something inside him that wants a kid."

"Don't bet on it. I haven't done a lot of reading on pedophiles, but I've done some and talked to a few people. A pedophile may be sick and need a lot of help, but don't bet they're stupid. I just think we'd be wasting a lot of time looking for somebody black. And we've got nothing so far that even remotely suggests that this thing is racially motivated. Now, we might spend a little time talking about the possibility that he has a woman working with him. The papers have already jumped all over that angle. Yes, Joe?"

Krease had started to walk up to the front of the room. "Far as I'm concerned, we'd be wasting time looking for a female involved in this thing, too. I didn't feel that way first off — I figured that a woman wouldn't have nearly as much trouble luring a kid into a car as a man. Kids just naturally gravitate to women more than to men at that age. But then I started thinking and going over some files and making some phone calls. Women are really strange when it comes to crimes involving children. They either really protect or really destroy. Now, the condition of the bodies doesn't suggest that the person who did this wanted to totally destroy, at least not Mark and Kristine, and while Jill had half her head blown away with the shotgun, I just don't buy a woman and a shotgun. Shotgun's not a woman's weapon, generally. I just think we better go after the most obvious, first. Then, if we exhaust that we can start talking about women and blacks or whatever."

The detectives stirred, and one of them spoke. "Would you believe a man in drag?"

8

It was a bleak, grey midmorning, with the clouds right down on the deck, and a cold drizzle pelted the green Mach I Mustang. McKee hung a right at the corner of Greenfield and Eleven Mile, and threaded his way through Berkley, timing the lights perfectly until he got to the one just this side of the Berkley Theatre. There went the perfect timing and the two-way.

"Creeper — Rhino. Give me your ten-twenty. It's quarter-to, and the place is filling up."

McKee, code name "Rhino," reached for the mike under the dash, turned the volume down a quarter-twist, and answered.

"Rhino — Creeper. On Eleven, right in front of the Berkley. Be there in a minute or so. You in place?"

The radio squelched. "All set. I've even got film in the camera."

Red changed to green above him, as McKee snapped the mike back under the dash, and eased the beast through the remaining few blocks of downtown Berkley, past the Sawyer-Fuller Funeral Home, to the parking lot on the corner of the next block. The corner lot was separated from the funeral home only by the side street. The undercover cop nosed the Mustang around so it faced the funeral home, giving him a good view of the Sawyer-Fuller parking lot. He let the engine idle as he removed his navy watch cap, ran his hands through his nearly shoulder-length hair, glanced to his right and across the street to the Roseland Cemetery, and lit a cigarette.

The Motorola squawked. "How do I look?" asked Hugh McMartin, code name "Creeper," from the dirty white van parked on Roseland's service drive, directly across from the funeral home.

McKee exhaled smoke into the mike as he replied. "Real good. The 'Maintenance' on the side is a nice touch."

Intelligence officers McKee and McMartin, along with two other men from their unit, were attending Kristine's services to see who showed up and "make" everybody who did. The Intelligence Unit worked mostly Organized and Conspiratorial Crime, and was employing the same kinds of surveillance here as on its other cases.*

McMartin's job was to get everybody that came and went on film. McKee and the other two officers drove the "chase cars," and it was their job to record all vehicle license plate numbers. The tag numbers would then be run through the Law Enforcement Information Network, providing names to go along with the license plates. Having done that, they would simply sit down with Kristine's mother, go through the list of names, and make sure everyone that showed up was invited.

By the time the services were over, forty-five minutes later, they had managed to get the plate number of every car in the Sawyer-Fuller parking lot and pictures of their owners.

But as good as they were, and they were pros, none of the policemen noticed the man with long sideburns and horn-rimmed glasses, standing a hundred feet from the funeral home, leaning against a brick building and watching. Hatless, wearing a nondescript blue-and-white-specked car coat with a fur collar, he just stood there, watching.

Kristine would be buried the next morning alongside her great-grandfather in the Oak Grove Cemetery at South Branch, nestled among the jack pine and white birch forest where she'd spent so many enchanting summers with her father. Before the amicable divorce, her parents, Debbie and Dan, had spent every available moment up there, and afterward Dan Mihelich had kept the cabin, so he and the children could enjoy the lake and the woods.

The 180-mile trip to South Branch late that afternoon was tiring, and the three Southfield detectives — McMartin had stayed behind to process film — slept at a mom-and-pop motel, just outside town.

They met with State Police Detective Harold Janiszewski the next morning about 6:45. Janiszewski had been sent up from the West Branch Post, because he was familiar with the geography and the people and might be needed.

It was quarter to nine when the three unmarked police cars parked

---

*Early on, no police officer seriously entertained the notion that the child killings had anything to do with the Mafia or other conspiratorial criminal activity. However, as events unfolded in the ensuing investigation, there was some thought given to the possibility that the children could have been victims of a child pornography ring connected to organized criminal activity, though not necessarily the traditional Sicilian Mafia. More will be written of this later.

along the highway at the cemetery entrance. They made no attempt to conceal themselves. Graveside services were scheduled to get underway at nine o'clock.

At 9:20, the black hearse led the string of a half-dozen cars off the main highway onto the winding, freshly snowplowed gravel road that led two hundred yards up a gentle slope to the graveyard. The detectives pulled in behind the small cortege. The road split at the top of the rise, and completely ringed the small graveyard. Tall jack pine, thrusting up from the heavy snow cover, protected the entire area, and the woodland was silent except for the closing of car doors, as the immediate family, maybe a dozen in all, including the preacher, walked slowly through an open gate to the freshly dug grave. The police cars went left and turned around so as to face downslope, effectively blocking the circle.

The ceremony was brief. McKee keyed the radio and spoke. "I'm going to keep with the mother and the boyfriend. See you back at the Post. Might as well run these tags, too, just for the record."

Debbie and the boyfriend were the first to leave, and McKee's green Mustang fell in a hundred yards behind them. They knew they were being dogged but didn't much care. McKee figured, correctly, that Kristine's mom just wanted to drive and clear out the cobwebs. It was a nice, slow tour of the backwoods. He wondered why all these backwoods roads were so well plowed. They certainly couldn't be used that much.

It was close to noon when McKee parked at the State Police Post at West Branch. There was a message at the desk for him to call Simmons.

"How'd everything go?" asked the Lieutenant from Southfield.

"Fine. Everybody seemed to belong. What's up?"

"Not sure, but you'd better head back. Creeper processed the film. There's somebody in it that we might want to talk to, if we can ever find out who he is."

9

From his spacious office at the end of what strikes the visitor as a third of a mile of narrow hall, lined with a score of cubicles for harried assistants, L. Brooks Patterson, the young and outspoken Oakland County Prosecutor, wing-tipped Johnston & Murphys propped on the desk corner, direct-dialed the Toronto offices of the Ontario Provincial Police. Somewhere the man, referred to by his assistants as "he who must be obeyed," had read about a new method of detecting fingerprints on human tissue and about the forensic lab specialist who could do it: Bud Hines. Would Hines, Patterson asked, fly to Detroit, all expenses paid, of course, to try lifting some prints off the body of Kristine Mihelich? The Toronto authorities were already informed, and, yes, of course, they'd let Hines come to Detroit. Was there anything else Oakland County needed?

Patterson didn't know it at the time, and wouldn't have cared if he did, but that phone call was to stoke up the fire a little bit between himself and Sheriff Spreen. Spreen, according to the Prosecutor, acted "badly" at the news conference during which Patterson announced that the Toronto fingerprint expert was flying in to look at Kristine. In Patterson's own words, "I remember the Sheriff's reaction. It was absolutely infantile." Spreen, not surprisingly, has a slightly different version. Spreen, who had already been excluded, to hear him tell it, from the entire investigation, also had his own crime lab. By his own admission, it was not exactly state of the art, but he did have a fingerprint expert by the name of Nelson Gelinas, who had studied under the Toronto people. Spreen couldn't understand why Patterson saw fit to call in Toronto, when all he had to do was walk across the street, literally, to the Sheriff's Office. Patterson justified the end-run by saying that even though Spreen's man had schooled under the Canadian expert, the importance of the case dictated that the teacher, and not the pupil, work on Kristine. If there were any latent prints on the youngster's body, the Prosecutor wanted the acknowledged top man in his field to lift them off. Nor, to make matters between the two worse, did the Prosecutor deign to even discuss the matter with the Sheriff, either before or after. Considering the flap it generated, it is somewhat ironic that the Toronto expert was not able to come away with any identifiable prints from the girl's body.

"You ready, Doc?" asked Krease as he steered Sillery to the front of the room filled with detectives. "Oh, wait a minute, Charlotte, you know Dr. Sillery, don't you?" He was pretty sure they'd met. Charlotte Day, lab specialist for the State Police, smiled tentatively in Sillery's direction and took the proffered, well-manicured hand. "And Dick Sharkey from our lab."

"Sergeant," said Sillery as he withdrew his hand from Day's and grasped Sharkey's.

"Nice to see you again, Ms. Day," said Sillery in a voice that sounded almost patronizing. Krease thought he perceived the kind of tension in the air you detect when two bitter enemies meet face-to-face in a small room. Joe really didn't think the two were bitter enemies, but he would've bet that one of the two was a touch intimidated, and it didn't seem to be Day, an attractive, middle-aged woman, with established credentials as a lab specialist, totally sure of who and what she was. Sillery, on the other hand, though Chief Pathologist for Oakland County, was image-conscious, with a fragile ego. It probably wouldn't take much to put him on the defensive.

Krease waited for a moment for the shuffling around to stop, and when they'd all settled down, he introduced Sillery to the group, more as a matter of protocol than anything else, for everyone in the room knew Sillery, or at least knew who he was.

Sillery retrieved some official-looking documents from his leather portfolio, placed them on Krease's desk, greeted everyone, and began going through a list of medical terms that meant little or nothing to anyone, save Day and probably Sharkey. Sillery droned on in a soporific monotone that reminded Simmons of a pilot going through his take-off checklist. Simmons wondered if he would ever get around to telling them what they wanted to know: how did Kristine die, and was she raped? Finally, Sillery explained that she'd not been starved, that there were no signs of dehydration, and that she had died of asphyxia, due to suffocation. No, he didn't know how the killer accomplished that.

In addition, there was no gross evidence to indicate that Kristine had been physically abused, no bruises or contusions save for one small blemish on her cheek, that the M.E. thought might have been a burn.

Neither the vaginal nor anal orifices showed signs of tearing. The lack of gross evidence of penetration, in the absence of other trace evidence, seemed to indicate she'd not been sexually molested.

"However," Sillery added, almost as an afterthought, "the slides showed sperm in both the vaginal and anal canals."

This seemingly contradictory revelation so stunned the room that no one spoke. Not surprisingly, it was Day who broke the silence. Krease won a bet with himself.

"What did you say, Doctor?" she asked incredulously.

"I said, Ms. Day," responded the other, in a manner that definitely sounded patronizing to Krease, who usually couldn't be bothered with noticing personality clashes, "I said that I found no gross evidence that the little girl had been penetrated, but my slides did show sperm in both her vagina and anus."

Charlotte started to follow up, but the M.E. cut her off.

"Let me try and explain it this way, Ms. Day," said Sillery, peering over the tops of his wire-frame bifocals, "the young male in a rutting mood is quite powerful when he ejaculates and can propel his seed great distances with such force that it's conceivable that some of the semen could have lodged in the vaginal and anal orifices, and could have indeed been imbedded well within those areas, perhaps through spasms, or involuntary muscle contractions of some sort, given that the child was undoubtedly traumatized."

"Holy Jesus," exclaimed Sharkey to himself.

Sillery, unflapped by the obvious disbelief of his audience, reached for the black leather portfolio, inserted his reports, and said, "That's pretty much it. I'm sure some of you must have questions. I'll try to answer them as best I can. Oh, by the way, I can't be exact about the time of death, but I'm going to give you an educated guess and say it was sometime after midnight on the twenty-first. She was killed within a matter of hours before she was found. Charlotte, either you or Sergeant Sharkey have the blood work-up yet? That ought to tell us how close I am."

Day, nonplused by Sillery's unexpected familiarity, which she wasn't sure she liked, responded simply, "No, not yet. Soon." Maybe Sillery had decided cooperation was more fruitful than confrontation.

"Doctor," Charlotte added, "I'm going to have to go over my slides again because I saw no evidence of sperm or seminal residue." Sharkey, who saw what was coming, smiled to himself.

"With your permission," Charlotte went on, "I'd like your slides, too. I'm sure I must have missed something."

"Of course. At your convenience," answered the M.E.

There were no other questions.

Back at the State Police lab, Day checked and double-checked her own slides and Sillery's and came to the firm conclusion that she'd missed nothing. Neither her slides nor Sillery's showed evidence of sperm. Joe Krease brought the discrepancy to the attention of the Prosecutor's Office, and the decision was made by Krease, Robertson, Patterson, and Patterson's chief assistant, Dick Thompson, to send both sets of slides to an independent lab in Baltimore. Day's original findings were confirmed. Whatever Sillery had seen on those slides, it wasn't sperm. The bigger question remained — if Sillery made a mistake on the sperm, what about the rest of the autopsy?

10

Stunned with sleep, Tobin swatted in the general direction of the telephone on the nightstand. The red numerals of the clock radio bore like lasers into his bleary eyes. It was 4:30 in the morning. After two more swats, the groggy police chief managed to get the phone to his ear.

"Yeah. Yes. Hello," mumbled Tobin. By this time, he'd levered himself up on one elbow. "What the hell? Yeah, this is Tobin, and this had better be good."

Jan stirred next to him.

"Yeah? How long's he been gone?" asked Tobin into the mouthpiece, swinging his legs to the floor. He groped for and found the lamp's pullcord. "You sure he didn't just get pissed off and decide to sleep in a closet, or under some boxes in the basement? Seen it happen before. 'Cause I sure don't want to get over there and find him hiding under somebody's bed. How about friends and neighbors, you checked everybody?" He waited for the police officer on the other end to reply. "Well, okay. Look, how long did you say he's been missing?" He listened. "All right . . . no . . . it doesn't look good to me, either. Better give me the address. Wait a minute."

Tobin pulled the nightstand drawer out and fumbled for some scratch paper and a pen. By now, the Birmingham Police Chief was fully awake.

"Okay, let's have it. Yeah . . . sixteen-one-eight . . . got it . . . Devonshire. Better give me the phone, too. Five-three-eight, one-four-two-eight. Okay. Stay put. I'm rolling."

"Sorry, honey," apologized Tobin, heading for the shower, more to wake up than get clean. He'd showered just before bed a scant four hours ago. "Got a missing kid, eleven or twelve. Looks legitimate. Gotta run. They're at the house now."

"Want something to eat first, Jerry? Let me get you a cup of coffee and some toast, at least," said Jan as she started to toss the covers back.

"Thanks, anyway, hon," replied Jerry, "but I can get something later.

I really gotta move," and with that, flipped the shower handle on. He finished the shower quickly and within minutes had dried, dressed, kissed his wife, turned out the light, and left. It was 4:53, the morning of March 17, 1977.

Tobin made the twenty-minute drive from his house in West Bloomfield in a little over ten minutes, and had no trouble finding the residence of Barry King. The home itself was not difficult to spot. It was the only one lighted throughout the downstairs, and the only one with a Birmingham Police car parked in front. The King house was modest by Birmingham standards. A story-and-a-half brick-and-sandstone bungalow with a two-car attached garage, it was sandwiched between more elegant homes but still maintained the character of the neighborhood. In summer, stately elms arched over the street to form a thick, green canopy. Now, in the throes of a Michigan winter, the giants were naked. Widely spaced street lights cast grim shadows on the street below.

Tobin pulled his car into the drive, checked out of service, and walked to the front door. As he was about to knock, the door was opened by the uniformed figure of Police Officer Don Studt, who had awakened him.

"Morning, Chief. They're both inside in the dining room."

"They okay?" asked Tobin, as he stepped inside and stood in the landing area while Studt closed and latched the door.

"Yeah," answered Studt in muted tones, "Better than I'd be under the circumstances, I guess." He led Tobin through the living room, into the dining area. Tobin noted that the home was not lavishly decorated, but warm, tasteful, and neat as a pin, with nothing superfluous or out of place.

Barry and Marian King were an attractive, middle-aged couple, dressed in street clothes that showed signs of having been worn for a long time. In their eyes, Tobin recognized the special kind of fatigue brought on by worry over a lost child. The Chief extended his hand and introduced himself to Mrs. King, who did not rise, then to Mr. King, who also kept his seat.

"Please sit down, Chief Tobin," said Mrs. King, in a surprisingly steady voice. "Would you like some coffee?" Tobin accepted and she took the few steps to the kitchen to get it. Tobin sat down opposite the Kings at a heavy, dark trestle table while officers Studt and Tim Gracey sat back down in front of their half-empty coffee cups, on either side. Mrs. King returned with freshly brewed coffee, retrieved a cup and saucer from a glass-fronted hutch, and poured. Tobin liked the Kings so far. He sipped his coffee and spoke.

"I know you've told these officers your story, Mrs. King, but I'm going to ask you to tell me, too. Each time you tell it you may remember something a little different, something that may not seem important to you but may be important to us. I should probably add that, depending on how successful we are in locating him, some other officers may also want to talk with you in great detail later on. What I'd like from you now is just basically an overview of the past twelve hours or so, but I'd like you to begin by telling me a little bit about Timmy. You know, what kind of a boy he is, good, bad, or indifferent student, whether or not he's athletic. What about his friends? How's he get along at home — any behavior problems with the family? How was he when you last saw him? That kind of thing, okay?"

Mrs. King put her hand on her husband's wrist, as he rested his hand on his coffee cup. "Well," she began, "I guess Timmy is a pretty average boy. He knows we love him a lot. He's a really good student, all As and Bs. He always does his homework, and his teachers think he's great. He's a very outgoing child, lots of friends, always bringing somebody home from school. Like with any other eleven-year-old, you have to get after him every once in a while, to pick up or do this and do that. But, he's a joy to have around, and he really likes his brothers and sister, he's the youngest. There's Cathy, his sister, who's seventeen. Then there's Chris, the next oldest. Chris is sixteen. And then there's Mark, who's a ninth grader. Sometimes the older ones kind of pick on him, but really all the kids are very close. He was just fine the last I saw him."

"Yes," Barry began, "When I got home from the office. . . ."

"Excuse me, Mr. King," interrupted Tobin, "What do you do for a living, if I can ask?"

"I'm an attorney with McFadden, Bates, Richards, and McCauley here in Birmingham."

Tobin reached for his pen and notebook and wrote down the name. "Now what were you saying about Timmy?"

"Yes, well, I got home from the office about, oh I guess it was shortly before seven, and Timmy was out on the drive playing with his skateboard and wanted to show me some new trick he'd learned with it. We talked about how good he was getting on it, and then I just came in the house. He seemed in really good spirits like he always is. That's about all, I guess."

"What about his health?" inquired the Chief.

"Fine," replied Mrs. King. "He participated in the usual sports, and we make sure the kids have routine physicals."

"What about the possibility that he just ran away?" asked Tobin, a little sheepishly. "Nothing you've said so far really gives me the slightest notion that Timmy's the kind of boy even to play a joke on his parents, but I want to make sure we cover all the possibilities, just to keep the record straight."

"No," said Mrs. King. "At least it's never happened before. Timmy's never gone anywhere without telling us, and if he decides he wants to shoot some basketball, or something, he always leaves a note."

"Where do you work, Mrs. King?" asked Tobin.

"At the Nancy and Me dress shop in Somerset Mall. Mostly Tuesdays and Wednesdays from eleven to three."

Tobin glanced at his watch. "You say you got home shortly before seven, Mr. King, and Timmy was playing in the drive on his skateboard. What next?"

"Well," the boy's father continued, "I had made arrangements to meet a client to sign a new will, and I had to take Marian with me. So I suggested to Marian that we stop and get a bite to eat, after."

"What about the other kids?" asked Tobin.

"Well," interjected Marian, "Mark is in a French play, and they sprang a surprise rehearsal on the cast, which caused a problem because he was supposed to babysit for some friends of ours, the Boyers. So I had the Boyers drop their youngest boy over here, and I figured we could have Chris, our sixteen-year-old, substitute for Mark. About ten after seven, Barry and I, and Chris and Kevin, that's the Boyers' boy, left our house, and we dropped the two boys off at the Boyers' house, and Barry and I went to his client's home to sign the will."

"Okay," said Tobin. "Now was Timmy home when you both left with Mark and Kevin?"

"Yes. Both Timmy and Cathy were home. Cathy was really excited because someone had given her tickets to see Jerry Lee Lewis, her first live concert show."

"What time was Cathy supposed to go to the show?"

"She said she was going to leave around eight o'clock, maybe a little before. But," Marian glanced at her husband, "he knew where his father and I would be, and he knew Chris was at the Boyers, and he knew we'd be home before nine."

Barry spoke. "That's right. Marian and I went to see my client, grabbed a bite at Peabody's, and got back here about ten to nine. A couple of the living room lights were on, and the front door was ajar, maybe a foot or eighteen inches."

"That's kind of strange, isn't it?"

"Well," Barry said, "Sure, maybe, I guess. But I really didn't think too much about it at the time. You know how kids are—sometimes they close a door, and sometimes they don't."

"And then?" prompted Tobin.

"Well, then we came inside and called to Tim and got no response. I told Marian he was probably just around the neighborhood someplace, and he'd be home shortly. She started calling the various friends he might be with. Finally I got the car and started just driving around looking. Nothing. So then about 10:15, I got back here, and called the police, and the woman who answered your phone said I should call back a little later, I guess because maybe he hadn't been missing for a long enough time. I called back shortly before midnight, and she told me to call back after shift change. I was getting a little upset with her because Timmy's long overdue, it's dark, and she's telling me to call back when the shift changes. So I said to her," King continued as his mouth grew tighter, "'What can they do for me that you can't?' That's when she referred me to an officer, who got here just after midnight and interviewed us."

King said, "Excuse me," got up with his coffee, and headed for the kitchen.

"Yeah, sure," replied Tobin. The chief detected the frustration; still, he marveled at the couple's composure. But there were still some embarrassing but necessary questions that had to be asked. In his years as a Detroit cop working corruption within the department, then as an investigator with the Michigan Attorney General's Organized Crime Task Force, Tobin had learned not to be fooled by appearances.

King resumed his seat at the dining room table with a fresh cup of coffee. "Refill, Chief Tobin?" The momentary break and short trip to the kitchen seemed to refresh the man.

"No thanks, Mr. King. Just a few more things I want to go over, then I'm going to get things rolling." He could see their relief.

"So," Tobin continued, "Cathy would've been the last person to see Timmy."

"Yes," said Mrs. King, leaning back and folding her hands on the table in front of her. "Cathy got home a lot later than we allow her to stay out, and of course, we were both up. It was around three o'clock when she finally got here. She told us Timmy had been here when she was getting ready to go out and had told her he was going outside to shoot some basketball, but then he came right back in because he said it was getting too dark. And Cathy said that was maybe about 7:20 or so, and he asked her for thirty cents so he could go up to the store at Hunter-Maple, and she said okay and gave him the money. She saw him go. She remembers because he poked his head into her room and told her to leave the front door ajar so he could get back in. Then she left at quarter to eight."

"And that accounts for the front door being open when the two of you got home a little over an hour later," said the chief, who reached up to run his hand through what little hair he had left. "Oh, before I forget, what about the skateboard? That still around?"

"That's gone too," answered Tim's father. "Looked all over the place. Just not here."

"Could he have taken it with him on the way to the store?" offered Tobin.

"Hard to say," replied Mr. King.

"Can you describe it for me?"

"Well," answered Marian, "the kids could probably do a better job, but it's bright orange, turned up the back, and it has two letters raised. It's the brand, but I don't know what the letters are."

"All right, I guess we can get that later. Can we talk with the other children if we need to?" asked Tobin.

"Of course. They should be getting up shortly."

"I don't think it's necessary we talk with them just now. Only if we need to, later," said Tobin, hoping it wouldn't be necessary.

Now, and how he hated this, he was going to have to ask those necessary questions. He'd asked them many times before, most of the time in much less comfortable surroundings, and of people with whom he felt a lot less comfortable. When children were reported missing, it was usually from broken homes or as a result of abuse. He thought of one particular case he'd worked as a sergeant in Detroit: a ten-year-old girl sexually abused by both parents. This certainly seemed a different kind of case, but the questions had to be asked.

"Mr. and Mrs. King, I'm going to have to ask you both a couple of, I'm afraid, very personal questions. Just to make sure we've covered all the bases. Mr. King, as an attorney, I'm sure you'll understand. First let me ask you if either of you have any enemies, especially you, Mr. King, in your line of work, perhaps an irate client?"

The Kings looked at each other.

"No," answered Barry, "at least none that I know of. Practically all my work is civil. I've had a couple of clients quite bitter about the outcome of a particular matter, but it's always been resolved to everybody's satisfaction, I guess. I guess I know what you're getting at, but, no, no enemies."

Mrs. King almost chuckled. "Gosh, none that I know of."

They appeared quite at ease with that one, thought Tobin. "You know," he said, "sometimes if parents fight, kids don't understand. We've seen it happen before—the parents have a fight, the child hears it, misinterprets some of the things that're said, decides it's his or her fault, and runs away. Or misinterprets and thinks that because the parents are yelling at each other, they don't love him."

"No, no fights, Chief. Marian and I have our share of spats, just like any normal couple, but they're few and far between, and we've even explained to the kids, the few times it's come up, that it's perfectly all right for a man and woman to disagree, and even raise their voices, but that certainly doesn't mean they don't love each other, or aren't happy married to each other." Barry was holding his wife's hand. "The children are well adjusted, and any disagreements in this house are resolved pretty quickly, with no hard feelings."

"Chief Tobin," Marian said, "Timmy didn't run away, I'm certain of it."

Tobin didn't think so, either, but didn't say so.

"Now, just so you both know, it's procedure for us to run checks on all family members in cases like this."

"Fine with us, Chief," she said. "Do whatever you have to do, just help us find our son, please."

Tobin got up from his chair. The Kings' sincerity was obvious, and as far as he was concerned, the interview was over. He glanced at his wristwatch. It was a little before 7:00 A.M., and Timmy King had been missing almost twelve hours. As he stood by the table, Tobin said, "What I'd like to do, Mr. and Mrs. King, is have officers Studt and Gracey stay with you. In case you get a call from Timmy or somebody else, they can go pick him up." He really wanted a cop there in case the Kings got a ransom call, but he didn't want to be quite that candid yet. "By the way, where did you say Timmy goes to school?"

"Adams."

"Good," said Tobin. "I'm going to head up there. He might show up. Thanks for your cooperation, both of you," said Tobin as Mr. King joined his wife at the front door. "Try not to worry—this is a top priority." Tobin shook both their hands and asked Studt to walk with him to his car.

When Tobin and Studt had reached the Chief's car, Tobin turned. "Don, I want you guys to stick with them. I don't know if they'll get a ransom call, but if they do, I want somebody here to handle it. Any kind of call. If that kid doesn't show up at school, we've got a big, big, problem." Tobin opened the car door and settled down in the seat.

"Yeah, I know — the other three kids . . . " Studt's voice trailed off.

"Nothing about that to the Kings," ordered Tobin as he hit the starter, "unless they bring it up. Then just handle it."

Tobin backed out of the Kings' driveway and headed up to Adams School.

11

Bob Jones thought he recognized the man sitting in his outer office, as he walked in from the hall. As Jones entered, the man in the chair jumped from his seat, startling the principal somewhat.

"Good morning," said Tobin, who draped his London Fog over the arm of the wooden chair and offered his hand.

"Yes, good morning. You're. . . ."

"Jerry Tobin, Birmingham Police." Tobin smiled.

"Ah, yes. Chief Tobin," replied Jones, almost with a sigh of relief. "Yes, I knew the face." He chuckled.

"Sit down, Chief," Jones said as he rounded his battle-scarred wooden desk and plopped his briefcase on the top. He slung his car coat on the coat tree and settled into the swivel chair. "Can I get you a cup of coffee? Instant, but it'll just take a minute to heat the water."

"No thanks, I'm all coffeed out. But go ahead."

Jones fiddled with the coffee makings on a small table at the rear of the room.

"Mr. Jones, Bob, if I may, I think we've got a problem with one of your sixth graders, Timmy King. He's been missing since around nine o'clock last night. I've got two of my men at the King house now, and we're still making checks, but it doesn't look good. I've got to think in terms of abduction, and I've got to ask you for your cooperation here at the school." Jones looked startled.

"Absolutely, you've got it. God, what can we do?" Jones allowed himself to think, fleetingly, of those reports about that little Berkley girl.

The young police executive gave Jones a brief sketch of the events leading up to his visit. But, while it was beginning to play heavily on his mind, Tobin did not allude to the three child abductions and slayings in Oakland County. There was no need to send out that kind of alarm, at least not here and now. "I'm probably going to want to talk with some of Timmy's friends," he said, "maybe some of those he especially hangs around with. I don't want to scare the kids, but this thing is pretty serious. Do you have any kind of information that might help us find the kid?" Jones swung around, spooned some instant coffee into his cup, poured the steaming water into it, and faced Tobin again.

"Well, Timmy is one of our favorites, one of those kids everybody likes. Lots of friends, good student, involved in a lot of school activities." Jones held the cup in both hands, and leaned back in the chair.

"Chief, what I'd like to do is talk to some of the kids first to narrow it down to the ones that might be able to help, then give the parents a call to make sure they don't have any objections. As a matter of fact, the kids know your liaison man Herb Duncan pretty well. He and I can both kind of feel them out." Jones sat back and waited for a response.

"Sure, I have no problem with that. Is Herb scheduled here today?" asked Tobin.

"Yes, in fact he's supposed to talk with Timmy's grade first hour," answered the principal.

Tobin had one of the best in Herb Duncan, a police officer who really had a way with kids and had been at it for a while, too. Duncan would hit the ground running with this because Tobin had called radio on the way to the school to tell them to hold the shift over and bring the day shift early. So Duncan would know all the particulars by the time he got to school.

"Good. That'd be fine. Work with Herb and find out anything you can. But I can tell you this, if Timmy doesn't show in a few minutes, this whole city is going to be crawling with police."

It was precisely 8:15 when the phone rang at 1618 Devonshire. Studt picked it up and spoke briefly, then handed the telephone to Tobin, who waved it off saying he'd take it on the kitchen extension. He figured it was Herb Duncan from the school, and didn't want to talk to him in front of the Kings, who were seated in the living room. He asked Duncan if Timmy had shown up.

"Shit," Tobin hissed into the mouthpiece. "All right, you started talking to anybody yet? Good, hang tight in there and keep me informed." The Chief walked back to the living room and sat down.

"I've just talked with Officer Duncan at the school. Timmy's not there," said Tobin in a soft, steady voice. The Kings showed no emotion. Tobin turned his gaze to Studt and Gracey, then back to the Kings. "First of all," he said to them, "again, I want these two officers to stay with you both, at all times, when you're at home. I don't know what we've got, just yet, but I've got to be honest with you — it's serious." Still, the Kings hadn't spoken. "Have you got a place where at least one of them can sleep? I want them to eat with you, answer the door and the phone, and keep the media out. Okay?" Tobin didn't wait for a reply. "I caught a radio broadcast on the way back from school and the media's already all over this thing. Remember, the phone rings, one of these guys picks it up. Okay?" Tobin stood up. "Now, I'm heading to the office, where I can get things rolling. Don, Tim, nobody gets in the front door, unless they're wearing a badge and a gun, okay?" It really wasn't a question, but the two policemen nodded and muttered, "Yes, sir." "Also," continued Tobin, who started to move toward the front door, but paused, "I'd like you, Mrs. King or Mr. King, to go over your phone lists again and make any calls that you might've forgotten earlier. By the way, Don," he added, turning to Studt, "I'm guessing that the media's going to call here. No interviews. None. Be polite but firm. Just tell them I'm the only one that can give out information, and I'm not here. I want to hold them off until we get some other things in place. Then, I'm probably going to want to call them myself. I don't know yet. Anyway, nothing for now."

"Yes, of course," said Marian, who'd risen from the loveseat. They were the first words either of the Kings had spoken since learning that Timmy hadn't shown up at school.

"Another thing, Mrs. King. I'm going to have Michigan Bell bring in some equipment to put on the phones, recorders that're activated automatically. I'll want an officer on the extension no matter who calls. Again, I want them to answer any phone calls. If it's a relative or friend they can just tell you, and if you want to talk, fine. If you don't, Tim or Don can handle it for you. If you do decide to talk, try to make it as brief as you can. I'd like to keep the line free."

"You think we might get a ransom call?" Barry asked. Marian grasped his hand.

"We certainly have to be ready for one if it comes. If it does, we hope to be able to get a trace on it."

"What should we do, I mean, how do we talk to such a person?" Marian asked.

"Do anything he asks," replied Tobin firmly. "Just listen closely to whatever he or she tells you to do."

"My God," exclaimed Marian, "you think it might be a woman who's taken my son?" Her eyes narrowed.

"We can't rule it out, Mrs. King," answered Jerry, who didn't believe it himself. "It's happened before, and again, we've got to cover all the bases." Marian released her husband's hand. "Anyway," Tobin went on, "if they ask for money, tell them you'll get it. I'll be talking with some banks this morning." He moved to the door. "Just so you both will know what is going to happen next, I'm going to notify all other police departments in the area. We're going to mount a house-to-house search and just keep spreading out. We're also going to look in garages, alleys, shopping centers, parks — we're not going to leave a stone unturned. I'm also going to be in touch with the State Police and the F.B.I. to enlist their help. Try not to worry," the Chief said as he walked out. How stupid that must sound, he thought out on the porch. To Studt, who had followed him out, he said, "Don, let's get that goddamned marked car out of here. Tell King, ask King if he'll move one of their cars out of the garage, so you can put the police car in and close the door." Tobin got in his car and left. The hunt was on.

12

Robbie always seemed to be running late. He glanced at his watch as he approached the conference room: 10:15 A.M. Well, he'd done the best he could, he thought as he turned the doorknob and entered. It was a small room packed with men, most of them seated at the rectangular wooden table. He recognized all but one or two.

Chief Tobin was just finishing a thought. "We've still got a city and a police department to run, and I want to keep as much of the activity away from their normal, day-to-day operation as I can. Hi, Robbie, I guess Joe's already told you what we've got, eh?"

"Yeah, sorry I'm a little late," said Robertson, leaning against the wall. "Go ahead, Chief. You can fill me in when you're done."

"Haven't been at it that long. I'm just letting our people, and yours, know what moves we've made so far. Very simply, we've got a missing eleven-year-old, and far as I'm concerned, it's an abduction. We've got people from a half-dozen shops out looking right now, plus a few of Spreen's men and the chopper. I was just telling these guys that I'm setting up a mobile command post in Poppleton Park, pretty close to where the Kings live, because I don't want to disrupt city business any more than we have to." Tobin paused. "Lieutenant, we could sure use your people."

"You got 'em," said Robertson. He liked the way Tobin had put it together so far.

"Great," replied the Chief, turning back to the others, "that's about it for now. Let's hit the street." As the others were getting up from their chairs to leave, he said, "Robbie, I'd like to have you meet the Kings, see where they live, what kind of people they are. Okay?"

"Sure. Give me just a minute to run a couple of things by Joe." He signaled Krease, who was talking with a couple of his men by the door. Krease walked to the front of the room to join his boss, as Tobin, already engrossed in conversation with two of his own men, led them a few steps away.

"Joe, there's no question in my mind about what we've got. How about you?"

"Nope," replied Krease. "Got to be the same one. Too much fits, at least so far. Lieutenant, where the hell are we going to put everybody? I'm assuming you're going to call in some more help," said Krease. It sounded more like a plea than a question.

"Got to, Joe. I'm going to call Hassinger and tell him we need twenty-five of the best State Police dicks we got. As far as what we'll do with them, that mobile command post that Tobin's talking about doesn't sound like it's going to hold even his people for long. Well, he and I can talk about that. Meantime, you need anything?"

"We're all right for now. I'm bringing everybody from the Northland office and we'll do the search. I don't know, though, it almost seems like a waste of time."

"Yeah, I don't think we're going to find the kid in somebody's garage, either. But people around here are mad as hell, and we've got to at least show them we're doing all the things you're supposed to do when a kid is snatched. Anyway, until we get this thing organized these cops have to be doing something. Might as well be looking behind trees, or whatever. Who knows, one of them might just turn up something."

Robertson's visit to the King household convinced him that Tobin was right about the family. They were, as Tobin had said on the ride over, remarkably well-composed, considering. And while no one had mentioned the other three child abductions and homicides, both Tobin and Robertson knew that it had to have crossed the Kings' minds. They read newspapers and watched television. How could they not know? Robbie let his mind wander. Faith. That had to be the answer, he thought, as Tobin drove him over to the mobile command post. Faith was what the Kings were all about. Timmy would be okay no matter what. It was a faith bordering on naivete.

Robertson had assured the Kings that the State Police would not rest until their son had been found. He could not promise more.

Poppleton Park was about ten acres of clipped grass and well-cared-for trees and shrubs just a mile from the King home. In the summertime it offered residents a tennis court and ball diamond, and it was a favorite retreat for young couples. Now, some fourteen hours after the disappearance of Timmy King, Poppleton Park would serve as a police command post. The laughter and whispers of young people were replaced by the clatter of the Oakland County Sheriff's helicopter, just now gently settling down about thirty yards from the mobile home that Tobin had requested from a local dealership. The chopper balanced itself six inches from the ground, then clunked down. Tobin and Robertson parked nearby as the pilot idled the rotors, and a figure popped from the plexiglas bubble, wearing brown Wellingtons, khaki pants, and a heavy brown leather flight jacket with a gold sheriff's badge on the left breast. The figure ducked low under the whipping blades, and in a half-crouch, quickly scooted out from under them, holding his brown baseball cap tightly to his head.

"Hi, Chief Tobin?" said the deputy as he swaggered up to where Tobin and Robertson stood.

"Yeah. How you doing, Deputy?" answered Tobin. Putting his hand to Robertson's shoulder, he said, "Lieutenant Robertson, State." "You've got the LEIN* on him?" asked Tobin of the sheriff's man, without waiting for the reply. "So you know what he was wearing."

"Yeah, we oughta be able to spot the red jacket, if he's still wearing it, since there's no foliage on the trees. We do a standard grid pattern, real tight and low as we can."

"Good," interrupted Robertson, who wanted to keep it short because a million things had to be done yet. "You guys spot anything out of place, give us a holler on the radio and we'll get some people over there right away."

"Fine, Lieutenant," said the young deputy, and with that he spun around, and in the half-crouch, scudded back to the waiting helicopter. With a thumbs up signal from both pilot and passenger, the rotors picked up rpms, and the machine fairly leaped into the air, leveling off at about two hundred feet.

Krease and three other detectives were in what was supposed to be the trailer's kitchen but for now was, in effect, a war room. A huge street map was spread over the kitchen table. Tobin and Robertson leaned against the sink, while Krease and the others seated themselves around the table on built-in benches. Two of the other three men were Robertson's—Waldron and Rivard—and the other was Tobin's—Detective Jack Kalbfleisch.

Kalbfleisch, who was in charge of the street teams, explained that Ferndale, Southfield, Berkley, Royal Oak, Troy, and of course, Birmingham, had two-man teams of detectives doing a house-to-house, starting on the Kings' street and fanning out toward all points of the compass.

*Law Enforcement Information Network.

Each had a LEIN copy, noting the boy's physical description and the clothes he was last wearing. The detective teams had special instructions to work closely with the helicopter in coordinating the search. The detective teams were not to limit their physical search to the streets and alleys. Every square inch of ground in the city was to be scrutinized, and Tobin had ordered that trash bags and cans be searched for articles of clothing, the skateboard, or anything else. The message was to talk to people, look around, and talk some more.

While Robertson and Kalbfleisch had never met personally before, he knew the solidly-built detective by reputation. He'd done some really good police work on the Srock case, and Robertson was pleased to have him coordinating the search.

Krease spoke. "Lieutenant, another thing. Timmy apparently had a paper route. We ought to. . . ."

"Absolutely," Robbie interrupted, "we'll put a team on it." He turned to Tobin. "Jerry, let's get a list of his customers from the Kings and have a team follow it and talk to all of 'em."

"Good idea. Jack, you take care of that. Better do it yourself, the Kings, I mean."

Kalbfleisch slid from the rear bench, opened the trailer door, and was gone.

"Almost forgot," said Tobin, as he moved to the seat vacated by Kalbfleisch. "We have a pretty darn good auxiliary police force. A guy by the name of Jack Strauss is the acting Chief. Jack's a civilian, but he's a top notch auxiliary policeman, dedicated and thorough. He'll get his guys together, a couple dozen of them, and then operate out of here. They live all over the city, and they know about places to look that we might not think of — sheds, old garages, back lots, that kind of thing."

"Where the hell we going to put all these people?" Rivard asked of no one in particular. "We've got twenty-five of our people, or will have by tomorrow, more than a half-dozen departments with two-and some-times four-man teams, and the Sheriff's people, not to mention Mort Nichols, of the F.B.I., and his people working with the Task Force."

Robertson agreed. "Chief, we're going to have fifty or sixty people that we'll have to find some place for, and this trailer just isn't going to hold everything and everybody."

Tobin replied thoughtfully, "Yeah, you're right . . . we've already outgrown this thing. I do want to keep us somewhat separate from the police station and city hall."

Robbie nodded, and Krease added, "Yeah, we don't want to be tripping over them any more than they want to be tripping over us. Just hamper the investigation."

"Okay," said Jerry. "Say, why not the Adams Street firehouse? They've got an upstairs with a good-sized recreation room and another smaller room where they got the pool table."

"What about the firemen?" asked Krease.

"Hell, just kick 'em out," grumbled Rivard. They chuckled.

Tobin said, "Robbie, let's go see Bob Kenning, our city manager and see if we can get ourselves a fire station."

13

"The people who run this city are really something, Robbie," exclaimed Tobin, as he wheeled into the Adams Street fire station, and around to the back lot. He killed the engine, and turned in his seat to face Robertson. "This is a pretty cooperative bunch of people. I mean, once in a while, I gotta do a little arm-twisting, but I can't believe the kind of support we're getting from Kenning on this one."

As he got out of the car Robertson thought that arm-twisting was probably something Tobin was pretty good at. Barely into his forties and Chief of Police in one of the most affluent communities in the Midwest, Tobin was aggressive, a smooth-talker, and a sharp dresser, with a master's degree in Criminal Justice and a reputation for arrogance. Tobin's progressive approach to police work had ruffled more than a few feathers. On the other hand, thought Robertson, there's nothing wrong with that. Some of these old guys need somebody to drag them kicking and screaming into the twentieth century.

Tobin reached the door, but hesitated before he opened it. "Bob damn near insisted we move into the fire station, and got mad when I mentioned rent. He said, 'You just worry about the kid. Let me worry about the money. What else do you need? I know you're gonna have lots of people on lots of overtime. I don't care. You just get the kid back.'"

The station was just about five minutes from the Mobile Command Post in Poppleton Park and about five minutes from the King house. Easy enough access, thought Robertson, as he followed Tobin down the hall to the Fire Chief's office. With a shopping center right across the street all the comings and goings over here should go relatively unnoticed. The Task Force had to be able to operate without causing too much disruption.

Chief Richard Nunley, a barrel-chested man with brush-cut white hair, was seated behind his desk, with the phone to his ear.

"Yeah, Bob, here they are now. Thanks for the call." Nunley was a living legend among firefighters, Robertson remembered. The myth about policemen and firemen being rivals is nonsense. The two professions have nothing but the highest regard for each other and work a lot closer with each other than most people believe. Policemen know that more firemen die in the line of duty than cops. Nunley greeted the two men and, without wasting time, led them down the hall and up the rear stairs. Robertson noticed the burn-scar tissue that began behind Nunley's left ear and ran down the neck to the shoulder.

As the three men stood at the top of the landing, Tobin focused on the two gaping holes in the floor, each bordered on three sides by low, brass railings. "Does this mean I can use one of those firemen's slides to get downstairs, if I want to?"

Nunley laughed. "Sure. I can see it now, 'Local Police Chief Breaks His Ass Using The Fireman's Slide.'"

The upstairs recreation room and dormitory was large, about seventy-five by forty-five feet. Off to one side was another, smaller room, with a pool table in it. Six wooden bunk beds were against the south wall on the carpeted area, with three single beds lined up just opposite them. On the east wall was a huge combination color TV/stereo, faced by several large upholstered armchairs. A large, low coffee table scattered with magazines sat in front of a long couch. Against the west wall were a dozen hooks with each firefighter's coat and hat hanging from them. The boots were placed neatly under each coat. The entire room, save for the magazines on the coffee table, was neat as a pin.

"Looks good, Dick," said Tobin, turning to Robertson. "How about it, Robbie?"

"Just fine," answered the other.

"Good," exclaimed Nunley. "It's done. What's next?"

"Well," said Robertson, "I wanna' tell Joe, my operations man, to start bringing some of our stuff up here, and I've got to call Michigan Bell. We need at least a half-dozen phones yesterday, so I guess we better get going."

Tips had already begun pouring in. The abduction had focused the media spotlight on Birmingham, and journalists, both print and electronic, were swarming over the city like locusts. The *Daily Tribune* ran the headline: B'HAM BOY, 11, MISSING, with a black-and-white photo of the Sheriff's helicopter taking off from Poppleton Park against a stark background of bare trees and a half-dozen police cars. The *Tribune*'s lead was: MORE THAN 50 POLICE OFFICERS SEARCHED TODAY FOR A BIRMINGHAM BOY, MISSING SINCE 8PM WEDNESDAY. The Detroit papers didn't headline it, but did give it a front page. Local TV and radio calls flooded the police switchboard, and any news organization with more than a one-person news staff had people there.

Somebody, probably Tobin, decided that Tobin should handle the media. Robertson was comfortable with that. Tobin was definitely presentable, with his prep school looks and manner, certainly knowledgeable, and after the Srock case, at least fleetingly familiar with the reporters who covered the metropolitan area.

Several dozen uniformed police were by now scouring the streets, aided by Strauss's reservists, and Krease had the plainclothes Task Force on its own house-to-house canvass. The Sheriff's helicopter was searching the area bounded by Twelve Mile to the south, Twenty Mile to the north, Lahser Road to the west, and Coolidge Road to the east, roughly eighty square miles.

The community was both angry and shocked. The Kings lived only three blocks from where Sheila Srock had been murdered fifteen months before, and things like this just weren't supposed to happen in Birmingham.

Robertson asked Krease to handle the move to the fire station, since he himself had some other administrative things to tend to. One was another call to Hassinger because District would have to be brought up to date. He also wanted more talk with Hogan. Krease was up to his neck in the investigation, and was less than ecstatic about having to ramrod another move, the second in the last six hours. They'd just gotten settled after moving all the paperclips and rubberbands from Northland to the Birmingham P.D.'s two-room Detective Bureau. The Task Force trying to stay out of Birmingham's way, Birmingham trying to keep clear of the Task Force, there was paper all over the place, and the phones were ringing off the hook. Frustration prompted Krease to step out of his usual understated character and bellow from the door:

"All right, let's everybody grab something and move. We gotta get all this crap outta here and over to the firehouse." He felt better.

Meanwhile, Tobin, who'd dropped Robertson off at his office, headed back to Poppleton Park. He had some things he wanted to bounce off his Chief of Detectives. He'd called him off the street, with instructions to meet him back at the CP.

Seated at the old kitchen table in the trailer again, across from Kalbfleisch, Tobin told him about the firehouse, and then, "Jack, I need some input on this thing—let's share some thoughts." Tobin looked at his watch. It was nearly 3:30. "Look, it's been over eighteen hours, with no ransom call. You think we're going to get one?"

"My guess is no," replied the burly detective. "My guess is we've got ourselves another child killer victim, and he's not interested in money, he's interested in killing children."

"Yeah," said Tobin, thoughtfully, "if the guy wanted money, we'd have heard something by now. He's got what he wants. All right, I don't see any sense in trying to keep the lid on. What I mean is, I'm kind of thinking about going very public with this whole thing. We've already got every damn reporter within a hundred miles poking around, so what's your feeling on a news conference? At least that way, if we level with the media and get the word out officially that we've called the Task Force in, hell, Jack, the public might help us solve this thing." Kalbfleisch started to respond, but Tobin cut him off again. "At least we can tell the reporters that if they quit bugging us, and play ball, we'll give them regular updates on whatever information we can give out. That'll stop the calls, and some of the bad information that's gotten out already. But I'm telling you, all we've got to do is start stonewalling those bastards, and they're just going to make it that much harder for us."

"Yeah," said Kalbfleisch half-heartedly. He leaned back against the window bench with both arms outstretched along the top of the seat cushions. "The only thing is, what the hell are you going to say at this press conference?"

Robertson listened to the six o'clock news on WJR while driving back to the firehouse to check on the move. He'd grabbed a quick sandwich at Alban's, which was practically next door to the drugstore Timmy'd gone to with his thirty cents, about twenty-two hours earlier. WJR led with the child abduction in Birmingham, followed by some sidebar stuff from residents and an unnamed cop, and then quite a bit of background on the other three abduction-slayings.

It was about 6:20 when he pulled into the rear parking lot. He entered through the back door and trudged up the stairs. There were about a dozen members of the Task Force milling around—a couple on phones, some writing, the girls typing. The City of Birmingham had given them a number of folding chairs and a couple of long folding tables. He walked over to Krease.

"Hi, Joe. All set?"

"Yeah, Lieutenant. Michigan Bell just left about thirty minutes ago. Those guys are really something. You know," said Krease, who'd perked up a lot since the move to the firehouse, "one of them was telling me that as soon as Tobin called, everybody dropped what they were doing and hustled on over here to set us up. I had 'em put a half dozen phones in the Tip Room over there," Joe pointed at the room with the pool table, "and four phones out here on these tables. Boy, it's nice to have some room to move around in."

"Looks like the place was made for you, Joe. Anything from the street yet?"

"Nope. Some of the guys are still out, and the ones that came back in are headed back out. I told them to grab a bite or knock off for the day, if they want, but nobody wants to go home yet. They're really fired up."

"Sergeant," called a voice from behind. "Jesus, Sergeant." It was Tom Cattel from Ferndale. Krease and Robertson turned. "We've just had a call from a witness, at least she thinks she might have seen Timmy talking to some guy last night around 8:30 or 9:00, talking to some guy standing next to a Gremlin in the Chatham parking lot."

Robertson and Krease looked at each other. Activity in the room stopped. Krease, who was not an excitable person, said, "Oh." Robbie smiled.

"Desimone and I are on the way over now," Cattel went on excitedly. "She says she was out of town yesterday and didn't see the papers until after she got home from work about an hour ago. Says she's been trying to get through, but the lines were always busy."

The woman who greeted Cattel and Desimone was named Edith Raubacher. She'd gone to Flint, Michigan, on March 17 to visit her daughter's family and hadn't gotten back to Birmingham until about 7:30 that night. She'd gone right over to the Chatham supermarket to do some shopping, and was returning to her car about 8:30.

"Then," she said in a soft voice, "I saw this boy, a young boy, talking to a man who was standing beside one of those funny-looking little Gremlin cars. I know that's what it was, because I always have to smile every time I see them on television. Anyway," she continued, "I just kept right on going to my car, and put the groceries in, and came right home and went to bed."

Cattel, who'd been sipping a cup of coffee Raubacher had made him, said, "Mrs. Raubacher, it was pretty dark by then. . . ."

"Oh, I know, Officer Cattel, but they were close to one of those bright lights that they have in the parking lot."

"Mrs. Raubacher, how far away from them were you?"

"Oh, I don't know," said the woman, hesitating, "I'm not real good. . . ."

"Well," interrupted Desimone, "ten feet, twenty feet, more?"

"I guess maybe from here to my front sidewalk. Farther than twenty feet—maybe not as far as the front walk, though."

"I'm guessing that from where we're sitting in your living room, the front walk is close to forty feet, maybe forty-five. That's a long way," Cattel declared.

"No, it wasn't that far, I guess. They were near the light in the next aisle over from my car. Perhaps twenty-five or thirty feet, officer." Raubacher sipped her tea.

"Okay," said Desimone. "Could you hear what they were saying?"

"No, I couldn't, but they were talking, I know that."

"Mrs. Raubacher," asked Cattel, "were they close enough that the man could have reached right out and touched the boy without taking any steps?"

"Yes. Yes, I think so."

Cattel jotted something down on a small note pad he'd pulled from his shirt pocket.

"Okay, Mrs. Raubacher," said Desimone, sighing, and reaching for his coffee, "exactly what was their position? To you, I mean?"

"Well, they were facing each other, but I was looking at them kind of from the side."

"Like were they turned, say, ninety degrees from you?" asked Desimone.

"No, I don't think quite like that. More of an angle, you know," explained the woman. "About like this," and she made a forty-five-degree angle with her hands on the table. "Okay," said Desimone. "Mrs. Raubacher, who was closer to you, the boy or the man?"

"Oh, the boy, of course."

"Could you tell if the boy was carrying anything, maybe holding something?" asked Cattel, trying for the skateboard.

"Well," she said, turning to him, "it looked like he could have been holding something. I couldn't really see his hands, but yes, I did see something sticking out from in front of his leg, part of it seemed to be almost touching the ground." Cattel jotted something else down on the pad. He looked from her to Desimone.

"Mrs. Raubacher," asked Desimone, "from the angle you described, I guess you couldn't see the boy's face clearly, but," he reached into his inside suitcoat pocket and pulled out a school photograph, "do you think you might be able to tell us if the boy in this picture might be the one you saw?"

Mrs. Raubacher studied the picture, close up, then at arm's length. "I guess it could have been, you know. It's hard to say."

"Look at it closely, Mrs. Raubacher," said Desimone, "and take your time. Keep the picture for a minute, while we keep talking."

"What about the man, Mrs. Raubacher," interjected Cattel. "If the boy was turned so you couldn't see all his face, but the two were facing each other, then the man was facing you as you were walking. That right?"

Raubacher looked up from the picture of Timmy she was holding. "Yes, I could see more of his face, but you know it was dark."

"But you did say they were standing right under the light," stated Cattel, looking down at his notes.

"Not right under the light, Detective Cattel. No, I didn't say right under the light. I said near the light. It was still kind of dark."

"Okay, I understand," said Cattel, clearing his throat. "Was it light enough for you to describe what the boy was wearing?"

"Yes, I think so," she said, putting Timmy's picture down on the table. "He had a jacket on, I know that. I really didn't notice his shoes, but his trousers were dark, and the jacket was, well. . . . " She thought a moment. "His jacket was lighter, but not much, sort of a red color with one of those small collars like baseball players wear."

"An athletic jacket, Mrs. Raubacher?" asked Desimone.

"Yes, like boys wear."

"Mrs. Raubacher," inquired Cattel, "you started to tell us about the man. Did you get a pretty good look at him?"

"Well, yes, I guess I did. Like I said it was dark, even with the light, but yes."

"Well, could you describe him, Mrs. Raubacher?" asked Desimone, a little impatiently. Raubacher appeared a little nervous, thought Desimone. Maybe he was pushing too hard. She squirmed in the chair.

"Well, Officer — er, Detective Desimone," she said, clearing her throat, "he was, sort of," she hesitated, reaching for the word, "swarthy, you know. Almost Mexican, you know, but not really. I mean he had Mexican, or Mediterranean features. His hair was full and dark."

"No hat, then, eh?" interrupted Cattel.

"No, no hat," she replied, glancing at him. "His hair was full and dark, and he had long, heavy sideburns. Sort of a long face, I think . . . kind of a long nose."

"Mustache?" interjected Desimone.

"No, no mustache. Just that long hair," she replied. "He was a pleasant enough looking young man, I guess, except for those long sideburns. You know, I don't like to see young men wear their hair that long, especially the sideburns."

"You say 'young man,' Mrs. Raubacher. How young a man would you say he is, I mean, over twenty, but less than say forty?" he asked.

She put her finger to the corner of her mouth. "I'd have to say he was a lot younger than forty, Detective Desimone. I'd have to say he was somewhere between maybe twenty-five and thirty years old."

"Good, Mrs. Raubacher, that's fine," said Cattel. "Now, what kind of a build would you say he has? I mean, was he a big man, little man, short, tall, heavy-set, or what?"

"He was . . . " she spoke slowly, "sort of average, I guess. Can I get either of you some more coffee?" she added.

"No thanks," replied Cattel, not wanting to disrupt her train of thought.

"Under six feet?" Desimone continued.

"Yes, but almost six feet, I'd say."

"Weight?"

"I'm not good at weight at all. . . . "

"No, you're doing just fine, Mrs. Raubacher," Desimone encouraged, "just fine. Well, was he, say, under two hundred pounds?"

"Oh my, yes. I guess I'd say more like 150 pounds or so, maybe a little heavier than that."

"Could you tell the color of his clothes, Mrs. Raubacher?" asked Cattel, drinking the last swallow of his coffee.

"Not really, I just think they were dark, you know, pants, and a lighter jacket. I couldn't really tell what color, with the light and all. . . ." She sounded apologetic.

"That's okay," said Cattel, smiling. "You've been a great help. I know it's difficult. Just another couple of minutes, and we'll be through for now."

"Yeah," said Desimone, who glanced at his watch and flipped his note pad to a clean page. "I don't think we asked you about the car, the Gremlin. Could you tell the color of the car, Mrs. Raubacher?"

"Oh, yes, as I said earlier, I always notice those little Gremlins. Well, this one was blue, with one of those stripes that looks like a hockey stick along the side," she said confidently and with some pride. "Yes, I know it was blue with the stripe along the side."

"And the stripe?" asked Cattel. "What color was the stripe?"

"Oh, it was white," she replied assuredly, "it was a white hockey-stick stripe."

"Okay, Mrs. Raubacher," said Desimone as he rose from the chair. "Listen, you've been, really a great help. We can't thank you enough for your cooperation." As she got up from the table he added, "One more thing, if it wouldn't be too much trouble. We might like to have you work with a police artist. You can tell him the man's description, just like you did with us, and he'll try and draw a picture of him, a composite, we call it. By the way," asked Desimone, as the three reached the front door, "we'd like to ask you not to tell anybody what you told us. In fact, we'd prefer you didn't even tell anybody that we were here. And, especially," said the detective as he reached for the doorknob, "please don't talk with any reporters."

"No, of course not, Detective Desimone. No, I won't say anything to anybody, you can be sure of that."

The two detectives walked to the car. As Desimone backed out, Cattel spoke. "Well, what do you think, Norm?"

"I don't know. It looks okay, but I'm not going to get excited about it till we see if her story holds water. Let's see what she tells the artist, tomorrow. She still didn't give us a positive make on Timmy, but that sure as hell could've been him, and that is the closest store to his house. But I just don't know."

"Me either," agreed Cattel. "But I'm guessing it's the best thing we got so far."

"Why's that?"

"'Cause it's the only thing we got so far."

It was getting on toward 11:30 when Cattel and Desimone plodded up the stairs to the Task Force squad room in the firehall. Krease was tied up on the phone. A half-dozen other detectives were in various stages of winding up the long day. Cattel and Desimone pulled chairs up on either side of Krease, who was seated at the end of the long table. He hung up, and looked at Desimone.

"Well, whaddaya got?" Joe asked, taking off his glasses and rubbing his eyes as he leaned back into the metal folding chair. Desimone told him.

"Yeah," said Krease. Fatigue was written all over his face. "Let's get her over here tomorrow to work with Powell."

Watson from the Sheriff's Department appeared from the tip room. "Sarge, you believe this shit?" He walked to where the three men were seated. He was holding a small piece of notepaper. He picked up a folding chair on the way over and set it between Desimone and Krease.

"Along about now, I'll believe anything," replied Krease. "What's the problem?"

Watson, seated, held the note in front of him, for reference.

"Some asshole just called, says he's got a good tip on the missing boy." Watson paused.

"Yeah, so?" asked Krease, impatiently.

"Well," continued Watson, "he says it'll cost us two million bucks to find out. Then he hangs up. No name."

"Oh, for Christ's sake," said Krease as he pushed himself out of his chair and headed for his coat. "I'm outta here. See you tomorrow."

14

"This place looks like a bookie parlor, Joe," laughed Robbie, as he and Krease stood in the Squad Room. All ten phones were either busy or ringing, and the six o'clock news the previous night had done it. Now everybody in the metro area knew that Birmingham had a missing eleven-year-old, and while there'd been no official reference to Timmy as the fourth victim of the Oakland County child killer, there didn't need to be. Everything fit, and everybody knew it.

Krease flopped his coat over the end of the table and reached for a phone. He put it to his ear, hung it up, and picked up the one next to it. To Robertson he said, "Lights. Lights are what we need on these things, so we can tell which one's ringing." After a brief conversation, he turned to Robertson. "That was Dick over at the lab. He's got those pictures of the tire tracks at the Kristine scene and says they came out real clear. Think I'll take them over to Goodyear and have some of their experts take a look. Be nice if they were some weird make or model, kind of narrow it down."

"Yeah, that'd help, all right," said Robbie. "By the way, I'll talk with Bell about lights for the phones. You've got enough to do."

"Thanks, Lieutenant. Yeah, we're gonna' want to talk with Amy Walters again, the gal at the drugstore where he bought the candy. Also, I've got to get the crews out to do the other businesses this morning. Maybe he stopped someplace else. Kids just kind of wander around and in and out. Who knows? And, like I was saying at breakfast, I've got to get Powell down here to do a composite with Mrs. Raubacher."

"Better give him a call quick, Joe," interrupted Robertson. "This snow and all, it's gonna' take him a while to get down here." Gary Powell was the State Police artist, and a renowned one at that, at State Police Headquarters in Lansing, normally about an hour-and-a-quarter drive from Birmingham. This particular morning, however, March 18, the city lay under a seven-inch blanket of snow. Thirty-six hours before, the day Timmy had disappeared, the temperature had been in the 70s.

"Good idea," said Krease. "Yeah, better get started, I guess."

"I've got a bunch of stuff to do at District. Well," he turned and headed for the stairs, "keep me advised."

Powell wasn't available. "Damn!" muttered Krease to himself as he hung up the phone. He looked around the room. "Cattel," he called, "Powell isn't available. Now, we've got to get your witness over here to-day while everything's still fresh. You got anybody local we can use to do the composite?"

Cattel thought for a minute. "Well, yeah, as a matter of fact there's a gal in Royal Oak. The school. She's pretty good. Used her before on a couple of occasions."

"Good," Krease said. "Get her on the phone, tell her you're bringing a witness down. Then give Raubacher a call. You and Desimone."

After making sure everybody had an assignment, Krease grabbed Detective Sergeant Louis Orlich and headed over to the Chatham Supermarket in the Hunter/Maple shopping strip, where Mrs. Raubacher had done her shopping. It was barely a mile from the Adams Street fire station, but even though the rush hour was over, traffic was miserably snarled because of the heavy snow. As Krease turned left onto Maple he said, "Maybe the guy Raubacher saw talking to the boy had done some shopping. I think what we have to do is ask the manager if we can get the names and addresses of everybody who came into the store that night and paid by check. Then we'll talk to each and every one of the people who were in there shopping between eight and eleven o'clock, or so. And later, if we get a good composite, we can go back and show 'em the picture." Krease stopped talking. He was pretty satisfied with what he'd said.

"Ever thought about getting into police work?" asked Orlich.

Shortly before noon, Cattel and Desimone, who'd spent the morning with Mrs. Raubacher and the artist in Royal Oak, returned with the composite. It had been touch and go, Cattel said, with both the artist and the witness. They had worked well for the first forty-five minutes, then Raubacher announced that she just didn't remember what the man looked like at all. To make things worse, the artist hadn't been very patient with her. It had suddenly dawned on Mrs. Raubacher that she was a linchpin in an enormously big investigation, a larger-than-life drama, and it scared her. Finally the two detectives had told the artist to leave for a while. The next twenty minutes they spent chatting with Mrs. Raubacher about her family, a favorite subject and a relaxing one. By the time the artist got back from her break, Mrs. Raubacher was eager to go to work. It took the witness and the artist, who by now were getting along famously (Mrs. Raubacher said later that the artist reminded her of her daughter) about forty-five minutes to produce a likeness composite. "It looks just like him. That's him!" Mrs. Raubacher had exclaimed, rather proudly.

In the Squad Room at the fire station, detectives were focusing on a tip that had come into the Berkley Police Department the previous night. A tipster had informed police that he'd seen a man, whom he knew slightly, load a stuffed duffel bag into the trunk of his car. The tipster was "pretty sure" that Timothy King was in the duffel bag and that the man, the duffel bag, and Timmy King, were headed up north to a place near Alpena. The State Police Post in Alpena had to be notified; at this point nothing could be overlooked.

It was now thirty-nine hours into the King investigation, and according to Reserve Police Chief Jack Strauss, "So many people were involved in the investigation, that additional personnel would have simply cluttered up the scenery." So Strauss and his people steered clear of the Birmingham Police Department and the Command Post in Poppleton Park. A few of them settled in the Task Force Squad Room at the fire station, to make sure they were available, if needed.

The neighborhood canvass had left few stones unturned. Krease's men were still talking with business people in the immediate area, and a few crews were still doing house-to-house, mostly to catch people they had missed before. Those police who always worked the suburbs were not surprised that many of the people whose doors they beat on actually invited them into their living rooms for coffee. Birmingham had rallied, and the cooperation and courtesy of her citizens was extraordinary.

It was a culture shock for the Detroit team, the elite Squad Seven homicide detectives, whose regular beat was the core of "Murder City." When they knocked on a door in the inner city, they did it while standing to the side. Squad Seven was used to talking through chained front doors, and when they did get into living rooms, it was rarely by invitation.

"Joe," said Waldron, "I've just been looking at the paper on Stebbins, Robinson, and Kristine. It's weird," he went on, scratching his ear, "Stebbins and Mihelich were both snatched on a Sunday, and Jill and Timmy both disappeared on a Wednesday. Wonder what the hell that means?"

Krease shrugged. "Probably nothing."

"You don't think it might be important?" asked Waldron, apparently not satisfied with the answer.

"Probably ought to run it by Tobias," said Krease, "but I doubt it's anything. Why don't you. . . ."

"Joe," it was Chief Tobin, who'd just hit the top of the stairs. "See you a minute?"

"Yeah, sure Chief," he said as he turned from Waldron and walked to where Tobin stood. Tobin put his arm on Krease's shoulder and walked him away from the tables and phones. "Joe, I want a full-blown news conference this afternoon."

"Okay," said Krease with a blank look. "Any special reason?" Joe wasn't at all sure it was such a good idea.

"I've been thinking," Tobin explained. "First of all, we must have a zillion reporters hanging around talking to people who aren't giving the right answers. Christ, the networks have even picked up on this now, and they have people on the way. I think we have to have press briefings on a regular basis, maybe even one in the morning and another one in the afternoon, if we want their cooperation. Another thing it's going to do is free up the telephones and some of our people. I've got people right now spending all their time just taking media calls."

"Yeah," said Krease, letting some of the Chief's reasoning sink in. "Yeah, that makes sense."

"Another thing," continued Tobin. "Jack says the composite's done, and I think it'd be a good idea to let as many people see what this guy looks like as we can. No better way than to put it in front of a dozen TV cameras. We'll give 'em the whole nine yards, the profile, the composite, and the Gremlin. There's a couple of million people out there and we might get lucky."

"Yeah," said Krease, a little more enthusiastically this time. "The only thing that concerns me is that once those lights go on, we're really on the spot. I mean, there are certain things I would just as soon not have get out."

Tobin nodded. "I know. But what we can do is get 'em all together and talk to 'em before they turn the cameras on. You know, background stuff. We'll tell 'em what we'll talk about, and what we won't talk about."

"You really think they're going to stick to any ground rules once the cameras start turning?" asked Krease skeptically.

"Sure, why not? Anyway, you can always refuse to answer. No law says they can't ask, but," Tobin smiled, "no law says we have to answer. Besides, I really think they will play by the rules."

Tobin had had considerable media exposure during his police career. He looked good and felt good in front of a TV camera. Joe, on the other hand, felt that if he never had to stand in front of another TV camera again, it'd be too soon.

"Maybe you're right, Chief," said Krease. Tobin or Robertson would do all the talking anyway, thought Krease, somewhat relieved.

"There is one other thing, Joe," said Tobin, "another reason for having the news conference. Barry and Marian King want one. Barry wants to make an appeal on television for Timmy to come home, and for the guy that's got him, to let him."

Tobin had scheduled the news conference at City Hall for 3:30, just a little over two and one-half hours away, with the media to be there at three for the backgrounder. That left Krease with a lot of things to do in a relatively short period of time, the first of which was to cancel any thought of lunch. Next was a phone call to Robertson, who'd gone back to District. Robertson already knew about the news conference. "I want you to handle the whole thing, Joe," he said. "I mean, you and Tobin. I just think it's a good idea to have somebody there from the Task Force, even though it's really Jerry's show, and it'll be a good chance for you to get your feet wet. After all, you're running the whole show. I'll just be a member of the audience."

"He's the boss," thought Krease as he tried to psych himself up for the news conference.

15

The investigators were literally faced with a life-and-death situation. Timmy had been missing for nearly forty-eight hours. If the killer's past M.O. meant anything, if he was following some perverse pattern, it could mean that the last hours of Timmy King's life were literally ticking away. Drastic measures would be necessary to save the youngster's life, if indeed, it could be done at all. The Oakland County Chiefs and the Task Force had discussed options. They figured they had anywhere between two and seventeen days left to find him.

As nearly as could be determined by the Medical Examiner, the other three children had been dropped sometime after midnight, within hours after they'd been murdered. The killer transported the children in some kind of car, van, or truck, possibly a Gremlin. And whatever kind of vehicle it was, it moved on the streets and roads of Oakland County. What if every car on the streets of Oakland County after midnight were stopped and searched by police?

The very contemplation of such a move on the part of the Task Force was heresy and blatantly unconstitutional, a violation of the Fourth Amendment proscription of unreasonable search and seizure. Even under these life-and-death circumstances, it would take a hundred years to find a judge to sign such a blanket search warrant. Yet the search of every vehicle that moved after midnight in Oakland County, though patently illegal, could possibly save the life of eleven-year-old Timmy King. The Chiefs were willing to take the risk, with one stipulation.

A call was made, and a meeting arranged with Dick Thompson, Brooks Patterson's brilliant and aggressive young Chief Assistant. If Patterson's office would give them some kind of written authorization, knowing full well it stopped far short of a bona fide search warrant, they'd take the plunge. Thompson researched the issue and issued this two-page memorandum over his signature:

March 18, 1977

Memorandum
To: Law Enforcement Officers Assisting in the Investigation of Missing
        Boy, Timothy King
From: Oakland County Prosecutor's Office

The Oakland County Prosecutor's Office has authorized all local law enforcement agencies assisting in the investigation of the missing boy, Timothy King,
to conduct the stop and search as is requested in the confidential memo to area
Chiefs from the Task Force. The purpose of the stop and search is to possibly
save the life of the missing boy, Timothy King, and apprehend his abductor.
In performing the stop and search pursuant to the requested action, police officers should conduct themselves in accordance with the following general rules:

1. If the stop is being made solely pursuant to the requested action of the
   Task Force, the vehicle stopped may be searched only to the extent necessary to determine if the perpetrator or victim is present in the vehicle,
   and such search shall be made as soon as possible after the stop.
2. Officers should detain a person only for the length of time necessary
   to obtain or verify the person's identification or an account of the person's presence or conduct and to conduct the necessary search, or otherwise determine if the person should be arrested or released.
3. Officers shall act with as much restraint and courtesy toward the person
   stopped as is possible under the circumstances. The officer making the
   stop shall identify himself as a law enforcement officer as soon as prac-
   tical after making the stop if he is not in uniform. At some point during
   the stop the officer should give the person stopped an explanation of the
   purpose of the stop.
4. Refusal to answer questions or to produce identification does not by itself establish probable cause to arrest, but such refusal may be considered along with other facts as an element adding to probable cause if,
   under the circumstances, an innocent person could reasonably be expected not to refuse. Such refusal is cause for a further investigation of
   the circumstances surrounding the stop.
5. Every officer who conducts a stop and search must be prepared to cite
   those specific factors which lead him to conclude that "reasonable suspicion" existed in accordance with the information contained in the confidential memo to Area Chiefs from the Task Force.

L. Brooks Patterson
Prosecuting Attorney

by: Richard Thompson
    Chief Assistant Prosecutor

The decision to inform the media, in confidence, of the stop-and-search was a testimony to the goodwill developed between police and reporters. Tobin and Robertson had a philosophy of dealing with reporters that was rather unique among law enforcement officers. For the most part, they trusted them, and the few they didn't, they simply didn't talk to. (One or two overzealous reporters breached that trust over the course of the long investigation and found themselves on the outside looking in.) Their trust proved justified, and the planned stop-and-search remained secret.

Birmingham had become a fortress. Long lines of cars, bumper-to-bumper, sat idling their engines outside school yards in the morning and afternoon, for parents no longer let their children walk to school. Kids themselves moved in large groups, and no child went anywhere alone. They talked with their parents and with each other about what they'd do if a stranger tried to talk with them. The family dinner table became a forum. Police liaison programs in the elementary schools were stepped up, and the "DON'T GO WITH STRANGERS" program was developed.

The man who had abducted Timmy King now had a price on his head. The Birmingham City Commission added twenty-five thousand dollars to the nearly sixteen thousand in reward money already being offered by the City of Berkley, through its Junior Chamber of Commerce for the arrest and conviction of Kristine Mihelich's kidnap-killer. Indeed, two state lawmakers from South Oakland County, Dave Campbell from Royal Oak, and Dana Wilson from Hazel Park, were proposing a one-million-dollar state reward fund for the arrest of persons who kill, kidnap, or molest children, to be parceled out in fifty-thousand-dollar chunks.

Tobin, in an effort to enlist as much help as possible, talked with U.S. Postal Service officials. Some eleven hundred letter carriers in South Oakland County were provided with composites of the man seen by Mrs. Raubacher, and with the profile worked up by psychiatrists, psychologists, and law enforcement personnel for the Stebbins, Robinson, and Mihelich cases. This was the information given to the Postal Service over Tobin's signature:

> As a result of investigation and consultation with professionals in law enforcement, as well as the medical field, here are some of the characteristics that may be associated with the person responsible for the abduction of local Oakland County youths.
>   1. Male — Possibly two (2)
>   2. Age: 25–30 years
>   3. Educated
>   4. Intelligent

5. Caucasian
6. Has the capacity to store or keep victim for a number of days without being detected.
7. Has a compulsion for cleanliness and very neat. His house and car are very clean. To the point of being a fanatic.
8. Little or no substance abuse involved, such as drugs or alcohol.*
9. His work schedule permits a certain amount of freedom of movement.
10. He is a white-collar worker.
11. He has abnormal sexual habits.
12. He may be undergoing psychiatric treatment or is desirous of same.
13. He lives or works in Oakland County.

Involvement of the letter carriers was known simply as "Operation Observation." It was the forerunner of dozens of other Special Projects designed to alert the community and ferret out the abductor. The composite of the man standing next to the blue Gremlin, along with the profile, was sent out to all newspapers. Amateur radio operators had been coordinating a civilian Mobile Watch program, made up of residents with CB radios, who patrolled the streets on Friday and Saturday nights. The community had been fully mobilized.

After the six o'clock news, just a few hours after Barry King had made his television appeal for the safe return of his son, the Birmingham Police Department switchboard exploded in a cacophony of sound and light. In a matter of hours several hundred tips came in. It seemed to the Birmingham Police desk sergeant that every one of the viewers who watched Detroit's 6:00 P.M. news was calling to tell him that they knew someone who fit the composite and the profile to a tee. And they were probably right.

Most police departments as a matter of course save the tapes of all incoming calls for a specified period. You never know when new information could give a whole new meaning to a conversation with a tipster. It was not until much later that Robertson discovered something that was to haunt him for a long time to come—someone at the Birmingham Police Department inexplicably decided to erase the recordings of the hundreds of calls that came in the days following the King abduction.

---

*It was felt that the killer demonstrated too much control to be using drugs, or alcohol, at least excessively.

16

"Lemme hear it again," said Krease, as he walked to the window behind Tobin's desk. The State Policeman stood staring out into the night, hands buried deep in his pants pockets, watching the beam of the streetlight bounce off the falling snow. He was looking, but not really seeing, except for a shadowy mental image of a man with a deep, well-modulated voice. He looked at his watch. Quarter to twelve.

Tobin punched the rewind button on the Ampex tape deck standing on his desk. The tape skittered back, then the machine clunked as he punched Stop and pushed Play. Robertson got up and joined Krease at the window as the Chief leaned back in his desk chair and the tape began again. Tobin raised his arms and clasped both hands behind his head.

The voice was clear and steady, almost mechanical. "I know about the missing boy — believe me, I know." The voice paused. It had an ominous, almost theatrical timbre to it. "If you want him back," another pause, longer this time, "then you can find him at Shain Park, one of his favorite places. But he won't feel like talking and don't call to him." There was a pause of two beats this time. Then, "He won't be able to hear you. You know what I mean."

Tobin punched the stop button. Robertson and Krease turned to face each other, Robertson muttered "damn," then both walked back and sat in chairs at the front of Tobin's desk.

"Well? What do you think?" asked Tobin, as he leaned well forward in the chair.

"What time did it come in?" asked Robbie.

"About 11:15," replied Tobin, checking the log in front of him. "Thirty minutes ago, just before I called you at the firehall."

Krease chewed on his lip. Robertson spoke. "I think somebody's giving us the slow jack. I mean, the guy sounds like he's rehearsing for some kind of play. It's almost like he's reading it. I'd be willing to bet he's yanking us around, playing head games. Shain Park, for Christ's sake, that's right next door. The guy may be crazy, but he sure as hell isn't stupid. I'm not even ready to bet he's crazy."

"Agreed," Tobin said, "but we sure as hell can't ignore it. How do you want to handle it?"

Robertson got out of his chair and walked to the window again. He thought a moment. "Look, why don't I just give Simmons a call, see if he can free up a couple of his Intelligence people and set 'em up someplace, maybe a second-story office or something, overlooking the park."

"All right, let's do it," said Tobin, who also got up from his chair, and walked around to the front of the desk. "We can put 'em up there in Kenning's office."

Robbie turned to Krease. "What's your feeling, Joe?"

"Chief, can you put some of your people on the street right around the park? Give our guys some back-up?"

"Oh, absolutely. No problem. On one condition," smiled Tobin.

"Yeah, what's that?"

"That both you guys get the hell out of my office, and go get some sleep. I'm serious. You both look like hell." The three cops laughed, something they hadn't done much of during the past forty-eight hours.

It was 1:30 A.M. by the time the trap was set in Shain Park. It was snowing harder now, and the moon was hanging high in the southeast, pregnant as it approached the full. Two Intelligence men were in Kenning's dark office, overlooking Shain Park. They had high-speed infra-red film in the camera, and with the thick cover of snow and the sodium-vapor streetlights, the four-acre park in the middle of town was surprisingly well lighted. The scattered bare trees posed virtually no obstruction to either human eyes or the camera. The panorama also offered a reasonably clean shot, if they had to resort to the M-1, which was fitted with a nightscope. It was unlikely that they would need it, but the child killer did have access to a shotgun, and had used it at least once. What if the caller *was* a little bit crazy or stupid and marched Timmy into the park at the business end of a shotgun? Who the hell could know? The M-1 was Timmy's life insurance.

Tobin had put four of his men on patrol around the park in unmarked cars, two cruising and two parked. One was in the Police Department lot, just a block over from the park. The other was in the public parking lot, at the southeast corner of the park, right across from the Community House. There were a half-dozen other civilian cars scattered throughout the lot, and the unmarked Fury with its lone occupant slouched down in the front seat was reasonably inconspicuous. If the anonymous caller did know something—if the call wasn't a hoax—then the six police officers would have a visitor sometime between now and dawn. They were ready.

"That was a nice waste of time! Jesus!" groused Kalbfleisch to Tobin as he stood by the corner of the Chief's desk.

"Well, Christ, Jack. We couldn't take a chance—you know that. Wouldn't it have been a fine mess if the guy did drop the body and we were all at home asleep? Sit down. Jeez, it's not even eight o'clock yet, and already you're loaded for bear," said Tobin to his Chief of Detectives. Kalbfleisch could really get cranky sometimes, particularly when he'd only had a few hours sleep. Kalbfleisch eased his bulk into the chair. "Look, got something I want to ask you. You ever heard of a guy named Hurkos, Peter Hurkos?"

"Who?" asked Kalbfleisch, frowning.

"Hurkos," repeated Tobin. "H-U-R-K-O-S. Guy's from California, some kind of mystic. Got a note here from yesterday, says call him at his home in California soon as I get in."

"Naw, never heard of him. Mystic, eh? Jesus, that's all we need. You gonna call him?"

"Might as well."

"Well, I'm not working with any mystic," declared Kalbfleisch. "Jesus!"

"Calm down," retorted Tobin with a smile. "I haven't even called him yet. Don't know what he wants. Oh, hi, guys," said Jerry, looking up. "You guys are here early." He was speaking to Robertson, Krease and Tobias, who were all standing in the hall just outside the office.

When all three men had found chairs, Robertson spoke. "Jerry, here," gesturing to Tobias, "hasn't seen the firehall operation yet. Thought we'd give him the two-dollar tour. Guess our man didn't show last night, eh?"

"Naw. Hopefully, that means Timmy is still with us. Say, any of you guys heard of Peter Hurkos, a mystic from California?"

"Yes," replied Tobias, leaning forward in the chair. "Guy worked the Boston Strangler case as a matter of fact, and eight or ten years ago he did some stuff on the John Norman Collins case in Ann Arbor, remember? Why?"

Tobin passed around the phone message. Krease spoke for the first time since entering the office. "Call him and tell him thanks but no thanks! Don't want any mumbo-jumbo mucking this thing up." Kalbfleisch smiled.

Tobias added, "I don't put a lot of faith in those guys. They're primarily entertainers, you know. Hurkos has made the talk shows, Vegas a couple of times, stuff like that. They're fun to watch, and a lot of people swear by them, but I can tell you, neither the Boston nor the Ann Arbor police give much credit to Hurkos for solving those cases."

Tobin smiled. "Jack here," he said, nodding at Kalbfleisch, "thinks Peter Hurkos could probably crack this case."

"Bullshit, Jerry," he burst out, as the others laughed.

"By the way," said Tobin, glancing at the notes he'd made to himself, "you all know Joel Smith, that reporter from the *News*. He's pretty trustworthy, and I've kind of given him the run of the place. Anyway, and I'm not too sure how this happened, he's been in contact with Marian King, something about an open letter to the public and to the kidnapper. She wants to publish it in the *News*. What do you think?"

"Well," said Krease, "I guess I don't have any problem with it, but I'd like to see a copy of the letter, first. Of course, we can't really stop her, or the *News*, anyway."

"I don't think it can do any harm," added Robertson, "but like Joe here, I think we should take a look at it before it hits the paper just to make sure there's nothing inflammatory in it, nothing that's liable to piss the guy off."

"Good," said Tobin. "Smith ought to be here any minute. Meanwhile, I'll call Marian and ask her if she minds if we look it over first."

"Yeah, but what about the *Free Press*?" asked Kalbfleisch, who didn't really care.

"Well, I don't see any real problem, Jack," replied Robbie. "They have a way of working these things out themselves. I never tell one reporter what the other one's got, just don't think it's right. Now, if Jane Briggs-Bunting comes right out and asks me if Joel Smith of the *News* is going to publish an open letter from Timmy King's mom, then I suppose I'll tell her. I treat 'em all the same way and try to level with 'em, but there's a lot of stuff I don't volunteer."

"This oughta really be something," Rivard said to Lloyd Sterns, as the two detectives stood in the lobby of an apartment building in Madison Heights, a blue-collar suburb a mile or so east of Woodward. Roger looked up and down the vertical rows of names and buttons and stabbed at the one identified "Pauline."

"Yes?" came the throaty reply from the wall speaker after a slight pause.

"Two friends who want to talk, Pauline—can you let us in?" answered Rivard.

"Not without some names and references. Sorry, I'm busy."

"How's State Police for names and references?" blurted out Sterns, a little impatiently. "C'mon, we called you around noon, remember?"

"Oh, yeah. Sorry, I forgot. Sure, c'mon up. Top of the stairs, down at the end to your left."

The two cops looked at each other. The inside door latch jumped in response to Pauline's buzz. Rivard pushed the door and Sterns followed him through and up the stairs. They stopped in front of number 214 and Sterns knocked gently. Both men stepped back a couple of feet to let her get a good look at them through the peephole. They heard the deadbolt slide back and the latch pop. They stepped forward as the door opened about three inches and a hand with long, well-manicured fingers slid the chain off its track.

She was tall, close to six feet in her three-inch heels, and a study in black, accentuated by short-cropped blond hair and milky white skin. She had the kind of lips that pout even when they smile and the teeth were sparkling white. More than ample breasts strained at a black glove-leather blouse tucked into a black, mid-thigh lambskin skirt. The blouse revealed a dangerous amount of cleavage, as any blouse might that had the top three buttons undone. The hose were black.

Without waiting to be asked, Rivard reached into his inside suitcoat pocket, pulled out his State Police I.D. wallet and flipped it open.

"Pauline, I'm Detective Sergeant Rivard. This is Sergeant Sterns." Sterns was still staring.

"Sure, c'mon in. Sorry. I've had a bunch of calls since I talked with you guys. Just forgot, I guess." The two cops entered the apartment and she closed the door behind them. "Have a seat," she said, waving to a red velour davenport. "Can I get you something to drink?"

"No thanks," said Rivard.

"Duty and all that stuff?" interrupted Pauline, flippantly.

"Little early for us, anyway," interjected Sterns, finally looking at the woman's face. It was a little after three.

"Coffee?"

"No, thanks, anyway," replied Rivard. "Just some talk, okay?"

"Sure? You know, cops are some of my favorite clients," she laughed.

The apartment was gaudy, with gold carpeting. Cheap vinyl-covered recliner chairs were at opposite sides of the room. They were separated by a heavy, wooden end table, on which sat several S-and-M magazines and two tattered scrapbooks. A color television with a twenty-five-inch screen sat at one end of the room. Hanging on the walls was an assortment of whips, chains, manacles, and collars. A wicked-looking hinged block with holes for head and arms sat ominously off to the side.

"What can I do for you?" asked Pauline, as Rivard and Sterns opted for the recliner chairs. She moved to the davenport and sat. Crossing her legs, she revealed that she was wearing a garterbelt.

From their street contacts, the detectives had learned that Pauline had once been Paul. The surgeons had done a good job. The voice was a little husky, perhaps, for a woman, but the rest of it was pure art. Pauline's figure blew the top off the one-to-ten scale, and the face was one you wouldn't be ashamed to be seen with, providing nobody knew her history and what she did for a living.

It was what she did for a living that brought the State Police to her door. Pauline provided a service for a certain, select group of people who enjoyed a special flavor with their sex. She was into bondage and discipline, for one hundred dollars an hour, though oddly enough, sexual intercourse was not on the menu. Her clients included doctors, lawyers, judges, cops, and clergymen. Some of her clients were women.

"Pauline," began Rivard, "you've heard about the child murders and the Timmy King kidnapping. Maybe you can help us. We know some of the stuff you're into, and it's a little off-the-wall. Not many people are into whips and chains and dog collars."

"You'd be surprised," Pauline cut in defensively.

"Maybe so," said Rivard. "Anyway, all the kids were snatched within a mile or so of Woodward, so, we're working the Woodward Corridor. A lot of your business comes from the area, doctors, lawyers. . . . "

"You guys really think a doctor or lawyer grabbed the kid?"

"Not necessarily," said Sterns, "but maybe somebody with that kind of freedom."

"You think the guy is wealthy, eh?" asked Pauline, uncrossing and then recrossing her legs. "You know, if you're thinking he's one of my customers, we're talking one hundred dollars an hour."

"Pauline," said Rivard, getting to the point, "all we figure is maybe somebody's talking to you when they unload their fantasies."

"I draw the line there. Anybody who does kids is no customer of mine. Yeah, I've got to admit I've got some weirdos. I mean, I got a priest who can't get off unless I tie him to the bed, legs and arms, then I gotta hold a crucifix in one hand, while I do him with the other," she said, smiling.

"Yeah, okay, Pauline, but does anybody ever show you any kiddie porn—pictures, books, letters, anything like that?" asked Sterns.

"No. I told you, none of my clients go that far. This guy you're looking for does that kind of thing with the kids?" The detectives ignored the question.

"Pervert," exclaimed Pauline. "If you guys get him, lemme have him for a half-hour. I'll do the same thing to him with the whip that the doctors did to me with a scalpel."

The detectives didn't doubt it. There is a strange credibility that some street people possess, perhaps because there's no pretense. They are what they are, and you can either accept them for what they are, warts and all, or not. Pauline knew what she was and lived by her own code. She didn't force it on anybody and didn't want anybody's forced on her.

"Well, we just thought you might be able to steer us in the right direction," said Rivard, getting to his feet. "All right if we leave you our card?"

"Sure,—Sergeant Rivard," she read the name off the card and rose from the davenport. "Sorry I couldn't be of more help. I sure hope you nail the son of a bitch, and I'll get ahold of you if I hear something. Maybe I'll see you guys off duty, sometime," she joked as she reached out to shake hands with the detectives.

"Don't think so, Pauline," replied Sterns with a grin, "can't afford your rates."

"Hey, free ride for you guys," she laughed. "Got a cage big enough for the both of you—throw in a couple of spiked dog collars, too."

It was late afternoon when the telephone rang in the King house. Marian looked at Studt, who nodded, signaling her to pick up the kitchen phone while he simultaneously picked up the special extension Bell had wired in. Studt sat on the stool behind the counter that jutted out into the kitchen. Marian walked to the wall phone near the front entryway.

"Hello," she said into the mouthpiece. "Yes, this is Mrs. King. What? Yes. Who is this?" Her voice was controlled. "Yes, of course." She turned to look at Studt, while she continued the conversation. She was stalling. The lady was good. "Yes, could you repeat that, please? Well, can you tell me where I should go? Okay, just a moment. Let me write that down." She never took her eyes off Studt, who was writing on his notepad. Then he mouthed silently, as he looked up from the pad, "just another few seconds, please."

Marian read the signal and spoke into the mouthpiece again. "Okay. Please, I didn't get that last part. Could you repeat it once more? Yes. I have it, thank you."

Studt nodded his head, signaling that enough time had gone by for Bell to lock in on the caller's location.

"We got him," exclaimed Studt, as soon as Marian hung up. "You did great, Mrs. King," he said with a smile. "Terrific. Now, lemme call our people."

"Do you think it was real?" she asked.

"Don't build your hopes, Mrs. King," said Studt as he dialed the Task Force. "I got a gut feeling the guy just wants an easy twenty-five thousand dollars. But don't worry, Detroit's already got a couple of men on the way there. They'll have him in a few minutes."

17

It was a few minutes before 3:30 as the brown and gold Pontiac inched its way along Pinecrest, just a quarter mile west of Woodward. The Roosevelt Elementary School, in Pleasant Ridge, was disgorging its charges as the sedan stopped along the curb, its engine idling.

Snow was piled a foot or more along the sidewalk edge and beside the curb. The winter sky was dark and heavy with more snow as the children, those who weren't being met by anxious parents, ambled home along freshly swept sidewalks. The driver leaned across the front seat and rolled the passenger window down, as a group of five youngsters approached, four boys and a pretty little girl. He waited until the kids got alongside the car.

"Say, kids," he called pleasantly. "Hi. Say, c'mere for just a minute. Any of you know where Oak Park Boulevard is? I'm supposed to see a friend who lives over there, and I'm kind of lost, okay?"

The children stopped their chattering and looked at the stranger. They slowed their pace, but didn't stop completely. They bunched up, two of the boys taking the little girl by the hand. She smiled nervously at the stranger and started to step closer to the car.

"No, Marcy, c'mon, let's go," said one of the two boys holding her hands, as he jerked her up short.

"Yeah," said a third youngster, who fairly pushed the little girl, as the tallest of the two boys holding her hands yanked her back onto the sidewalk. The group broke into a slow trot, bumping and pushing each other along the sidewalk, dragging Marcy with them. At a distance of about thirty feet, they stopped. One of the boys took off his mittens, fumbled for a pencil in his coat pocket, and as he turned to glance back at the sedan, which was just pulling away from the curb, he jotted something down on the cover of his geography book. The car drove around the corner and stopped again, near the entrance to the playground in front of the school.

Three boys, about eleven or twelve years old, were pitching snow-balls through the gate at classmates clustered together on the school steps.

Again the driver, a nice-looking man in his late twenties or early thirties, dressed in a suit and tie, stopped the car, leaned across the front seat, and called out.

"Say boys, c'mere for a second, will ya? I wanna talk to you for a minute."

The boys stopped and turned.

"Look," the driver continued, "I'm not from around here, and," he produced a notebook, "I'm supposed to see a friend who lives over on," he hesitated and looked down at the notebook, "on Oak Park Boulevard, but I musta missed it some place."

The youngsters began to advance cautiously on the car, still holding their snowballs. Two of the boys got within twelve feet of the car and stopped. The other lad bravely stomped through the drift at the edge of the sidewalk and approached to within an arm's length of the window.

"What'd you say, Mister?" Then, taking a deliberate step back, the boy said, "You sure look like the guy on. . . . "

The driver quickly turned away. "Yeah, never mind," he said, as he rolled the window up, slipped the car into gear, and rolled away.

"God damn it, I feel like a real slime," Savage said to his editor. "I've got some real problems with this," he added bitterly as he viewed the tape. He squinted at the edit monitor. "'TV reporter entices children to his car.' Shit. I think it was a dumb idea, and it's gonna get us in a whole shit-heap of trouble. Not to mention I coulda got my ass blown off by some irate father."

"Aw, calm down, Tom," said Savage's producer, whose idea it had been to stage the mock abduction attempt in the first place. "I think we're doing the public a real service here. After all this crap about how parents are supposed to tell their kids not to talk with strangers, here you got one to come right up to the car. Some of the kids did what they were supposed to, though. You got a message from a Lieutenant Sullivan from Ferndale P.D. Seems like they got a couple calls about a man answering your description and driving a piece of crap Pontiac like yours, trying to snatch a couple of kids."

"God damn it," exploded Savage, turning abruptly from the viewer and pushing his way out past the producer. "Charlie, some people are content just to go through life letting other people think they're assholes. You, you gotta go out and prove it."

"You know that extortion call, Lieutenant, the one to the Kings? Well, Detroit nailed a kid—kid, hell, he's eighteen," exclaimed Krease. "Those guys were on him practically before he hung up the phone. They don't screw around, huh?"

"Any reason you want to see him, Joe?" asked Robertson.

"Naw—Detroit says he's just after the money. You know, those Detroit dicks are a whole different breed. Christ, they're putting people away left and right. You drive a blue Gremlin in Detroit, you better have a toothbrush with you, 'cause you're going to spend the night in jail, or at least as long as it takes for them to clear you," he chuckled. "I don't know how many damn Gremlins we've stopped out here already. Surprised it hasn't hit the fan yet. You know, somebody hollering about illegal this and illegal that."

As the two men walked out of the Sandwich Shop in downtown Birmingham, Krease said, "Hey, you see the early evening edition yet? Somebody said they published the King letter."

Robertson shook his head. "Let's grab a copy, then head on over to the firehall for a minute to check the tip room and then get the hell home."

"Sure, Lieutenant. Like the last five nights?" Joe grinned.

"No, really, Joe. We've all been working these fourteen to sixteen hour days. Christ, we've got to ease up. Some of these guys are going to start picking at each other. You having any problems with 'em yet?"

"Nope. I tell 'em after eight or ten hours to get out of there. They tell me okay, then I see 'em back there in a couple of hours. They want this guy, bad. A lot of the men are pretty frustrated, but they won't quit. Hard on the families, too."

The two walked into the pharmacy at the corner of Maple and Woodward for an evening *News.* Krease put the paper under his arm, and as they went out the door, Robertson picked up the conversation again. "Seriously," he said, "we aren't going to be able to investigate anything, if we've got a bunch of zombies walking around. Let's start cutting down on the hours."

They got into Krease's car and headed toward the firehall. Neither man spoke for a few minutes. Both noticed a marked Birmingham Police car behind a red Gremlin at the stop sign just a block west of Hunter, on Maple. The police car hit his flasher and the Gremlin pulled to the curb and stopped. Joe pulled by just as the cop who was driving got out, then leaned back into the front seat to pick up his flashlight. His partner was already punching the Gremlin's tag into the computer. Joe slowed, as Robbie rolled his window down. The cop, flashlight in hand, turned.

"That you, Lieutenant?" he asked, surprised.

"Hi, officer. How's it going? What's this, about number one hundred for you today?"

"Christ, I dunno. Lost count."

"Looks clean, Tom," said the officer still in the car. He'd just gotten the license plate information back from the secretary of state.

"Yeah, thanks, Walt," Tom said. "I'll just see if he's carrying any passengers." He turned back to Robbie. "Lieutenant, we stopped a guy 'bout an hour ago. Blue Gremlin, the whole nine yards. Guy looked a lot like the poster, too. He was out of the car before we were, big smile on his face. 'Officer,' he says, 'any way you guys can give me some kind of pass? I've been stopped twenty-three times in the past four days.' We had a good laugh about it."

"You hear that?" Robertson asked, as he turned to Krease. "Anything you can do about that?"

"I don't know, Lieutenant. We'll take a look," Krease answered good-naturedly.

"Well, gotta get to work, Lieutenant. See ya later." The uniformed cop turned and walked to the waiting Gremlin, his flashlight beam stabbing through the rear window, then into the backseat.

Krease pulled slowly by, then spoke. "One of the men was telling me two days ago, they followed this Gremlin buzzing around town with the hatchback window up. They pull him over, run the check, and then ask the fella why he's driving around town in the dead of winter with the back window up. And he says to them, 'so you guys can see that I ain't got nobody in the trunk.' I'm telling you, we're getting nothing but cooperation, even from the suspects."

As they pulled into the firehall parking lot, Robertson said, "This whole thing is one for the books. Even the businesses around town are calling us asking for the times and dates of the abductions and murders of the other kids, so they can send us records of all their employees who might've been sick or on vacation then. Never seen anything like it before."

In the Squad Room, Krease dropped the evening edition of the *News* on the table, while draping his overcoat over a folding chair. "Want another cup of coffee, Lieutenant?"

"Yeah, I suppose. I'll get it, then we can sit down for a couple of minutes and see what kind of letter Mrs. King writes." Robbie stopped in the tip room on the way to the coffeemaker, while Krease chatted with a detective team who'd just come in.

"Two hundred and twenty-eight tips so far today, Joe," Robertson said to Krease, as he came back to the table with styrofoam cups of what passed in the Squad Room for coffee.

"Yeah," Joe replied, "we been running close to three hundred a day. I'm afraid we been losing some, too, they just been coming in so damn fast."

Robertson left Krease talking with his men and sat down with the paper. He didn't have to bother opening it up. The letter was right at the top of the front page under the headline: MOTHER'S PLEA FOR TIM'S SAFETY. There was no byline, only some remarks by an unnamed editor: "The following letter to the public—and to the kidnapper of her eleven-year-old son—was given to a *Detroit News* reporter Saturday by Mrs. Marian King of Birmingham. Her son, Timothy, has been missing since Wednesday night."

The letter began:

> I am expecting at any moment for the side door to bang open and hear Tim say, "Have we ate yet? I mean, have we had dinner yet?" When that happens, I will run for his favorite Kentucky Fried Chicken and mix his glass of Ovaltine. Then, when he has had the usual eight Oreos and some plain milk to dunk them, Tim and I will go on our delayed shopping trip. We had planned to buy a much-wanted light blue warmup suit with the money he has saved from his newspaper route. Wherever Tim is, he is distressed about worrying me. He has always left notes or called to tell me where he is. He is impatient to return to rehearsing for his role as "Mike TV" in the upcoming production of "Willie Wonka and the Chocolate Factory" at Adams School. He is also eager to play on his basketball team, try out for Little League and his new career as a soccer player. There are no words to express how much we all miss Tim. We can hardly wait to see him, hug him and hear his latest collection of jokes. It is my hope that Tim is not frightened or hungry and that his cold is not any worse. I appeal to all of you from the bottom of my heart—help bring him home to us very soon. Do whatever you can to help find him, and call the Birmingham police with any possible information which might be useful. We are overwhelmed at the outpouring of love and support from neighbors, friends, and concerned persons. The magnificent efforts of the Birmingham police and their associates from all of Michigan are beyond any expectations. We are eagerly anticipating Tim's safe arrival. Someone, please, give him all our love until we can do that ourselves.

Robertson reread it twice more, took a slug of coffee, got up and stretched, and walked over to where Krease was standing. Krease was listening to Dave Piche, from Berkley.

"Beats the hell out of everybody, Joe. They've looked at the tapes a dozen times. Guy might as well be from another planet. Oh, hello, Lieutenant."

"Hello, Sergeant, what's going on?"

"Well, I was just telling Joe, you remember that guy leaning against the building at Mihelich's funeral? Well, we're still trying to make him. Her family's looked at the surveillance tapes a dozen times — nobody knows who the hell he is. They can put a name on everybody else, even some of the neighbors they barely know, but not this guy."

Krease spoke: "All right. We need a still of this guy. Should be easy enough for our people to freeze a still on the tape."

"You know, Sarge," added Piche, "you put a pair of glasses on our composite. . . . "

" . . . and draw in a cigar, and you got a guy that looks like Groucho Marx," interrupted Waldron, who'd just come in off the street.

"All right, look," said Krease, drawing a sip of coffee, as the others took chairs. "We've got to find out who and what this guy is. We've got three kids dead, six, if you count Cadieux, Srock, and Allen. And while we're talking about it — and this is just an educated guess — I don't think Cadieux, Srock and Allen fit the same mold as Stebbins, Robinson, Mihelich, or Timmy. Their ages for one thing. Too old. And, well, the way they died and the way he left them. I just don't think so. Think about it. I guess what I'm saying is the person responsible for them isn't the one responsible for Stebbins, Jill, Kristine, or Timmy. I'm not saying Cadieux, Srock, and Allen aren't important. Hell, we've had a team on them for months."

Pausing, Krease let that sink in. No one disagreed, and he continued. "I want this guy, and I don't give a shit what we have to do to get him. Let's eliminate him, we been screwing around with him long enough. Now, what we're going to do is this." The others, including Robertson, leaned back in their chairs, folded their arms, and listened. Krease was running out of patience. It had been nearly two months since the surveillance films from the Mihelich funeral had revealed a medium-sized man with long sideburns and glasses leaning against a building near the funeral home, just watching people come and go. In that time, some of the best detectives in the business, turning over every rock, had been able to find out nothing about him. Now, with another child gone and some similarities between the loiterer and the man Mrs. Raubacher had seen, it was time to give the man-nobody-knows top priority.

"Okay," Krease began. "First of all, I want a good still off that film, or tape, or whatever the hell they call it. Then, I want five hundred copies. I want the street worked like it's never been worked before, especially the Woodward Corridor, until we come up with the guy." Krease looked at his watch: a little before nine. He got up from his chair. "Look, you guys, I'm tired as hell. I'm going to go over all this stuff at the regular morning briefing tomorrow. Lieutenant, you going to stick around here for a while?"

"No," said Robertson. "Well, maybe for a few minutes. You want to take the *News* with you, so you can look at the King letter?"

"Yeah, I guess," Krease muttered, sounding depressed.

Robbie waited until Krease got his coat, then, without his own, walked out of the Squad Room with him.

"Look, Joe," said Robbie, as he put his hand on Krease's shoulder. "I know you're pretty frustrated about the guy at the funeral. Don't be too hard on yourself. Look," he said, as the two descended the stairs, "you been doing one helluva job with this thing, but you've got to start cutting back on some of the hours, not only for the detective teams, but for yourself as well. Sometimes you have to step back and remove yourself from a situation for a few minutes, so you can clear your head."

"Yeah, I know, Lieutenant, but I've really been sitting on my ass with this character from Kristine's funeral. Should've been on Piche long before this."

"Piche's a good man from what I hear," Robertson pointed out, as the men stood outside the door. "I can pretty well tell you he's been looking for him, but, like you say, with all the other stuff going on, the guy probably just fell through the cracks. That's all right. You're on him now. We'll get those pictures out, like you say, and don't worry, he'll turn up. By the way," asked Robertson, changing the subject, "how are those regular morning briefings working out?"

"Pretty good," answered Krease with a little more enthusiasm. "We do some real brainstorming at those sessions before the guys hit the street. Besides sorting out our priority tips and assigning them, I kind of give everybody a chance to bounce ideas around, discuss theories, that kind of thing. They get a chance to give everybody else their input, maybe even shoot holes in the other theories. I figure it's time pretty well spent. Sometimes we're only in there for fifteen or twenty minutes, sometimes it's an hour. But I think it's worth it. Another thing, it gives the guys a chance to get to know each other, learn how the other guy thinks. A lot of them never knew each other before."

"That's good, Joe." Robertson smiled. "Now get the hell out of here and get some rest."

"Yeah," said Krease, as he started for his car. "Thanks, Lieutenant." He stopped. "Oh, wait a minute, I forgot. . . . "

"Joe," Robertson spoke firmly, "believe it or not, this Task Force really can survive without you for the rest of the night." He smiled. "But only for the rest of the night."

"Okay," laughed Krease as Robbie moved to block the doorway. He turned back to his car. "Lieutenant?"

"Yeah?"

"Thanks again for the pep talk. Haven't had one of those in twenty years."

The impact of the Timothy King abduction was felt from the Squad Room to the classroom. In a manner of speaking, every parent in the community was being held hostage, and child safety meetings were held at local schools, including Timothy's own Adams School. Speakers cautioned parents to get back in touch with their children, monitoring their movements twenty-four hours a day, and while they emphasized the good in most people, they also focused on the bad in some. Both school officials and law enforcement officials emphasized the dangers of speaking to strangers, approaching their cars, or otherwise getting involved with them. And, added these officials, the message to children must be reinforced periodically. Speakers stressed the importance of a close parent-child relationship, close enough to let the child feel free and comfortable in reporting any accosting episode. As Lieutenant Isaiah McKinnon of the Detroit Police Department's Sex Crimes Unit told Ferndale parents, "There are certain things about sex crimes that we have to tell kids that normally we wouldn't." Added Douglas Graves, a psychiatric social worker, "If you prepare a child, you give them a feeling of strength. They say 'I know what to do.' They may worry, but they are reassured and they know how to react and they're not preoccupied with it." McKinnon and Graves went on to list a number of precautionary measures. Some of the children were abducted while on their way to party stores and drug stores: don't send them to the store alone. Children should be wary of motorists who stop and try to engage them in conversation, no matter what the subject matter. As Sergeant Thomas Allred of the Ferndale Police Department said, "I'd rather have motorists think we have the most discourteous children in the area." Parents were told to warn kids against hitchhiking or accepting rides, even with family friends, and to steer clear of parking lots, public restrooms, vacant buildings, or other isolated areas. In addition, children were being warned to report any suspicious cars and to write the license number down on the sidewalk with a sharp rock, if necessary.

These were the very things Barry and Marian King had discussed with Timmy a dozen times over.

18

"Aw, that guy is just a frustrated cop," declared Kalbfleisch, sitting around the table in the Squad Room with Krease, Robertson, and Tobias. Assorted other detectives were going about the business of taking tips, and either going out to, or coming back from, the street. It was 10:30 in the morning, March 21.

"Maybe, Jack," said Tobias, "but he's a pretty good psychiatrist, written some good stuff, too. Plus, he has got that suicide hotline and has done some pioneer work in that area — saved a few lives, from what I hear. I guess all I'm trying to say is he's a giant step above your garden-variety shrink or mystic."

"I'm not so sure," growled Rivard, who'd walked over from the tip room and pulled up a chair, "if you're talking about who I think you're talking about." Rivard turned his chair around backwards so he could rest his arms over the back. "Bruce Danto, right?" He stuck his tongue out between his lips and gave Danto a Bronx cheer.

"What the hell's your problem with him, Roger?" asked Tobias, a little perturbed. Tobias and Danto were, if not drinking buddies, at least close professionally. "Christ, he's already helped us with the profile, and he's been in on this since Stebbins."

"Sure, for all the publicity it gets him. Christ, you see the papers this morning?"

"Both you guys, hold on a minute," said Krease in an effort to head off what could have become a full-fledged argument. "First of all, Jerry's right. Danto's a pro, and he has given us some pretty good input on the profile."

"I've got nothing against Danto personally," said Rivard in a calmer voice, "I just think if we open this thing up and ask for *his* help, you'll have every shrink and mystic in town hanging around here, sprinkling sand and reading tarot cards."

Robertson, who up till now had just been sitting back and enjoying the scene, laughed. "Now, let's not get carried away, everybody. You're right, Rog, we sure as hell don't want mystics hanging around. We're polite to them and thank them for their interest and usually tell them we'll call them if we need them. Nobody is going to turn this into a dog-and-pony show. But Danto's different, a respected psychiatrist. Yeah, I know he's a media groupie, but what the hell, so's Brooks. But Brooks is doing one helluva job for us." He paused. "Let me just share a couple of thoughts with you about Danto." Robbie leaned back in his chair and folded his arms. "First, any help Danto's given us so far is strictly his own idea. I mean, the guy's about the only one who's called us so far that's willing to stand up and be counted, put his name and career on the line. Sure, the media's all over him. They call him to see what he thinks about all this, and he responds. Then the media comes to us and says 'Danto says this,' or 'Danto says that,' and that puts us in a position where we either have to respond or stonewall. Hell, the way I figure it, if we at least ask him to work with us, it'll make him feel like he's part of the team. I mean, right now, he's got us by the balls. I don't think he means anything sinister by it, in fact, I'm sure he doesn't. But nevertheless, we're right in the middle, it's just one of those things." Krease and Tobias nodded agreement. And while Rivard wasn't nodding, his eyes showed that Robbie was getting through.

"Makes some sense to me," added Krease, who was tapping the table top with a wooden pencil.

"Besides," added Robertson. "I guess Danto's had some kind of police training, went to an academy out in Macomb County, so he's got some idea of how we work."

"Yeah," said Tobias, who kept folding and unfolding a piece of scratch paper. "Really, Rog, Danto's all right. There was a case down in Ohio where he sent some kind of message to a killer, you know, in the newspaper, asking him to give himself up." He stopped construction of his paper airplane long enough to look Rivard in the eye. "I'll be damned if the killer didn't do just that. Turned himself in to Danto. I've got the clipping some place. I'll show it to you."

"Naw," said Rivard contritely. "There's no problem, I guess. We sure haven't got anything to lose, anyway. Whatever it takes to get this animal off the streets, I'm for." Rivard got up from the chair and slid it back under the table. "Well, I'm gonna hit the street." He turned and started to walk away.

"By the way, Rog," said Robertson casually. "Seeing as this whole Danto thing was your idea, why don't you call him and tell him we want to talk?"

Tobin and Robertson decided to call a meeting of top law enforcement brass, primarily the South Oakland Chiefs, but also high-echelon people from the Sheriff's Department, the Prosecutor's Office, the F.B.I., and of course, the State Police. It was five days after Timothy King's abduction, and save for Mrs. Raubacher's description of the man with the blue Gremlin, they had virtually nothing in the way of substantial leads. This in spite of the fact that a dozen local law enforcement agencies had provided them with up to three hundred detectives. Both Tobin and Robertson felt they owed the local chiefs at least an update on the situation, because it was they after all, who were providing the manpower, at considerable inconvenience to their own communities. Tobin and Robertson also felt that a gathering of all the top brass from the different agencies involved would give them a sense of the unity in the project, a chance to measure the solidity of the foundation on which the Timothy King investigation was built.

Robertson and Tobin had also discussed the fact that they were going to have to start reducing the number of investigators working the case. They had little choice. Some two hundred fifty police officers and fifty detectives had been working fourteen- to sixteen-hour days, and as Robertson had told Krease, without some relief the investigation would disintegrate. The meeting, which had been scheduled for 2:00 P.M. at the Birmingham Community House, would be a proper forum for just such an announcement, and the media were to be excluded.

The Community House was packed. Robertson would say later it was probably the largest gathering of law enforcement people he'd ever seen. Both Tobin and Robertson spoke, each from a different perspective. Tobin, as the chief law enforcement officer in the jurisdiction, besides being concerned with the safe return of Timmy King, had the primary responsibility, over and above the police work, of making sure everybody's car was gassed, and indeed, that everybody had a car, and a telephone, and some place to sit, and so on. Tobin was the man all other chiefs were committing their resources and manpower to. It was his turf, and he, ultimately, would answer to the community. With two strikes against him because of his youth and ambition, Tobin could not afford to step on any individual or collective toes. Mostly, he was successful. Until much farther down the line, there would be no public criticism of either Tobin or the Task Force. Robertson, when he took over the Task Force, was highly respected for both his policework and his administrative effort. But in terms of public image, he was unknown and therefore had nothing to either prove or disprove. Tobin was in the trenches; Robbie was well back behind the lines. The two men were totally unalike in personality. Where Tobin was perceived as arrogant and a hotshot, Robertson was perceived as people-oriented and laid-back. So Tobin spoke to the Chiefs more on the administrative politics of the case and Robbie more to the investigative mechanics. Both did their jobs well, and the Chiefs left the Community House, once the media had had a crack at them, with a feeling of unity and resolve.

The ride out to Bloomfield Hills and Danto's house through some of the most affluent areas in the Midwest gave Robbie and Krease time to reflect on the past five days. The snow flurries had stopped about noon, but there was still a six-inch cover on the lawns on either side of Quarton Road. Even with a blanket of snow, you could guess that the lawns were not mowed, but manicured. The homes were sheltered by gigantic evergreens, giving them a Christmasy look even in March.

Robertson and Krease talked mostly about the meeting they'd just come from at the Community House, sharing thoughts about the unbelievable complexity of the case, with all the different law enforcement jurisdictions involved. They talked about how the Kings were doing and about the printout of all the Gremlin owners in Oakland County they'd just received from AMC.

"Slow down a minute, Joe," said Robertson, squinting at the mailbox number as Krease came to an almost complete stop at the entrance to a long wooded lane that led up a hill, the crest of which hid the house. "I think this is it."

Krease backed up slowly, then made a wide turn around a four-foot snowbank and into the lane. The freshly plowed blacktop lane, banked on either side by large drifts, led over the crest of the hill and down another one hundred fifty feet to where the drive circled in front of the house. The four huge columns at the front entrance were obscured by the forty-foot blue spruces growing in the island formed by the circular drive. Krease pulled up behind a black Mercedes sedan.

"Whew!" Krease exclaimed. "I guess we're in the wrong business."

"Well," Robbie said, "it hasn't got as many windows as the Chrysler Building, and it's smaller than Buckingham Palace."

The door opened as they approached. They greeted the maid who

stood just inside, identified themselves as State Police, and were ushered
into a living room that reminded Robertson of the Great Hall in *Gone
With the Wind*, only this one was carpeted off-white. A small figure sat
cross-legged on a large white divan.

"Dr. Danto? Lieutenant Robertson. This is Detective Sergeant Krease.
Thanks for seeing us."

The man, who had remained sitting, uncrossed his legs and in his
stocking feet walked toward them. The doctor was wearing a red and grey
warm-up suit. His hair was dark and wavy, and he wore wire-rimmed
glasses. He extended his hand, adorned with two large turquoise rings.

"Gentlemen, good of you to call," he said politely. "Have a chair.
Can I get you anything?" He glanced at his gold Rolex. "It's a little after
five, maybe you'd like a drink? I mix quite a vodka martini."

"Thanks anyway, Doctor, none of the hard stuff. Maybe some coffee."

"Bruce, call me Bruce, please." Speaking to the maid, who was hovering a few steps in back of Krease and Robertson in the slate entryway,
Danto said, "Olivia, could you take the coats and then please get us some
coffee? Just bring the service and leave it at the top of the steps." Olivia
nodded and silently swept away, swallowed up by the hall.

Danto waved the two detectives down into the sunken living room
and to a couple of expensive upholstered chairs with wooden arms, set
at angles in front of the divan and at either end of a long coffee table.
The psychiatrist fell back onto the divan and into a little nest he'd made
for himself with several fluffy pillows. "Feel free to kick off your shoes
and sit like this. Good for the soul. The Indians knew what they were doing. Well, what can I do for you, as if I didn't know?"

"Well," Joe replied, "first we just want to say thanks for all your efforts. You've spent considerable time with our people on the profile without our even asking."

"Glad to," interrupted Danto. "After all, it's what I do. Pretty well,"
he added, waving at his surroundings. He put both hands back on his
knees. "But most of this stuff is straight out of the textbooks. This man's
a loner who can't succeed as an adult, can't relate to adults, and uses kids
to salve his ego. And as for the killing, he's like a child playing with something he knows is forbidden, just because he can get away with it. Then
he leaves them clean and neat to disguise in his own mind the enormity
of his crimes."

"I never heard of a pedophile killing before."

"True," admitted Danto. "Most pedophiles don't kill. My guess is he's
just afraid they'll turn him in. And as you know, I believe he responds

to the season, the winter, for reasons that beat the hell out of me. Look," continued the psychiatrist, settling back into his nest of pillows and counting on his fingers, "you've got Cadieux, Srock, maybe Allen, Stebbins, Robinson, Mihelich, now King, all but King dead, and I'm betting he's number seven. Right?" Robertson and Krease nodded. "Now, if you don't count Allen, they all disappeared and were killed during the winter. Right?" They nodded again. "In fact, I have a theory you may have read about in the papers."

"The *Free Press* interview you gave to Jane Briggs-Bunting?"

"Yes. I believe that it's snow, or the forecast of snow, that prompts him to abduct children."

Krease said, "But hell, it could be coincidence. I mean, those things. . . . "

"Sure, could be," Danto cut in, "but I've done a lot of work with these people, psychotics, and my guess, my educated guess," he emphasized, "is that it might not be coincidence. Seasons might just have something to do with it. Maybe his father beat him in the wintertime for not shoveling the walk, and he's trying to get back at him. I don't know. Everytime another psychotic killer pops up, we have to rewrite the book."

"You say psychotic, Bruce. Do you think he's got a psychiatric history? Is the guy seeing someone like yourself?" asked Robertson.

"It's a good bet. Well, I don't know how good a bet, but I'd say there's a fifty-fifty chance he's talking to somebody. I think we ought to follow up on any possibility."

Krease leaned back in his chair, crossing one leg over the other and studying the psychiatrist. "Bruce, I believe you've also said in the papers that the killer might be trying to communicate with you, that that's why he dropped the body on Bruce Lane. Mind elaborating a bit?"

"Well, I guess I'm the only one that feels that way. The killer may have chosen Bruce Lane after he read what I had to say about him in the papers. He may be trying to tell me something. I've done a little detective work myself," he said. "I checked through the Michigan Psychiatric Society list of all the psychiatrists in the state. Only three with the first name Bruce." Robertson and Krease looked at each other again, then met Danto's gaze.

"And," Danto went on, "I'm the only one in this area, so who knows? Worth a shot, don't you think?" Without giving the two State Policemen a chance to answer, Danto pressed on. "I'm obviously pretty familiar with behaviors which are the result of subconscious impulses, and I think he might be trying to leave us some clues." He paused and stared at the floor.

"What else, Doctor?" inquired Krease.

Danto looked up. "Well, and this is a long shot, I've written the Michigan Psychiatric Society for permission to ask some of my colleagues in the tri-county area to provide me with some of their files on patients who might fit the psychological profile. My request is being processed, but, again, it's a real long shot because of the confidentiality between doctor and patient. Even in cases like this, with a child killer, most psychiatrists are touchy. I am myself. Not many things sacred left in this world, and we doctors like to hold that hallowed ground."

"We can understand that," said Robertson, "but it sure would be nice if they could break the rule, just this once."

"But then where do you stop? You set a precedent. On the other hand, there was the recent Tarasoss decision in California. A psychiatrist notified his patient's family of the patient's intention to harm a woman, but he didn't tell the victim or the victim's family. The patient killed her and her family sued and won. The California Supreme Court said that a therapist who is aware that one of his patients is going to harm someone must come forward with the information."

"Excuse me, Doctor." It was Olivia, the maid, who'd finally brought the coffee on a tray.

"Oh, fine, Olivia. Just set it down here. That's all for now."

The maid smiled and left the room.

Krease and Robbie picked up their coffee and sipped it.

Robertson said, "Bruce, if you are right about the killer trying to communicate with you because you've talked about him in the papers. . . ."

"Yes?"

"Well, you said something about how he picks up kids like a squirrel picks up nuts in the wintertime. You referred to him as a squirrel."

"And there's a Squirrel Road east of Pontiac! You think it might be worthwhile to stake it out?"

"It might be worth a shot. We've got nothing to lose and everything to gain."

They finished the coffee, said their thanks, and left. It was a little before 6:30 as Krease and Robbie pulled around Danto's circular drive, onto the lane, and out to the road.

Robbie called the Criminal Investigation Section (C.I.S.) at the Armory on Eight Mile Road, then the Pontiac Post and arranged for four cars to spend the night on Squirrel Road, two of them painted and moving, two of them unmarked and parked.

Squirrel Road was a lonely stretch of north-south blacktop that ran from the Bald Mountain Recreation area south to Auburn Heights. The rolling, wooded countryside was pretty by day and desolate by night, with only an occasional cluster of a half-dozen homes.

It was 3:18 the morning of March 22. A bright moon in its third phase lighted the snow-covered fields from high in the southwestern sky, and the constellations and Venus blazed through an unusually clear and frigid night. Detectives Stan Doubleday and Joe Koenig watched the only pair of headlights they'd seen all night approach from the north. Doubleday pulled the unmarked car just off the shoulder, where a dirt road tracked through the woods from the east.

"Hey, got a customer," said Doubleday.

"Yeah. Shit, about time."

Stan keyed the two-way. "We got company. You guys got him?"

"Yeah," squawked the Motorola. "We're on his tail. We'll follow for a minute before we hit the flasher. Let him get a little closer to you."

As the police car hit the flasher, the car, which was only traveling about thirty-five or forty miles an hour, slowed to stop. Doubleday watched as the uniformed trooper got out and approached the driver's side. Then he and Koenig got out. Doubleday stood by his open door, his right hand resting on the butt of the .38 special he wore on his right hip. Koenig walked to where the trooper stood, his own hand buried in his car coat pocket, wrapped around his Smith & Wesson.

The driver had already rolled his window down as Koenig stopped beside the trooper.

"Evening sir. State Police," the trooper said. "See your driver's license, please?"

"Sure. Say, what's the problem, officer?"

The state policeman took the license.

"Mr. Harold Carter Macauley, is it? Pontiac, eh?" He looked from the license to Macauley, then back down at the license again. Then another look at Macauley while he shined the flashlight into his face.

"Say, Officer," said Macauley with a worried look, "what's the problem?"

"If you don't mind, sir, we'd like to ask the questions. Mind telling us what you're doing out here, sir, at almost 3:30 in the morning?"

"Yeah, sure." Macauley squinted into the flashlight. "I'm just looking, you know, thinking maybe I can catch the child killer," he stated matter-of-factly.

"Oh," managed Koenig, masking his surprise, as he pushed himself back from the window ledge.

He took a step back and nodded toward the flashing lights of the

State Police car. A second uniformed officer got out of it, walked to the front of the car, and stood, leaning against the right front headlight. Koenig took a half-step toward Macauley, still seated in the car. "What child killer's that, sir?"

"Well, you know, the one you're. . . . "

"Sir," Koenig cut him off, "mind stepping out of the car for a minute, please? Turn it off, and bring the keys with you. Like to see what's in your trunk."

"Okay," Macauley said, laughing nervously, "but I don't need a key." He started to reach across the front seat.

"Real slow, Mr. Macauley." Koenig reached for the door handle, opened it, and took another step back. "That's good."

Macauley slowly popped the glove box open and pressed a yellow button. Koenig heard the trunk latch release.

"That's fine, sir. Now, if you'd just slide out real easy."

The man eased himself out of the car and stood against the door opening.

"Better turn it off, Mr. Macauley, and just give me the keys for a minute. Now, let's have a look in that trunk."

Both men walked to the rear of the vehicle, a clean, almost new Buick sedan. Macauley swung the trunk lid up, and the uniformed cop leaning against his car moved forward a couple of steps. Koenig bent forward as he shone his flashlight into the nooks and crannies of the trunk: a spare tire, a tool box, a pair of battery cables. "Okay, sir," he said as he backed away. Macauley slammed the lid down.

Koenig, Macauley, and the uniformed cop walked back to the front door of Macauley's car. Koenig stood there dangling the keys. "Pretty clean car," said Koenig. "New?"

"Well, kind of. Actually, I picked up a new 1976 a couple of months ago. You know, inventory they didn't sell. Got a pretty good deal, too."

"Yeah," replied Koenig, "you keep it real clean, even with all the snow and slush. You got kids, Mr. Macauley?"

"Sure, three of 'em."

"Hard to keep a clean car with kids. Noticed your backseat is real clean, the floor, I mean. Front, too. What's your secret? I got a couple kids, they're always putting junk in the car. Gum wrappers, all that kind of stuff."

"Well, I dunno, I just like neat and clean. The world's a real mess, junk all over the place, litter everywhere," the man rattled on. He started to lean into the car.

"Hang on just a minute, please, Macauley." Macauley turned back to Koenig. "What's that on the front seat of the car?" He pointed at a small black object on the passenger's seat.

"That's just my tape recorder," he said with a nervous laugh. "Like to fool around with it, you know, record different stuff."

"Mind if we take a look, sir?"

"Aw, look, it's nothing important, okay? Just some junk I recorded."

"Maybe we'll just see later." Koenig moved to within a foot or so of Macauley, who was looking more interesting everytime he opened his mouth. "You say you're out here looking for the child killer?"

"Sure. I could use that twenty-five grand you guys are offering. Figured I might as well collect it as somebody else."

"Really," replied Koenig, looking at the uniformed officer again, then back to Macauley. "And you just happened to come to Squirrel Road, huh?"

"The Doc's got it all figured out," he nodded.

"Doc? What Doc's that, sir?" asked Koenig.

"That Danto fellow who's on television all the time, and in the newspapers. He says the guy who took that kid . . ."

"What kid's that, Mr. Macauley?" asked the detective, continuing his cat-and-mouse game.

"That kid from Birmingham. You know, Timothy King," replied Macauley calmly.

"Oh, that kid. Okay," Koenig nodded.

"Well, Danto says the killer. . . . "

"Oh, I thought the guy just took the kid, didn't know he'd killed him," Koenig said, baiting him.

"Well, sure, I mean," he stammered, "I don't know if he's killed him yet, but he did kill the other three, you know, and I figure he's killed Timmy too. So anyway, I just figured I'd be out here to catch him dumping the body."

"That still doesn't tell me why you picked Squirrel Road, now does it?" Koenig repeated.

"Well, like I was saying, Danto said the man who took the boy is like a squirrel gathering nuts. And he said that the man who killed the little girl dumped her on Bruce Lane because that's Danto's first name." Macauley sighed. "So I figured it out that the guy who took the little boy is gonna kill him and dump him out here . . . on Squirrel Road."

Koenig looked at the uniformed state cop, then back at Macauley again. He flipped the key ring to the other policeman.

"Mr. Macauley, I think you better come along with me and my partner in that car over there. The officer here can follow us in your car."

19

Krease took the call from C.I.S. at his home at 3:47, just minutes after the Squirrel Road arrest. Mindful of the politics in the case, he got Spreen out of bed to tell him that Macauley had been plucked from his turf, and would he like to be in on the interview?

Spreen had arrived and was seated with Koenig, Doubleday, and Macauley at the far end of one of the long tables. When Krease got to the firehall, Spreen quickly got up, bigger than life in his cowboy boots and hat, and intercepted the State Policeman. He extended a huge right hand to Krease, while his left arm swung around Krease's shoulder to steer him away from the group.

"Thanks again for the call, Joe," said Spreen in a half-whisper, as he led Krease into the tip room. "Joe, this is the guy we're after. Jesus, I mean, the guy really looks good. Says he's out there to catch the child killer. Christ," he spat, "he's him!"

"Well," Krease managed, "I guess we better have a talk with him and find out. Let me get some coffee first, okay?" yawned Krease. "Jesus, why do these things always happen in the middle of the night?" Krease stepped out of the tip room. "You guys want some of what's left of yesterday's coffee? Mr. Macauley, how about a cup of coffee?"

"Sure, okay," replied the interviewee. Doubleday and Koenig declined.

"Black?" asked Krease, stepping over to the table where the coffee pot and cups sat.

"Yeah, fine. You're Krease, aren't you, the one these guys have been talking about?"

"Detective Sergeant Joe Krease, State Police. Coffee's pretty bad, but it's all we've got."

"Look, Sergeant," interrupted Macauley, "it's really late. How long's this going to take?"

"Dunno," answered Krease, taking a sip from the styrofoam cup. "How much you got to say?"

"Yeah, Mr. Macauley, you better start saying it, right now," growled

Spreen from his other side. Macauley turned to look at the big man in the cowboy hat, then back to Krease.

"I'm tellin' you, this is really stupid. I'm just out there to try and nail this guy you're lookin' for, maybe collect a little of the reward money. I've got expenses to meet, gotta pay for that car, you know, and other stuff."

"Like that tape recorder?" interrupted Koenig. "Say, now that the Sergeant and the Sheriff are here," he continued, "why not listen to what you got on the tape?"

"I told you, it's nothing, just some dumb stuff."

"Why don't we be the judge of how dumb it is," said Krease. "You don't mind, do you?" He reached for the recorder in front of Macauley and punched the play button.

It was Macauley's voice: "Now, it's a little after two, the morning of March 22. I'm turning south on Squirrel Road from Dutton . . . proceeding at thirty miles an hour on Squirrel . . . the moon is bright, probably don't even need headlights with all the light reflecting off the snow. I'm the only car on the road." The voice droned on in a monotone.

"What's all that, Mr. Macauley?" asked Krease, punching the stop button. "Sounds like you're keeping some kind of diary."

"If I caught the guy, then I'd have it all down," Macauley said, looking down at the tabletop, embarrassed. Krease hit the play button again. "Uh-oh," said the voice on the tape, "looks like trouble here. I'm stopping now . . . car pulled across the road, guy standing there in my headlights, holding, yeah, looks like police I.D. Another car behind me . . . flashing red light. Another cop." Then there were other sounds under Macauley's voice, unmistakeably high-pitched voices.

"Just my kids," said Macauley referring to the voices. "You know, they were fooling around with the machine the other day. Guess it didn't erase the way it's supposed to when you record over it," he laughed sheepishly.

"Like kids, do you, Mr. Macauley?" asked Spreen.

"Sure, doesn't everybody?" he replied, still looking down at the table and scratching the rim of his cup with his two forefingers.

"We're not concerned with everybody, Mr. Macauley," said Spreen.

Krease interrupted. "Okay, Mr. Macauley, I can see another couple hours here, maybe you want to call your wife."

"Does that mean I'm under arrest, or something? Maybe I ought to call a lawyer."

"Well," replied Krease thoughtfully, "arrest might be too strong a word at this point. You can call a lawyer if you wish, but I really don't see a need. We just want to ask some questions about your family, where you work, that kind of thing. I can promise you, if we even get the slightest notion that you need your lawyer, we'll even pay for the call. We just want your cooperation so we can get this thing over with and go back home to bed. What do you say?"

Macauley looked at his watch. "There's no real problem, I guess." He tried the coffee. "My wife doesn't much care when I get home, anyway. We're going through a divorce. I mean I'm still living there with her and the kids, but only because I can't afford to get my own place yet. Don't have a lawyer, anyhow," he added.

"Well, we'd see you got one anyway, if you needed one," said Krease. "Look, why don't you start out by telling us a little bit about yourself and where you work, so we can check with your boss and see where you were on certain days."

Macauley was cooperative with his questioners, providing them with details of his marital problems, his job running a shaper at a little machine shop just north of Pontiac, and his dream of becoming a private investigator. He'd taken a mail-order course on becoming a P.I., and finding the child killer was to be his first big case. Distraught over the breakup of his home, he was trying to be a hero in the eyes of his kids. A few quick checks proved the truth of his story, and by nine o'clock he was on his way home.

Spreen was genuinely disappointed and told Krease he was going to have one of his unmarked cars follow Macauley around for a few days anyway. Krease didn't object — Spreen generally did what he wanted, and if he had the manpower to tail somebody who'd already been cleared, who cared?

The tip lines at the Birmingham Police Department and the Adams Street firehall had rung approximately twenty-five hundred times since Timmy King had been abducted, and there was no sign yet of either Timmy or the man who took him. The appeal for information provided the perfect opportunity for revenge for the irate wives of philandering husbands, for feuding neighbors, and for disgruntled employees. But until the husbands, neighbors, or bosses could be contacted and checked, each name had to be treated as a possible suspect and duly processed. Widespread fatigue and the short overtime budgets for many of the local police agencies involved forced Tobin and Robertson to institute rather dramatic cutbacks in manpower. What had been a three-hundred-man force was now reduced to a hundred men. Both Robertson and Tobin knew that, despite the urgency of the case, other, unrelated police work had to continue in Oakland County. Services could no longer continue to be disrupted in those communities which had so graciously given of their time and money by way of their police departments.

It was argued that more, not fewer police officers were needed; after all, neither the boy nor his abductor had been found. The logic did not escape the men who made the decision to cut back, but the problem was that all officers were working incredibly long single shifts. So the call went out for other suburban law enforcement agencies to release some of their detectives, a fresh crew to work with the Task Force. Livonia was the first of many agencies to respond to the call. If the Task Force could be beefed up enough to run a double shift, it would be ideal. So even as the cutbacks were being made, the foundation was being laid for a much bigger manhunt.

The rusted-out Maverick with two teenagers in it turned south on Gill Road off Eight Mile.

"Hey, what the hell ya' doin', asshole? This ain't where we're supposed to go," exclaimed Charlie.

"What do you mean? This is Gill Road, ain't it? And that's where we're supposed to pick her up, ain't it? Jesus, can't you follow directions?"

"I'm tellin' ya, Mike, it's the next street up. She said the next street up from Gill."

"You sure?" asked Mike.

"Yeah, I'm sure. C'mon, turn this piece of junk around. Shit, we're supposed to be there at eleven o'clock." He reached up to turn on the dome light and looked at his wristwatch. "Jesus, we're already twenty minutes late."

"Yeah, yeah, don't be gettin all crazy. Lemme just find a good place to make a U-turn." The Maverick, which had rattled its way about three hundred feet along Gill Road, slowed, then edged into the driveway entrance of number 20147. After checking traffic from both directions, Mike swung across both lanes in a U-turn.

"Hey, Mike, you see that?" Charlie leaned forward to focus on something in a shallow ditch on the east side of Gill. "Jesus. Hey, stop for a minute, will ya? Stop the goddam car!"

"What the hell you talkin' about?" demanded Mike, who hit the brakes anyway, causing the car to skid to a stop on the gravel road.

"Just back the car up a little, will ya? There's somethin' in that ditch. Christ, didn't you see it in the headlights?"

"Aw, Christ, all right. Just calm down, will ya?" Mike threw the clunker into reverse, and it jerked backwards, wheels throwing gravel.

"Yeah, there, stop. There in the ditch . . . Jesus!"

The Maverick lurched to a dead stop, throwing Mike hard against the back of the seat.

"There, asshole," yelled Charlie, frantically pointing down into the ditch lighted by the Maverick's headlights.

He had opened the door and was half-in, half-out of the vehicle. Mike was leaning forward and peering into the ditch. "Holy shit!" he spat, as he opened his own door and stood looking over the hood of the car, one hand still on the steering wheel. "What the hell you think it is, Charlie?"

"It's a goddam body. Looks like a little kid." Charlie boldly took a few steps closer toward the prostrate figure and stumbled over a discarded skateboard lying just off the roadway.

20

Robertson was a little less than halfway to his home in Livonia from the Birmingham fire station as he flipped the car radio over from country music to the 760 spot and the 11 P.M. newscast on WJR. He'd stayed late with Tobias and Krease in the Squad Room, roughing out a questionnaire for the families of the victims in an effort to ascertain any common denominators.

"The search for a missing eleven-year-old Birmingham boy continues, while fatigue forces a cutback in the number of detectives working the case. Task Force spokesman and Birmingham Police Chief Jerry Tobin told WJR that fatigue on the part of overworked investigators, strained overtime budgets, and the press of unrelated police services, are reasons for the cutbacks. Tobin says that for the past several days, up to three hundred detectives and police officers were looking for the boy, but that number will now be reduced to approximately one hundred officers. Tobin also told our newsroom that police have no new leads in the disappearance of Timmy King, last seen six days ago, and who many observers believe may be the next child killer victim. . . ."

Robbie snapped the radio off. He'd had enough of the child killer for one day.

It was nearly 11:30 when the Lieutenant pulled into his garage. The downstairs of the house was dark. Dee's already gone up, he thought, as he flipped the switch for the kitchen light.

"Hi, I'm home," he called through the house.

"Hi, yourself," came the reply from upstairs. "I'm not in bed yet, just getting ready. Want me to fix you something?"

"Naw, that's all right, honey. Think I'll crack a beer and unwind a little before I come up."

He was interrupted by the ring of the telephone. He stepped to the wallphone and lifted the receiver. "Yeah, hello. Oh hi, Doug, what's up?" He reached for the refrigerator door, opened it, and snared a can of Stroh's, the phone cradled to his left ear, and popped the top of the can. "Damn. . . . well, okay. Yeah, I got a map in my briefcase. Sure. You called Krease, yet? All right, I'll give him a call. Livonia's good, yeah, they'll do a good job. All right, Doug, thanks." He hung the phone up, took a gulp of Stroh's, set the beer down long enough to shuck off his car coat, and walked into the living room to turn the TV on, just loud enough so he could hear it when he went back into the kitchen to call Krease.

"Yeah, Joe, look. Radio just called me from District. They got a body out on Gill Road. That's over here in Livonia . . . wait a minute." He stretched the phone cord into the dining room, opened and reached into the briefcase he'd laid on the table just after coming in and pulled out a map. "You get off the freeway and take Drake south to Eight Mile, then hang east maybe three-quarters of a mile and you come to Gill. It'll probably look like a policemen's convention by the time you get there. Naw, I'd just be in the way. Livonia runs a tight ship. Turner's a good man. Look, Joe, I'll get ahold of Tobin, and then I gotta let some of our people know."

Robertson took another swallow of beer and dialed Tobin's home number. Tobin elected not to go to the crime scene but to send Kalbfleisch. He himself would call Studt, who was living with the Kings, and tell him to keep the family away from the television set. There would undoubtedly be blanket coverage at the scene, and Tobin didn't want them to hear that Timmy was dead before anyone was even sure it was him. Tobin would wait for word directly from Kalbfleisch at the scene, then if the news was bad he would go to the King home to be with the family.

Dee, having heard parts of the telephone conversation from upstairs, came down to join her husband. "What's all that about?" she asked, joining him on the davenport in front of the television set. Robbie, leaning forward, elbows on his knees, both hands around the can of beer, told her. His eyes were glued to the television set, waiting for the news break he knew would come.

Krease, aided by all the flashing red lights, had no trouble locating Gill Road.

"Well, at least the media aren't here yet," he thought to himself. The flashing red lights had drawn some passing motorists, and he had to skirt a half-dozen cars that'd pulled off to the side of the road to watch all the action. Krease thought to himself how they all ought to be home in bed. The occupants had left their cars and were now clustered at the corner, quietly milling around behind the police lines. Krease parked in front of the first car next to the entrance, got out, and walked by the bystanders, thinking to himself, "Here we go again!" He flashed his I.D. to the Livonia cop standing by the marked car pulled across the road. After asking the cop, whom he didn't know, if anybody was there from the Task Force, Krease walked down to where several uniformed and plainclothes policemen were standing, about a hundred feet from where a Livonia Fire Department Rescue Unit was parked near the body.

"Hi, Sarge," said Kalbfleisch, who turned at the sound of loose gravel as the State Policeman approached.

"Hi, Jack. How'd you get here so fast?"

"I live a lot closer than you do, Joe. They fill you in?"

"No, not much. I talked a little with Robbie."

"The paramedics say the body was still warm. You know, dead but warm, so they tried to revive him, but he's deader'n hell."

"Is it Timmy?" asked Krease, knowing the answer.

"No doubt in my mind." Kalbfleisch, shaking his head looked over at the drop site again. "Red hockey jacket, the green corduroys, fits the physical description, and a skateboard right next to the body."

"How was the body . . . ?"

"On his stomach, left side of his face to the ground."

"Dressed?"

"Like I say, red hockey jacket and all. Looks like he just laid down to take a nap."

"Yeah," replied Krease somberly.

"The son of a bitch is playing games with us," said Kalbfleisch as he pulled his collar up around his neck, cupped his hands together, and blew on them. "The bastard's moving on us, Joe. This isn't Oakland County any more, you know—we're three hundred feet south of Eight Mile in Wayne County."

"I know. I was thinking about that on the way over here. Maybe he's smart enough to know that everything in Oakland County that moves is being stopped and searched. He thinks 'I'm gonna outsmart you bastards and dump him in Wayne County.' Things are hot for him in Oakland County, and we haven't exactly been low profile."

Krease looked at the activity going on by the Rescue Unit and changed the subject. "How long's the lab been here, Jack? I hope those are our people over there."

Kalbfleisch looked over to the half-dozen men picking their way around a small, dark form lying in the ditch, well lighted by several large floodlights set up in the middle of the street.

"About thirty minutes, I guess. Maybe forty-five. Yeah, those are your guys from District, five of them, I think. Want to take a walk over there?"

"I'll wait till they're done. There's plenty of time."

"There is that," agreed the Birmingham detective looking again at Krease. "Joe, ever want to take off your badge and go after somebody?"

"Know what you mean, Jack. We don't have that luxury, though." Krease changed the subject again. "What about the M.E.?"

"Spitz is on the way. Now, there's a coroner!"

Krease laughed. "You musta heard about the sperm thing on the Kristine case." He went on quickly, "You guys done any neighborhood canvass yet, Jack?"

"We've got a half-dozen guys working both sides of the street since an hour ago."

"Good," said Krease. "Got to wake some people up around here tonight—if they aren't already awake. Christ, somebody must have noticed something. I hope we don't draw a blank here like on Bruce Lane."

"Wouldn't count too much on it. Say, looks like the lab people might be finished," said Kalbfleisch, who was starting to shift from one foot to the other to warm himself. "Let's go over and take a closer look."

"Might as well. I want to talk to the paramedics, anyway."

The two policemen spent only three or four minutes with the rescue team. Timmy's body had been warm enough to indicate that there might be a chance, and they had tried everything in the book to bring him back, even at the risk of disturbing evidence on or around the body. After all, a paramedic's first priority was to save lives, not solve crimes. They acted properly and in no way compromised the investigation by disturbing the immediate area.

Krease and Kalbfleisch finished with the rescue team and walked the few feet to where a group of five men was huddled around Timmy.

"Hi, Sarge, Jack," greeted State Police Detective Sergeant Nowak.

"Hi, Mike. Okay if I step over there and take a look?" Krease asked of the lab expert while moving closer to the body. "You find anything?"

"Nothing except the skateboard here." Mike held the skateboard out in front of Krease. "I'll bet a dollar to a dime it's cleaner than a whistle, too."

"No bet," said Krease.

"We're wrapped up for now. We'll take another look tomorrow, or I should say, later today, in a couple hours when there's daylight. Medics say he's fresh. I guess they told you they tried to bring him back."

"How fresh, Mike?" Krease asked.

"I don't know. What'd they say?"

"Well, they said it wasn't like minutes. Maybe a couple hours, though. Couldn't put an exact time on it. They're not doctors. I just wanted to get your feel for it. Spitz ought to be here any minute, then we'll know for sure."

Schoonover, another of the Northville Lab experts at the scene, stopped making notes on a clipboard and looked past Krease. "That looks like the M.E.'s car now."

The others turned as the car came slowly at them down Gill Road and eased to a stop just a few feet from where they were standing. Krease and Kalbfleisch walked toward it, as the driver got out.

Werner Spitz was a rather distinguished-looking man, nearly six feet tall and slender, with short gray hair. He wore a parka over his business suit.

"Good evening." His German accent was pronounced.

"Hi, Doc," Krease returned, shaking his hand.

"I'd like you to meet Jack Kalbfleisch—Birmingham." The burly detective shook hands and asked Spitz if he'd been briefed.

"Yes. Well, I don't know all the details, leading up to tonight, except what I read, but yes, I know what you're up against."

"Well, we're trying everything we know," said Krease. "Our lab people are all finished—he's ready for you now, I guess." He turned to look at Timmy's body in the ditch a few feet away.

The lab crew acknowledged Spitz's presence by nodding, as they parted to allow him access to the body. Spitz turned to Krease before he got down on his haunches. "Joe, stay close. We can talk while I work and save some time that way. I'd like to get him downtown as soon as I can, you know." Spitz was already into his examination, lifting first one limb then another, checking the rigor. Without looking up, he said, "Joe, judging by the lividity, I'm going to guess he's been dead for. . . . " He hesitated, stood up, and walked around to the other side of the body. "Well, I think somewhere between six and eight hours." He looked at his watch. "Nearly 2:30. I'd say sometime between 6:30, well, let's say between six and eight o'clock last night." He got down on his haunches again and touched the dead boy's forehead. "It's pretty cold out, so that would speed up the process a little. I might be able to do better than that, but I'll have to go inside later." The pathologist turned the boy's head slightly and ran his finger over a slightly discolored spot on the left forehead. Without looking up, he said to Krease, "Looks like a small abrasion."

"Do you. . . . "

"No. I don't think it's a blow or anything like that. It could have happened when he dumped him, if he dropped him from a couple feet. I am not sure. I will take a closer look, of course, when we get him back." Spitz rose to his feet with a groan. "Getting old, Joe," he said, throwing his shoulders back to stretch. Then he stared down at the boy's jacket and stooped to pick up something so small Krease couldn't see it. He seemed to have trouble grasping it between his thumb and forefinger.

"What have you got, Doctor?" inquired Krease, kneeling himself.

"I don't know. It looks like some kind of hair — not his, not human, as a matter of fact. Too heavy and short, more like a . . . a cat, or something."

"What the hell?" Krease muttered.

"Yes, maybe a cat. It's pretty cold out, and the body was obviously warm."

"You telling me that a cat came over here and slept on the damn body?"

"Yes, that is what I'm telling you, Sergeant. Something like that, anyway."

"Any chance that hair could have dropped off the guy who put him there? Maybe he's a cat owner, or something," asked Kalbfleisch, who'd been standing on the road, watching and listening.

"I don't know," replied Spitz. "I'm a pathologist, not a magician." He managed a chuckle. "You understand all of this is preliminary. I must examine everything closely before I can give you anything definite. It wouldn't be a bad idea to have your lab people try and identify it, though." With that, he took out a small plastic Ziplock bag, opened it, and dropped a few of the strange hairs inside. "Here. You give this to them." He handed the bag to Krease.

"You about done, Doc?" asked Kalbfleisch, who walked over and stood beside Joe.

"Yes. Just one more quick look, here." He bent over to lift one of the dead youngster's arms, then the other. He pulled the jacket back a little, just off the wrists. "You know, we may have some slight indentations on the wrists. Noticed something on one of the ankles, too. Might be that he was tied." He rose to his full height. "Well, that's enough for now. I must get him back so we can go inside. Damn!"

Kalbfleisch said, "Look, can you give us a guess on how he died?"

"Well, Detective Kalbfleisch, I don't see any gross evidence of violence, no apparent wounds, anything like that. Till I know more, I'm going to say somebody helped him run out of air."

"You mean, suffocation?"

"Yes, that is exactly what I mean. Probably just one hand over the mouth, the other pinching the nostrils. Look," the pathologist said a little impatiently, "that's all I can tell you right now. I have a lot of work to do yet. Let's get him downtown." He beckoned to a couple of attendants who had followed him over in the M.E. truck and pulled unnoticed in front of the Rescue Unit. They walked over to the body, carrying a fold-up gurney. One had a folded white sheet in one hand. Spitz directed them as they placed the body on the opened sheet, which they folded carefully, so as not to lose anything that might have been on the body. They popped the gurney open, gently placed Timmy on the cart, and carried it over the gravel to where the truck was parked, its rear doors opened.

"Well, gentlemen, I had better get to this grim business."

"Okay," said Krease, "but when. . . . "

"It is going to be at least a couple hours, but it's priority, you know that. I should have something for you shortly. Just give me a couple of hours. I'll call you soon as we know something."

"All right, Doc, thanks, you know. . . . "

"Yes, I know, Sergeant. I know."

Krease was in no mood to play Twenty Questions with the media. He'd noticed reporters gathering as the night progressed, bunched together at the entrance to Gill Road. Joe had to go right through them to get to his car, and not surprisingly, Wade was the first one to nail him, or try to, as he approached Eight Mile.

"Sergeant! Sergeant, Channel 7."

"Yeah, I know, Vince," replied Krease tiredly. "All right, look, I'm not prepared. . . . " Wade's crew hit him with the lights, triggering the other crews to do the same.

"Sergeant, have you identified the body? Is it Timmy King?"

Krease stopped. He could do little else — they had him surrounded. He squinted into the cameras. "Yes, we do have a body."

"Is it Timmy King, Sergeant?" a print reporter interrupted.

Krease, perturbed at their impatience, began again. "Yes, we do have a body, and no, we do not have a positive identification yet." Technically, that was accurate.

"Does the body fit the general description of Timmy King?" persisted still another reporter.

Joe turned slightly to face the questioner. "Well, it appears to be the body of a young male, Caucasian."

"Sergeant," it was Wade again, "was he wearing a red jacket? What about a skateboard?"

"All right, look," Krease said in a voice that betrayed nearly twenty-four hours without sleep, "you guys, c'mon, gimme a break. You turn your cameras off, I'll talk to you for a minute. Otherwise, the interview's over, okay?" The lights went off again. "The body answers the general description of Timmy, red hockey jacket and all."

Wade asked, "Sergeant, what about the skateboard? Somebody said you found a skateboard."

"Yeah, Vince, we picked up a skateboard. Look," he addressed the whole group, "you guys are going to say what you're going to say, anyway, but just remember, until the postmortem is finished, we really can't say anything definite. If it is Timmy, and," he hesitated, "it undoubtedly is, we'd really rather not have his parents find out on television. We've been straight with you right along, and you've been straight with us. Let's just keep it that way. Now look, it's late and we've got a helluva lot of work to do yet. We'll let you all know as soon as we have something. There'll be a briefing tomorrow."

Reporters and cameramen stood aside and let him go.

21

"God, I hate this part of being a cop," Tobin thought to himself as he pulled out onto Maple Road and headed toward the King house. His throat was tight and dry. He snapped the car radio on and turned the dial to the all-news WCAR.

" . . . and the body, dressed in a red athletic jacket and green pants, is believed to be that of the missing Birmingham youngster, eleven-year-old Timothy King. . . . "

"God damn it!" Jerry exclaimed aloud, his voice cracking with emotion as he pulled into the Kings' driveway.

"However," the WCAR newsman went on, "police at the scene refused to confirm or deny the dead boy's identity. . . . "

The Chief switched the radio off, killed the engine, and got out. All the lights were on downstairs, as he walked up on the front porch and knocked twice. Studt opened it. The two men looked at each other, but neither spoke as Studt followed him into the living room. Officer Gracie, who was standing, nodded at Tobin. The Kings were seated on the couch holding hands and said nothing as Jerry seated himself near them. His voice caught. "Mr. and Mrs. King, I. . . . " He faltered, and began again. "Mr. and Mrs. King, I'm afraid I have some very bad news."

Barry King, who had been a pillar of strength through the whole ordeal, suddenly buried his face in his hands and began sobbing. Marian seemed to take a deep breath as she blinked the tears back. She didn't speak, but put her arms around her husband and held him close. As she caressed the back of her husband's head, she spoke softly.

"Yes, Chief Tobin, please go on." She took a deep breath, "When Tim, Officer Gracie, came, we knew that something was the matter." Gracie came to her and put a hand on her shoulder. She grasped his arm. "Tim, thank you." Barry King stood and wiped his tears. Studt, with an arm across his shoulders, led him into the dining room.

Marian's head was bowed. "Please, Chief Tobin. The boy on Gill Road, it is . . . my son, isn't it?"

"Yes, ma'am, I'm afraid it is. I'm so. . . . "

Marian seemed to gain strength, now that the worst was over. "No, it's all right. Please. The waiting is over." She paused. "What must we do next?"

"Mrs. King, someone, perhaps a close friend or relative, will have to go downtown with us soon and identify him."

"Yes, I know. I must do it . . . it must be me."

"It doesn't have to be."

"Yes, please, I'm Tim's mother. I have to, I want to be the one."

"I admire your strength, Mrs. King, both of you."

"Now, I must tell his brothers and sister."

"Yes, I know," said Tobin, who wished he could say more. "Mrs. King, please know that we're going to do everything to catch the man who did this to your son."

"Yes, we know you will. Would you mind terribly, Chief Tobin," she rose from the couch, "I'd like to be with my husband."

"Of course, but just one more thing, please. I'd like to have one of the officers continue to stay with you and your husband for a couple of days, in case anybody calls."

"Like my son's murderer?"

"Well, anybody, I guess," Tobin answered, somewhat taken aback by Marian's bluntness.

"Yes, of course. I don't know if either Barry or I could have survived these past six days without Don and Tim. They've become part of our family."

"Thank you," Jerry said, and Marian stepped over and hugged him. He held her for a moment, looking over her shoulder at Studt and Gracie, sitting on either side of Barry King at the dining room table. Then she turned to go to him, and Jerry let himself out.

The Wayne County Morgue, with its dirty, grey marble exterior and cold interior, is one of the grimmest buildings in Detroit, not only because of the business that goes on there, but because it was designed that way. You're not supposed to be comfortable in a morgue. Bodies are identified over a nineteen-inch black-and-white television monitor. Straight-backed wooden benches provide the only comfort for strangers waiting their turn to stare into the starkness of the monitor to identify wives, husbands, friends, relatives, acquaintances, and their own children. Medical Examiner

Werner Spitz says, "We don't want people to stay too long grieving. Grief is contagious, and if one person starts wailing, pretty soon everybody is standing around either grieving or trying to comfort those who are. Grieving is for the funeral home. This is a place where we must conduct a very grim but necessary business."

It was into this cold atmosphere of marble and tile that Marian King, accompanied by Birmingham Police Sergeant Jack Kalbfleisch, State Police Detective Sergeant Joe Krease, and the family priest, came on Wednesday morning, the twenty-third of March.

Spitz, in spite of his thirty-some years as a pathologist, could never quite suppress his emotions when parents had to identify their children. This one was particularly difficult for Spitz, who had a boy just a couple of years younger than Timmy King. After briefly greeting Marian King and offering his condolences, he called the picture up on the monitor and stood back with Kalbfleisch and Krease. The picture wavered, then froze into focus. She put her hand to her mouth, suppressing a gasp, but did not speak.

"Mrs. King," Spitz said, placing a hand on her shoulder. She turned quickly and faced the pathologist.

"Mrs. King," he asked again, "is that Timothy King?"

"Yes." She quickly looked again at the black-and-white picture of the boy, covered except for his face, with a white sheet.

"Yes, that's my son, Tim. Please, may I go now?" she asked, as Krease and Kalbfleisch took her by the arms.

"Certainly. I know it's difficult, but I have a document for you to si —"

"Can't it wait, Doc?" asked Krease. "She's —"

"No . . . that's all right, Sergeant." She composed herself. "Let's do it now."

It was close to 4:30 when Robbie left the Birmingham City Hall, where he, Tobin, and Livonia Police Chief Bob Turner had announced to a room packed with reporters that Timmy King was no longer missing. He went over to the Squad Room, grabbed a cup of coffee, and walked over to the work table where Krease was sitting with Kalbfleisch.

"How'd it go at the morgue this morning?" he asked.

"Okay, I guess. She's one strong lady," answered Kalbfleisch. "Funny, you know, you'd think that Mr. King was the stronger of the two. I mean, he's the one that did all the talking before. But now when the chips are down, she takes over."

"Oh, I don't know, Jack," said Robbie. "Who the hell knows. That's probably the way it'd be in my house. I'm not so sure any man is a match for a woman, when push really comes to shove, especially when it comes to kids. I guess I'm surprised, but I'm not surprised, if you know what I mean."

"Yeah, you're right," admitted Kalbfleisch. "I never really thought much about it, I guess, till now." He changed the subject. "Joe and I were just talking about the neighborhood canvass on Gill Road we did last night."

"I don't know what the hell to make of this, Lieutenant," Krease cut in. "We've got this woman, she's either nuttier than a fruitcake, or maybe we've got ourselves something."

"Oh?" said Robbie, taking another swallow of coffee, as his eyes widened.

"This woman is swearing up and down that the car that dropped the body off tried to run her down and chased her all over the road. They're bringing her in with them. She lives just a couple houses down from where the body was. And she says she knows who was driving it!"

Robertson started to respond, but Krease reached for a heavy, cardboard envelope and continued: "We also got one hundred fifty copies of the stills of the guy at the Mihelich funeral. I'll distribute them at the briefing tomorrow. Some of the guys already got 'em."

22

O'Brien and Sholtz, the two Oakland County detectives, steered her in, one on each arm. "Gentlemen," O'Brien announced, as Krease and Kalbfleisch rose from the table, "Gentlemen, this is Mrs. Ballantine. Mrs. Rita Sue Ballantine." Rita Sue smiled faintly as Krease acknowledged the introduction. She let O'Brien take her coat as she shrugged out of it.

She was tall, leggy, and full-breasted, inexpensively dressed in a skirt and sweater, both of which appeared to be a size too small. The face, which was pretty but showed some miles, was framed by heavily sprayed, freshly coiffed red hair.

"Have a seat, Mrs. Ballantine," Joe said, pulling a chair out from the table and holding it for her.

"Thanks, Sergeant. Call me Rita Sue, okay? 'Mrs. Ballantine' reminds me too much of that son of a bitch I married."

O'Brien said, "Sarge, Rita says they had a little argument last night. That's why she happened to be out walking at that hour."

"That right, Rita Sue?" Joe cut in.

"Yeah, I just got home from the beauty parlor — they're open nights, ya know — and he starts hammerin' on me, wantsa know how come I'm not there with his dinner ready. Hell, this is the first time in a month he's been home before me. He's usually hangin' around with that little tramp at the bar."

Krease smiled, figuring he was in for a real treat with this one. "So you decided to just go out for some fresh air, eh? That's why you were out walking around at that hour, because you were mad at your husband?"

"Yeah, sure." The woman settled back in the chair. "I'm out walkin' along Gill, and I hear this car comin' up behind me, but he don't pass right away, just keeps followin' me, and I can hear the tires crunchin' on the gravel."

"How long would you say he followed you?" asked Kalbfleisch.

She looked at him. "Oh, I dunno, seemed like a long time. Maybe a couple hundred feet."

"Okay."

"Anyway, pretty soon he passes me up, not real fast, kinda slow. So I look to see who's drivin', and he's lookin' right at me. Jesus, I think to myself, what's your problem, buddy? He's still lookin' right at me, and I'm startin' to get a little pissed, you know. I mean, maybe this guy thinks here's this broad walkin' late at night, maybe she's easy." She paused, fishing around in her purse. She pulled out a rumpled pack of Marlboros and took one out. Sholtz, the only smoker in the crowd, pulled out a Zippo. She French-inhaled deeply and sighed, throwing her shoulders back.

"Go on, Ma'am," urged Krease.

"Well, so the guy is giving me the look, you know, then he speeds up, goes up the road a ways, pulls over to the side, and stops. I stop, figuring I'm gonna walk to the first house and knock on the door if he don't pull away. Well, he finally does pull away, then stops again and gets out of the car. It's dark but I can hear the door open."

"How far away from the car were you?" interrupted Krease.

"I dunno, maybe fifty, sixty feet."

"Close enough to see him?"

"Well, no, not really. But," she quickly added, "I see just this form standin' at the back of the car like he's gonna open the trunk or somethin'. Then he walks around to the door, gets in, and turns the car around and starts comin' back toward me again. Heading right for me, coming fast right at me. I think, 'God, he's gonna run me down.'" She took another drag on the Marlboro. "But then, he slows right down when he gets up to where I'm still standin'. Course, I'm walkin' by now, headin' right for home."

"Is your house before where he stopped, or down the road past where he stopped?" asked Kalbfleisch.

"It's a couple houses past where he stopped," she answered. "Like I say, he's goin' real slow when he goes by, and he's lookin' right at me again."

"Get a good look at him, did you?" asked Joe.

"You bet I did."

"How about the car?"

"Yeah, that, too."

"How about the license plate, Rita Sue. You see it?"

"Yeah. Well, no, maybe not enough to remember," she replied tentatively, looking down at her hands.

"Could you tell what color the car was?" Krease pressed.

"Naw, not really. Dark color, I guess. I mean if it was white or somethin', I woulda noticed."

"What about the driver? You think you might be able to recognize him if you saw him again?" asked Kalbfleisch.

"Damn right I would. Yeah, I'd be able to tell for sure."

Joe got up from his chair. "I'm going to get some pictures. Be right back." He disappeared into the tip room and pulled a half-dozen composites, including one of the child-killer suspect, from a desk drawer. Nine times out of ten, if you show a witness a picture of a suspect, then ask "Is this the person you saw?" they'll say yes. But if you show them several pictures, they're a little more careful. If the witness could pick the suspect from several pictures, it was more solid. Back in the squad room, Krease laid the composite on the table, face down.

"First, I'd like to have you describe the man you saw in the car, then, I'll let you take a look at some drawings." She nodded.

"Well," she said, leaning back and folding her hands in her lap, "I'd say his hair was dark and heavy, kind of long and shaggy at the neck, you know."

"He wore glasses, too, right?" interrupted Kalbfleisch, trying to trap her.

She turned slightly. "No, no glasses." To Krease she said, "Kind of a narrow face, long sideburns, kind of a good-lookin' guy."

The detectives looked at each other. Krease turned the pictures over. The child-killer suspect composite was buried next to last. "Now I want you to take a very careful look at these." He took the first one off the pile and handed it to her.

She studied it.

"Nope, this ain't him," she stated flatly.

"You sure?"

"Yep, I'm sure."

"Okay, how about this one? Take a good look."

She studied number two and quickly handed it back. "Him, either. Not even close."

"Got a narrow face and lotsa hair," reminded Kalbfleisch.

"I'm tellin' ya, this ain't him."

"Okay, okay. Just want to be sure."

"Yeah, I know," she repeated, taking the third composite from Krease.

"Take your time now, Rita Sue. No rush," he said.

She shook her head, handing the next two drawings back. Krease turned over the child-killer suspect. "How about him?" he asked calmly. She held the drawing in front of her, studying it but saying nothing. Finally Krease asked, "What about it, Mrs. Ballantine? That the man you saw?"

She put the picture down and reached into the pack of Marlboros, taking another one out. Sholtz went for his lighter. She leaned to the side so he could light it for her.

"Yeah, that's him," she said, inhaling deeply as she reached for the picture and held it up again, exhaling smoke at it. Joe took the picture from her, and put it back on the pile of drawings. The detectives looked at each other, then back at Rita Sue.

"You sure, Ma'am?" asked Kalbfleisch. "That guy's been in jail for the past three years."

"Yeah, that's so much bullshit, too," she snapped. "C'mon, that's the guy on television, and that's the guy I saw followin' me." She snatched the picture from the pile and held it in front of Kalbfleisch's face. "I know what the hell I saw, and this," she shook the picture in front of him, "is what I saw, okay?"

"Okay," Krease laughed. "All right, that's the guy on television, the one we're looking for. We just have to be sure, that's all. Look," he glanced at his watch, "it's getting pretty late. Officers O'Brien and Sholtz here will take you home. We're probably going to want to talk to you some more, and I'd like to ask you to take a polygraph test. It's just routine. We do it with all the witnesses. Maybe we'll even have you talk with a hypnotist to see if you can give us a license number."

She got up from her chair. "That poly-thing, whatever you said. . . . "

"Polygraph."

"That one of those lie detector things? You guys think I lied? eh?" she demanded, looking a little affronted.

"No," Joe laughed. "But you know, sometimes people get a little mixed up in these kinds of situations. Especially after going through something like you went through."

Nice touch, Joe, thought O'Brien to himself, smiling as he held the woman's coat.

Because the four Oakland County victims had lived within a mile of the notorious Woodward corridor, the strip along Woodward from Six Mile north to Twelve Mile was given top priority status in the search for the child killer.

On any given night, you could drive down Woodward and see any number of youngsters, mostly boys, working the curbs with their thumbs out. Chickens, they were called, and a few were as young as thirteen. The going rate was ten dollars, twenty if the kid was slim and blond. Many of the youngsters did well – it was good money for ten minutes in the front seat of a car at the shoulder of the road. The clientele, most of whom wore three-piece suits during the day, came to Woodward at night, seeking pleasure along the curbs and in the bars and restaurants.

Police teams working the strip come to know the haunts well and use them as coffee and lunch stops, their eyes catching more in a glance than most absorb in a long, lingering look. It was in one of these restaurants, catering to both gays and straights, that a four-man crew from C.I.S. stopped to meet for a predawn breakfast after working the bars and the streets all night. The four detectives, Tom Meekins, Don Anderson, C. J. Anderson (no relation), and Jim Sherman, found the place surprisingly full, considering the hour. There were only two open stools at the counter as the four cops seated themselves in a rear booth. The crowd was mostly street people, with a cabbie or two and a pair of uniformed Detroit beat cops at the end of the counter near the door.

Meekins noticed him almost immediately. He continued looking around the waitress, distractedly putting in his order when it was his turn. He couldn't take his eyes off the man two seats down from the beat cops, a nondescript sort of a man, minding his own business and working on a wedge of pie along with his coffee. Meekins nudged Anderson, who was engaged in small talk with the other Anderson and Sherman seated across from him. Meekins said softly, "The guy down near those two cops . . ." He reached into his suitcoat pocket and pulled out a picture, looked down to study it, then handed it to Anderson.

"Well, I'll be a son of a bitch," Anderson exclaimed softly, handing the picture across the table to the others. "Christ, that's him. Even the same coat!"

C. J. and Sherman turned in their seats briefly. "Sure as hell is," nodded C. J. "It's the guy at the funeral! How we gonna handle it?"

Meekins flagged the waitress. "Honey, forget about the breakfast. Look, the guy at the counter over there, two down from the uniforms, he got a name?" He showed the waitress his badge. She turned slowly and then back.

"Yeah, sure, the guy's name is Ben. I mean, I don't know him, 'cept as a customer, you know."

"Last name?"

"I dunno, he don't talk much."

"He come in here a lot?" interjected Sherman.

"No, well, maybe once a week or so. I dunno, I don't work the counter that much."

"All right, thanks. Look, we're going to leave a couple of bucks for the coffee and a little something for your trouble, okay? Thanks, honey."

The girl picked up the two dollars, turned, and walked quickly back toward the kitchen.

"All right," said Meekins softly, "C. J., Jim, why don't you guys get up and go outside and just stand there by the door and wait. Me and Don'll bring him out."

Meekins and Anderson walked over to where the man was seated at the counter. Anderson quickly flashed his badge to identify himself and Meekins to the Detroit cops, then silently turned to join Meekins, who'd seated himself next to the suspect. "Excuse me, sir. I'm Detective Meekins, this is Detective Anderson. State Police." He showed his badge. "We'd like to talk to you for a couple of minutes."

"Why?"

"Can we have your name, sir?"

"Sure, it's Benjamin Ward. Look, what the hell's this all about? I ain't done nothin'."

"We'll ask the questions, if you don't mind, sir."

"Everything all right, officers?" asked one of the uniforms.

"Yeah, sure, thanks, guys. Everything's fine. Just want to ask this man some questions."

"Okay, we're right here." The Detroit cop smiled.

"Look, Mr. Ward. Let's just go outside."

"You guys busting me? Shit, I ain't done nothin'," he protested as he picked up his check, looking first at one plainclothesman, then the other. He fished out a couple of bills and dropped them on the counter.

"No, we're not exactly arresting you, Mr. Ward, unless you really don't wanna go with us," said Meekins, leading him out the door. "We'll bring you back to your car later. Is it in the lot here?"

"Yeah," said Ward, tentatively," right over there." He pointed to a small, late-model compact car that was not a Gremlin.

"Good. Nobody'll bother it here. Say, you don't mind if we kind of have a look inside as long as we're here? I mean, we can get a warrant and all that if you'd rather we didn't take a look. Maybe you've got something in there you don't want us to see."

"Yeah, s-sure," Ward stammered. "Say, what the hell's this all about?

You guys are supposed to tell me. I mean, are you charging me with some kinda crime?"

"Ah, you've been watching television, haven't you, Mr. Ward," commented Anderson. "No, we don't mind telling you what this is all about." He took the picture from his coat and led Ward under a sidewalk streetlight.

"This you, sir?"

Ward took the picture and scrutinized it. "Where the hell'd you get this?" he asked, startled.

"You happen to attend the funeral of a little girl about three or four weeks ago?" The suspect looked down at the sidewalk, then back up at Anderson. "Y-yeah," he stuttered. "Yeah, maybe I did."

"You know her?" asked Anderson.

"N-no, not really. No, I didn't know her," he replied meekly, looking down at the sidewalk as Anderson led him back to where the other three State Police officers were shining flashlights in his car.

"Shouldn't leave your car unlocked, Mr. Ward. This ain't the best of neighborhoods, you know," said Sherman dryly.

"Anything in the car?" asked Anderson.

"Naw, looks all right," answered Meekins.

"Well, Mr. Ward here says he went to Kristine's funeral, all right. Didn't even know her, either," said Anderson, leading Ward over to their unmarked car.

"Mr. Ward," asked Meekins, "now, why in the world would a person go to the funeral of a kid he didn't even know?"

"I dunno, just curious, I guess."

"Well," Meekins said, "so are we. Let's go!"

23

With the discovery of Timmy King's body, the involvement of Wayne County in the case, and the earlier request that other suburban police agencies send some of their investigators over, office space again became a problem. The Adams Street fire hall had served the Task Force well, but the investigation had outgrown it. Robertson and Krease sat down with Tobin, who promised to make some calls. An hour and a half later, the two men were on their way to check out the Valley Woods School, a ten-minute drive west of Birmingham. The elementary school was certainly big enough, about seventy thousand square feet, twenty-six classrooms, a large library, a multi-purpose room, and, best of all, a fully equipped kitchen. The school was vacant, due to declining enrollment, and the Birmingham School District was trying to sell it. Meanwhile, the Special Homicide Task Force could use it rent free. Robbie couldn't believe their luck. Another welcome feature was the location: just south of Fourteen Mile and west of Evergreen, the place was secluded, set back off the road and surrounded by trees. It was an easy place to miss, unless you knew exactly where you were going. The Task Force could come and go with minimum disruption to the community.

Benjamin Franklin Ward passed the polygraph test. According to State Police Detective Sergeant Chet Romatowski, the polygraph examiner, Ward was telling the truth when he said he was not involved in the Kristine Mihelich abduction and murder. Or the Timothy King abduction and murder. Ward stated that he was home alone on January 2 and March 16 — the days the children had disappeared. He also was apparently telling the truth when he told investigators that his only reason for showing up at the girl's funeral was curiosity. When he saw the crowd gathered at the Fuller-Sawyer Funeral Home, he had just decided to hang around and see what it was all about. He gave the police permission to search his car, which they did at the scene and then again when it was taken to the Ferndale Police Department, and permission to search his home in Detroit. They found nothing that would even remotely link him to either crime. Ward was kicked loose, so to speak, investigators having been thoroughly convinced that Benjamin Franklin Ward was perhaps a little "weird," but certainly he had nothing to do with the Oakland County child slayings.

Two other quick notes about Ward. Prior to Ward's apprehension, two officers had foolishly shown only his picture to Mrs. Raubacher, who had seen a young boy talking to a man, next to a blue Gremlin the night Timothy King disappeared. As they showed her the picture, she exclaimed, "That's the man!"

The second interesting point was that by this time, all but the most senior investigators simply wanted Ward to be the child killer, and many had psyched themselves into believing that indeed he was. Chief Assistant Oakland County Prosecutor Dick Thompson himself fell victim to his own exuberance. Later Robertson would say, "I don't think Joe and I were that excited about Ward, but Dick was actually writing out the wording for the warrant. He was just so positive Ward was the man. Some of the other guys in the group were so sure they were planning a victory party. There was great jubilance, and then, boom! he passes the polygraph. Dick says, 'I don't believe in those damned polygraphs anyway.'"

Rita Sue Ballantine didn't exactly pass her polygraph test, but she didn't exactly fail it, either. She passed the part about the car following her down Gill Road the night Timothy King's body was dumped. But the polygraph results were inconclusive as to the make of car and the description of the driver. As a matter of record, Rita Sue changed her description of the vehicle that followed her (in another interview with detectives at District just prior to the test, the vehicle had undergone a metamorphosis, and became a four-door sedan).

Two other things occurred almost simultaneously. The *Detroit News* offered a twenty-five-thousand-dollar reward for information leading to the arrest and conviction of Timothy King's murderer. The money was offered through the *News's* Secret Witness Program, which had an impressive track record, having helped solve forty-six homicides. The reward, the largest ever offered by the *News,* matched the twenty-five thousand dollars offered by the Birmingham City Commission a week or so earlier. Over and above that, another $17,600 had been posted in the Mihelich case by the Berkley Jaycees; there was four thousand dollars offered in the Robinson case, and another five thousand in the Stebbins case. Ten thousand five hundred dollars was posted for the January 1976 slayings of Cadieux of Roseville and Srock of Birmingham.

Meanwhile, in Lansing, the State Capital, a one-million-dollar reward fund aimed at obtaining convictions of persons who killed, kidnapped, or molested children age sixteen or under was being proposed by a couple of South Oakland legislators, State Representative David Campbell, a Republican from Royal Oak, and Democratic Representative Dana Wilson, of Hazel Park. The money would be channeled by special appropriation to the State Police and would be doled out in fifty-thousand-dollar lump sums. Campbell and Wilson had been tossing the idea around since January, but now it was off the drawing boards and into the legislative hopper.

Oakland County Sheriff Johannes Spreen and his undersheriff, John Nichols, had been burning the midnight oil trying to determine how they might help in the search for the child killer. The Sheriff's Department had cooperated fully and assisted in every way, and Spreen had given freely of his manpower and his budget in the search for the child killer. But he wanted to do more.

"Great pressures will be placed on police departments this summer. Any time a child is more than five minutes late, you can bet the parents will call the police," Nichols told *Tribune* reporter William Willoughby. "In normal times, the police would tell the parents to wait an hour and call back if the child is still missing. But because of these abductions, the police will have to start looking for the child immediately. The result," Nichols went on, "will be that police will be putting out many brush fires, and they won't be able to do any real work."

That awareness prompted Spreen to request emergency authority to hire between twenty and twenty-five additional deputies to assist local departments in street patrols. Spreen had actually been fighting for such an "emergency powers" mandate from a recalcitrant Board of Commissioners since 1973 with little success. While he labeled the request "emergency," he did not hide the fact that the additional manpower would become a permanent part of his patrol. "A visible force that will deter all crimes," he said.

Meanwhile, school cafeterias and multipurpose rooms were serving as clearinghouses for the concern, fear, and tensions of an anxious citizenry. Panels of experts, of one ilk or another, were called in by school officials to meet with parents in hopes that an exchange of ideas and a sharing of thoughts would result in new ways to protect children. In Berkley, Dottie and Gregory DeQuinn organized a meeting of parents and officials at Berkley High School. School officials, police, and a psychologist appeared in a panel discussion to answer questions and discuss ways that parents might better protect their children, and ways that children might better protect themselves. Greg DeQuinn echoed the feelings of the community when he said, "We tried so hard and wanted to believe that abducting a child would be harder now. This [the King abduction and slaying] just goes to show that we need to work harder with our children so they are aware of the dangers. We don't want to scare our children to death, however, and have them go through life frightened of anyone new. We hope that we can find a common point on where to draw the line."

On that last score, many school officials, including those in Berkley, warned repeatedly against placing too much stress on avoiding strangers, feeling, like DeQuinn, that common sense had to prevail. Warnings had to insure the child's safety but still allow him or her enough social latitude to develop into a healthy young adult.

In Ferndale, the hometown of the child killer's first victim, Mark Stebbins, police organized a meeting of parents and concerned citizens at City Hall. Police Chief Donald Geary called in Detroit Police Inspector Isaiah McKinnon, commanding officer of the department's Sex Crimes Unit as the principal speaker. Ruth Stebbins, Mark's mother, also attended the meeting, and much of the huge turnout was due to her diligent work in distributing flyers to businesses and banks in Ferndale. In painful hindsight, Ruth Stebbins would say that some of the tips passed along to parents at that meeting might have saved her son.

Some rather interesting theories on how the child killer might operate were batted about at the meeting. The official police profile of the killer described him as a "sophisticated person" who could be posing as a priest or a police officer, someone children would trust. One person at the meeting speculated that the killer might be a substitute teacher who made the rounds of several South Oakland schools and was known by many children. Geary said he'd pass that information on to the Task Force. One woman suggested that the killer could get a child over to his car by accusing him of shoplifting or throwing snowballs at the car. Another concerned citizen suggested that a hypnotist could easily lure a child into a car, and still another offered that a woman was the killer, or at least working with the killer. It was thought that children would be more apt to trust a woman than a man.

Case No. 2116-77, Autopsy No. A77-472.
OPINION:
This 11-year-old white boy, Timothy King, died of smothering. Injuries of the face included scrapes at the margins of the mouth, a scraped

area of the inner lining of the mouth, and a bite mark on the tongue. Also, a scrape was noted in front of the left ear lobe. Abrasions on the left forehead are believed to have resulted after death when the body was dumped from a short height. Areas of indentation and discoloration on the wrists and one ankle suggest binding. The anal canal was grossly dilated and abrasions of the lining of the anal canal were present indicating sexual abuse. No sperm or evidence of semen was present in swabs from the anorectal area, nor was sperm or semen found in swabs from the oral cavity. No other injuries were present on the body.

The stomach contained partially digested food. Particles were apparently that of fowl. This was ingested very shortly before death. The large intestine contained identifiable fragments of kernels of corn, ingested possibly two days before death. In consideration of the findings at the time of examination of the body at the scene, the time of death is estimated at approximately 6-8 hours prior to the body being found. The body was dumped at the scene approximately 2 hours or less before being found. The clothing and external surface of the body, including fingernails and toenails, were exceptionally clean. Extensive toxicological studies, including carbon monoxide, were entirely negative.

The typewritten opinion was over the signature of John E. Smialek, M.D., Deputy Chief Medical Examiner. There was much more to the report, but the bottom line was that the corpse of Timothy King, forensically speaking, was "unremarkable," and revealed little. The hair found on the body proved indeed to be animal hair, but no other conclusions could be made about its presence on the body.

"Discussion?" prompted Krease, looking at the men seated with him at the table in the Squad Room. Each had just read his own copy of the M.E.'s report . . . just a matter of hours before King's funeral. Robertson, Krease, Rivard, Tobias, Kalbfleisch, Waldron, Tobin, and Turner were present.

"Yes," replied Robertson. "I think we ought to hold back a lot of this stuff from the media. No sense in giving them too much information, stuff like what he had to eat, and so on. No sense in letting the killer know that we know that sort of thing. We're going to have to give the media some information, like that he was sexually abused, because they're going to ask, but I just think we ought to keep some of the details to ourselves."

"That's good," agreed Tobin. "There's so much goddam misinformation already hitting the streets, even with the regularly scheduled press briefings, that I'm beginning to think that the less information we give out, the easier it's going to be for us. Hell, we've already got people scared to send kids out in the snow, because of that goddam snow theory of Danto's. Christ, the story's already around that Jill was shot instead of smothered because she'd started menstruating and was unclean to the killer until the snow cleansed her blood on a massive scale. Can you believe this shit?"

"I'm for telling the goddam media as little as we can get away with from this point on," Turner declared. "We can always give 'em the old 'no comment during the ongoing investigation' routine. I'm for playin' it close to the vest."

At the regularly scheduled press conference several hours later, Chief Turner surprisingly went right down the list and told the world that Timothy King had chicken, his favorite meal, just before he was killed.

24

The King family received hundreds of letters of condolence from across the nation, and some six hundred people attended services for him at the Holy Name Church just outside Birmingham. Many of them were strangers, representatives of a community in grief. The church was full and many who came had to stand outside.

Scores of people, including many in the media, wept openly during the service, and many of Timmy's friends walked up to touch the casket. The family, Barry, Marian, Mark, Christopher, and Cathy, held hands as they left the church.

Surveillance and security at the funeral were extremely heavy. While the high visibility command officers who ran the Task Force elected not to attend services — they felt the family was entitled to at least that much privacy — there were no less than twenty-six surveillance officers, some from C.I.S., in attendance. (Many off-duty police officers involved in the case were there, too.) Everyone who came within a hundred yards of the church had their picture taken on film or videocassette. But the technique used at the Mihelich funeral, of trying to pick out the person or persons whose presence was unexplained, proved impractical. What had worked at Kristine's comparatively small funeral was unworkable at this one, where hundreds of strangers had come to share the family's grief.

The community was trying to cope with the tragedy in the only way it could — by trying to prevent another child from being taken. The gathering of parents, school officials, and police in Ferndale precipitated other similar efforts in a dozen south Oakland County communities. Just forty-eight hours before the King funeral, Holy Name Church staged a panel discussion called "Coping with a Community Crisis," featuring a psychiatrist, a psychologist, and a clinical social worker. Diane Vincent, the Director of the nonprofit, multipurpose agency Common Ground, said immediately following the King funeral that the organization was making a citywide effort to bring together "educators, police, the PTSA, clergy, city officials, mental health professionals, business people, and the press" in hopes of establishing seminars for the dissemination of child safety information. Three Boy Scout troops at Birmingham's First Presbyterian Church and First Methodist Church organized a "Crime Against Youth" meeting at which an F.B.I. agent was invited to speak. A coalition of representatives from twelve communities touched by the child killer began pushing for what they called an "Officer Bill" program in all elementary schools to educate children about child safety.

Meanwhile, a number of activities were being promoted to keep the memory of Timothy King alive. Timmy's sixth-grade classmates at the Adams School decided to buy a tree and plant it in front of the building. This they would do, not by donations, for they wished to put forth some effort, but either by doing odd jobs for citizens in the community, or perhaps a car wash. Several groups and organizations launched and contributed to the Timothy King Memorial Fund, the proceeds of which would be used to maintain the school playground that Timmy loved so much. As Spike McKenzie, a friend of the Kings put it, "Tim practically lived in the Adams playground, so it is appropriate that the money given in his memory be spent improving the playground."

In addition to the programs being contemplated, a number of programs aimed at protecting children were already underway. The Birmingham Mobile Watch was a group of citizens with CB radios in their cars, who patrolled city streets at night and on weekends to spot any suspicious-looking characters around stores, playgrounds, or parks, anyplace where children congregated. The Helping Hand program designated safe havens for children with signs in the windows of homes. A child accosted by a stranger need only look for the sign of The Hand on someone's window and seek refuge there.

While all this was going on in the community, the Task Force was burning the midnight oil.

"I don't know," said Tobin between bites of filet at the Sly Fox. "I bet we could offer a million-dollar reward and not be any further ahead." He gestured at Robbie and Joe with a fork. "Look, we already got fifty grand, plus, we're probably going to get that thing in Lansing pushed through, the million-dollar fund which'll mean we got another fifty thousand on top of what we've already got." Robbie and Joe nodded agreement. "I mean, if somebody's not going to drop a dime for a hundred-thousand-dollar reward, I don't see 'em turning over for twice that, or ten times that." He took another sip of wine. "Plus we don't want to get into a situation where somebody's withholding information just because they think we'll raise the ante."

Robertson pushed his plate aside. "Yeah, I guess I agree with that thinking. Christ, you'd think somebody'd give us something for that kind of money!"

"Well, maybe the guy who's holding that kind of information doesn't need that kind of money," said Krease, picking at his fries. "Just for the sake of argument, let's say somebody like Danto, with all his dough. Shit, what's he need with another fifty thousand, or even a hundred thousand?"

Robertson smiled. "Old Joe here isn't too sure about Danto." He paused. "Come to think of it, I guess maybe I'm not either. Maybe we ought to find out a little more about him, tag him for a while, or something." His voice trailed off. Tobin grunted assent.

"You see the Birmingham paper today?" Jerry asked. He grinned. "Your friend is blabbing it around about how he's afraid there'll be more killings. Says he thinks the killer is angry because the Robinson funeral home was closed to the public. He says he's concerned that this angers the killer, who wants to see the children all laid out as part of his ritual."

"Hell, for all we know Danto could be right," said Robertson with a sigh. "Who knows what makes the guy tick. Look at Ben Franklin Ward, a guy who gets a kick out of going to funerals of people he doesn't even know. There's just a lot of weird shit in the world that we can't even imagine. Trouble is, something might be for real but sound weird to us, you know, because we live in an entirely different world. It puts a different spin on things." Krease and Tobin chuckled.

"What else does Danto say in the paper?" asked Robbie, signaling the waitress for more coffee.

"Well, I've got the paper right here," Tobin said, finding it on the seat beside him. He scanned it. "Yeah, here. 'Dr. Danto says he thinks the killer has attended. . . . ' Okay, here we are: 'I think it may be part of his game — he needs to humiliate the child in a sexual manner. This has been evident with the boys, and I suspect also with the girls. He also humiliates the parents by depriving them of their child. The real victims here, psychologically, are the parents because they are deprived of their child.'" Tobin put the paper down. "Then he goes on to say he doesn't think the guy is schizophrenic. Says he's very deliberate, clever, and intelligent."

"Well, I'd have to agree with that," said Krease.

"On the subject of things that are driving me crazy," said Robertson, "I wish there was something to do about the written reports we're getting.

Some of the ones from the local departments, well, you can hardly even read them. I know they can't all look like they were prepared by State Police, but we need to be able to go back to a report six months later and know what the hell happened!" He was interrupted by Krease's beeper.

"Dammit! First time in a week I get a chance to relax and actually eat dinner. Be right back!" Krease left to make the call.

"Anything important?" inquired Tobin when Joe returned a few minutes later.

"Could be. That was Waldron. We better go," he sighed, reaching for his wallet to pull out his share of the tab. "Looks like we've got ourselves another witness!"

"Here, ma'am, you can just have a seat right here." Wayne held the chair for her. "This is Detective Sergeant Joe Krease, Lieutenant Robertson, State Police, and Jerry Tobin, the Birmingham Chief of Police. Gentlemen, this is Mrs. Lenore Marzolino." The woman was late middle-aged, with neatly trimmed grey hair. She sat as Tobin asked if she'd like some coffee.

"No, no thank you, Chief Tobin," she replied in a voice that betrayed some nervousness, "unless maybe you have some decaffeinated."

"I think we can find some. My secretary usually has a jar around," said Tobin, ducking out the door of his office.

"Sorry, Mrs. Marzolino," apologized Krease, "we're just in the process of moving from the Adams Street fire station to a school out west of town, so we have to use the Chief's office here for your interview. Sorry it's so crowded."

"Oh, that's all right. I've really never been in a police station before."

"I wish I could say the same," Krease said. She smiled.

Tobin was back almost immediately.

"Here you are, Mrs. Marzolino," he said, placing the cup and saucer in front of her, and then taking a seat behind his desk. "Now, Sergeant Waldron here says you may have seen the man we're looking for. Can you just start from the beginning?" He reached into his drawer for a small tape machine. "Mind if we record this conversation?"

"No, I guess that's fine. I've never done this before, you know."

"Well, we have, lots of times." Robertson spoke for the first time. "Just tell us the story, like you'd tell it to a son or a daughter or your husband."

"Well, it was the night that the little boy disappeared from the drugstore. I had to get some things, so I was in there."

"Was it crowded?" Krease asked.

"Well, I don't know, there were other people in there, I don't know how many."

"A dozen would you say, ma'am?"

"Yes, I-I think. Yes, maybe a dozen or so. I really wasn't paying that much attention. But. . . ."

"Did you see a little boy in there, ma'am?"

"Well," she thought for a moment, "there were several children, I think, when I went down the aisle where they have the candy and things, but I really didn't notice them. I just went back to the pharmacy to get my prescription. I had to wait for it, so I sat down. They have several chairs back there so a person can sit and wait. So I was waiting, and when I do that, I just like to watch the people who come back there."

"You're a people-watcher, then?" smiled Tobin. "Me, too."

"Yes, I guess it's kind of rude, but I like to do it anyway," she confided, clearly more comfortable.

"Is this when you saw the man?" inquired Robertson.

"Well, sort of," she decided. "He was walking down the aisle where the candy was. He just walked down the aisle and was going to go out the back door. I really didn't notice him that much, I guess. You know how you might look at somebody, but you really don't notice the face."

"So you really didn't get that good a look at him?" asked Robertson, raising his eyebrows.

"Well, not when he was coming down the aisle. I probably wouldn't have given him another thought, except that when he got to the door, he sort of just stood there and turned around to look back at the aisle he'd just come from."

"You mean, where all the candy was?" asked Tobin hopefully.

"Yes. When he stopped and looked back, you know, turned his head, his mouth moved like he was trying to say something. But he didn't."

"How long would you say he stood at the door, looking back toward the aisle?" asked Waldron.

"Not long, just a few seconds, perhaps. I don't know." She sipped her coffee and smiled.

"Do you think you could draw us a picture?"

"Oh, I can't draw, Chief Tobin," she laughed.

"Well," Jerry smiled, "we have people who can, Mrs. Marzolino. If you could just sit down with one of them and describe to him the kind of face this man had. . . . By the way, how did you know that we'd be interested in this person you saw?"

"Well, I wasn't sure, until one of your men knocked on my door and said you were looking for a suspect."

"We tracked everybody who'd gotten a prescription there that night," Tobin explained.

"Oh, my, that's really clever. It's just like on. . . ." She stopped. Tobin smiled.

"Yes, on television, Mrs. Marzolino. Now, could you describe the man you saw?"

"Well," she took a long pause and shifted in the chair. "I've seen the person you're looking for, I mean, the one that's on the television, and he looks something like him."

"Something like him?" repeated Krease. "How much like him?"

"Quite a bit, I think. His face was at kind of an angle from where I was sitting, but, yes, quite a bit, I think. His hair was heavy, and he had those long sideburns. I think his nose was bigger, though. Yes, it was. His nose was bigger."

"Mrs. Marzolino, if we can get our police artist down here by 9 o'clock, could you take an hour or so tonight and sit with him, so he can draw a picture of the man you saw in the drugstore?"

"Why yes, I suppose so, if you think it'll help."

"I think it might just help, Mrs. Marzolino."

State Police artist Gary Powell was rousted from a pleasant evening, and arrived at the Birmingham P.D. shortly before nine o'clock. By ten the Task Force had a picture. Mrs. Raubacher, who until this moment had been the only witness to come forward, was shown the picture at 10:30. She agreed that the second drawing bore an even more striking resemblance to the man she saw talking to the boy in the parking lot than her own composite. By 11:15 copies of the new composite were on their way to both Detroit papers, plus the *Tribune*, and the *Eccentric*.

The Task Force had a new drawing of an old suspect.

25

It was late on a grey afternoon when Bill Reese, from Akron, Ohio, pulled off the freeway and headed through Livonia on Eight Mile Road. He'd been driving all day through crummy weather and was tired, looking forward only to a very dry vodka martini, a quiet dinner, and maybe a little action in the Holiday Inn lounge. He did have a full day tomorrow — a dozen people to call on at the Big Three. Maybe he'd be better off to forget the action and get to bed early.

He picked the map off the front seat and tried to read it while negotiating the beginning of the inbound rush-hour traffic. He'd worked the territory once, about six months ago, and could've sworn the Holiday Inn was on Eight Mile just east of the freeway. He'd gone too far, or was it not far enough? It was late, traffic was miserable, the weather stunk, and he was lost. He'd thought he'd ask somebody at that gas station at the next corner, but couldn't even pull in, too many cars in the driveway. He rounded the corner onto the sidestreet, leaning on the horn to warn the tow truck nosing its way out of the pump area into the street. He glared at the driver of the truck, who gave Reese the one finger salute, which made him even madder. He'd ask someplace else, he thought, as he slowly proceeded another ten yards down the sidestreet to where two boys were walking across somebody's front lawn. He stopped at the curb.

"Hey kid!" he hollered, leaning across the front seat. "C'mere a minute, will ya?"

Startled, one of the boys turned abruptly and hollered "Screw you, mister!" and both boys took off on a dead run.

"Nice people here in Detroit," thought Reese disgustedly. He started to turn his head to check traffic before pulling away from the curb and saw it about the instant he felt it. The jolt startled him and he could feel his seat belt grab as the rear of the car was thrown up on the curb. He regained his composure long enough to see the tow truck back up a couple of feet and stop. He'd been bashed in the left rear, at an angle, as though the truck had crossed over into the other lane to take aim, then rammed him. Still rattled, Reese saw the truck door fly open, and the driver leap out.

"You goddam pervert child molester son of a bitch!" He took three giant strides and yanked Reese's door open. "I'm gonna' kill you!" Reese, a corn-fed Ohio farm boy who'd wrestled his way through college on a scholarship before joining the Goodyear sales staff, still pumped iron in his basement three times a week. He let himself be pulled from the car because he knew what was coming next. He saw it start from low behind the truck driver's body. Reese slipped under the roundhouse right, twisting half-around and to his left, and in a cat-like move, grabbed the truck driver's right wrist. He jerked it down and, twisting from the waist again, powered the man's arm up behind his back in a hammerlock until he heard the elbow snap and the man yelp and curse. Reese kept the pressure on, forcing the man hard against the open door frame while applying a choke hold with the left forearm.

"You fucking maniac! What are you doin', you crazy son of a bitch! I'll break your fuckin' arm," Reese screamed, applying still more pressure on the hammerlock. The reply was a gurgle and Reese let up a little, primarily because he caught sight of a flashing red light. He watched the Livonia police car jerk to a halt not six feet from where he had the man pinned against the car but could think of nothing to say as the two officers leaped out of the vehicle and pulled them loose from each other.

The tow-truck driver, grimacing in pain, began sputtering wildly, "This son of a bitch here tried to pick up a couple a kids! I seen him! He's the goddam Oakland County killer!"

"So Livonia keeps both of them for a couple of hours," explained Krease, as he related the incident to Robertson. "They call us of course, we run a check on the tire salesman — hell, he's clean as a whistle. Poor bastard! What's he know, from out of town, just coming up here to try to make a living and asks somebody for directions. Bang! His whole world comes crashing down around him!"

"The whole area's really on edge," Robbie commented. "I hope we don't have more people trying to take the law into their own hands. Never seen people so spooked."

"Not only that," Krease chuckled, "but Turner says the two of 'em had to be separated again at the police station. The tow-truck driver said *he* was going to file assault charges, and they had to break 'em up again!"

"Well," said Robbie, "I think the panic will wear off in a couple of weeks, even if we don't catch the guy by then, but everybody's going to be a lot more cautious."

"Hope so," Krease said. "Anyway, what do you think about this place?" He waved his hand at their new office in the Valley Woods School. "Let's take a walk through. You haven't been by in a couple days. Still got a lot of stuff we haven't found a place for, but it's coming!" Krease and Robertson were in an office together, just down the hall from the main entrance. The Operations Area was the former principal's office, pretty much turned over to Jack Strauss and his radio communications equipment. Right behind Operations and across from the Command office were several small rooms that would be used to interview anyone coming in off the street with a tip. There were a half-dozen classrooms off the hall beyond that; one was designated the tip-receiving room and another the tip-processing room. Long, cafeteria-type folding tables had been placed in these rooms for telephones and the mountains of paperwork these two operations generated. Another of the classrooms would house Phil Hogan's computer. And still another was set aside exclusively for the detectives from Detroit, although Robertson would say later it was a mistake, since it caused some carping amongst the other officers.

Robertson and Krease stood in the door of the tip-processing room, where a half-dozen men were busily talking on phones, writing, and sorting. A couple of them looked up, nodded, and went right back to work.

"Joe, bring me up to date. I haven't had a chance to even get out here, let alone know what the hell's going on. How many tips have we got, ballpark, I mean?"

"We're up around seven thousand and still climbing."

"Jesus! You playing catch-up?"

"Afraid so, Lieutenant. Say, Bert!" Joe walked to the nearest of the detectives. "Bert, what are we running on tips now?"

"Well, lemme see, here." He shuffled through some papers on the table. "Well, as of midnight last, we had 7,123 tips received and, let's see," he studied the sheet in front of him, "thirty-three hundred processed so far. I'll be glad when Hogan gets that goddam computer hooked in, ought to speed things up a bit. It's real slow, Lieutenant, but we're doing the best we can."

"Yeah, I know," agreed Robertson. "Just keep plugging away. That computer might make things a little easier, but it's not going to solve the crime. Only thing that can do that is good, old-fashioned police work."

"By the way, you guys see the paper today?" Bert asked, changing the subject.

"No, why?"

"Danto's written a letter to the killer, kind of an open letter from doctor to patient. It's really something."

"I'll bet," said Krease.

"Got a paper up front, Joe?" asked Robertson.

"Yeah, should be one in the office. I suppose we ought to take a look."

Danto was a free agent. He had no official status with the investigation, but on that one occasion he had been asked to help with the profile. He was, after all, a recognized authority in the field of forensic psychiatry, and, as such, a lot of people listened to him. Robertson sat down at his desk in his new office and read the *Detroit News* article headlined "Psychiatrist's Plea to Timothy's Killer":

> I am writing to you as a doctor to a patient.
>
> You and I know you are acting in a manner foreign to the whole purpose of being a human being, and you are setting into motion your own human response to act against your best and human interests.
>
> I'd like to speculate about you and share some of the impressions I've formed since you first began to devise your game.
>
> That's right. I said "game."
>
> I'm going to assume that you've been abducting and killing children for at least the past 13 months. I also believe you hadn't played the game before that, otherwise you would have had a record of this behavior and would have been detected by the police some time ago.
>
> I think that certain events triggered your "death game," and now you find yourself locked into a pattern of destruction which you can't stop.
>
> The triggering events, I believe, were the death of the Redford babysitter in December of 1975 and the murders of Sheila Srock and Cynthia Cadieux in January of 1976. I think those events touched off a chain reaction within you, and your specific childhood hurts bubbled up to the surface.
>
> I feel your murdering Timothy King, Jill Robinson, Kristine Mihelich and Mark Stebbins was an attempt by you to subject them to the same kind of sexual perversion and humiliation you experienced by a substitute parent in your own childhood.
>
> You then get to the point of either feeling that (1) killing the child is necessary to save him from the life of pain you knew, or (2) you are using the child as a sacrificial lamb in order to punish your parents for abandoning you. You kill the child and thus deprive your victim's parents of their most precious achievement.
>
> Smothering the child, you believe, is the least painful and most tender method of murder. You achieve a greater definition, in your mind, of ten-

derness, when you wash the body and gently lay out the victim on a public roadside. In this way, you hope to deny the terrible game you are playing.

But, you've erred.

Someone knows who you are.

That someone is YOU.

What I'm telling you is that since you started out with a human image, you are setting yourself up for the worst possible retribution you can create.

You've gone from being pursued by one police department, to police agencies in three counties, the State Police, and the FBI. I think this shows what you are setting yourself up for.

It is for this reason, that I'd like to help you in a way a doctor helps a patient. You need such help to stop what you're doing.

You have a chance — right now — to achieve victory in a greater game. You can become a hero by way of being the only person . . . who can stop you.

Robertson handed the paper to Krease, who read it. When he was finished, he remained silent. Finally, Robbie spoke.

"Well, Joe," he drawled, "might as well send everybody home. Danto's on the case. Looks like all we gotta do is sit here and wait till the killer walks through the front door with his hands up."

"Yeah," Joe agreed dryly. "Well, good. I haven't arrested anybody all day."

The first public criticism of the investigation had come from Tom and Karol Robinson, Jill's parents. Divorced, they nonetheless maintained an amicable relationship, and though Jill and her two sisters, ten-year-old Alene and six-year-old Heather, lived with their mother, their father maintained contact with the family. Joe invited both into his office at Valley Woods, after giving them a tour of the building and explaining each facet of the operation along the way.

They were an attractive couple — Krease could not help but wonder what went wrong with the marriage as he invited them to take seats. She was a pretty woman, neat and trim, dressed in a simple but tasteful skirt and blouse. Tom looked like the college professor he was, balding, with a salt-and-pepper beard, black woolen turtleneck and tweed sportscoat.

"Please, sit down." said Krease.

"Thank you," she said. "Please, we'd like to make this as quick as possible. Sergeant, I just don't know what to think."

"I know how you must feel," Joe said reassuringly. He'd read the interview in which they had told a team of *News* reporters that they felt the Task Force lacked leadership, or at least coordination. Karol had noted that a Task Force detective had told her he'd never even seen a report from Troy on Jill's death. In a word, the Robinsons felt that with the spotlight on Timothy King, Jill's death wasn't being given enough emphasis. Joe had agreed to the meeting to try to assure them that everything possible was being done. "I guess I can understand why you might think, because of all the publicity surrounding the King boy, that we've forgotten about the others, including Jill." He leaned back in his desk chair. "Please try to remember that we honestly believe that the man who killed Timmy also killed Jill and the others. I think what's happened, Mr. and Mrs. Robinson, is that there's been an awful lot of publicity about *all* the cases, and Timmy just happened to be the last one and is getting all the news coverage. That doesn't mean *we've* forgotten the others."

"Yes, we know that, Sergeant," Tom Robinson interjected a little testily, "but what about the fact that one of your people told Karol that he hadn't even seen a report on my daughter's case!" Without waiting for Krease to respond he continued, "I mean, I'm sure that individual officers are sparing no effort, but where the hell's the imaginative leadership, the coordination? Jesus, if these murders are somehow connected, you'd at least think you'd concentrate on them on a more equal basis. One kid's life is certainly as valuable as another's. Who knows, if the cases are all connected like you say they are, when a clue will turn up that might be the key to the whole thing?"

Joe listened, then leaned forward as he responded. "There's no question about that, Mr. Robinson, that's exactly the way we're approaching this thing. As far as your wife being told that we've not seen the report on Jill's death, that's not really true. I mean, it's entirely possible that the officer you talked with had not personally seen the report. But I can assure you, we are working with Troy on the case. As a matter of fact, we have one of their people in our detective team, Bill Maur, who is quite familiar with Jill's case."

"I know, Sergeant, and I must tell you I'm perfectly satisfied with the way the Troy police are handling the case. It's just that, well, there's some negative. . . ."

"It seems like there are so many negative connotations about the whole thing," Karol cut in. She rubbed her forehead. "You know, negative connotations about Jill's life. Like her portrayal by police and the media as being a runaway. I never felt she was running away. We did have a little scrap before she disappeared, but what mother doesn't have words with her daughter? At that age they're pretty headstrong, and you can't tell them anything, but then you hug and make up. I never felt she was running away. I think she was probably on the way to her dad's house in Birmingham. It just seems like," her voice caught as she took a deep breath, "like my daughter had to die before anyone would pay any attention to her." Tom reached over and put his hand on her arm.

"Well, whatever mistakes that we've made in the past," Krease said, "I can assure you will not be repeated in the future. And I'm sure we've made our share. This is a terribly difficult case, and you see," he continued in a steady voice, "we're charting new ground here. There has never, in the history of criminal investigation — as nearly as we can determine — been a case quite like this. And to be quite honest with you, the investigation is especially difficult because of all the different agencies involved. And while those problems are ours and not yours, please try to understand that we're confident that we'll catch your daughter's killer. And one more thing. I want both of you to feel perfectly comfortable to call me anytime you have any questions. We want a continuing dialogue."

"Well," said Tom Robinson, rising from his chair, "I guess I'm satisfied that you people are doing everything you can. I saw a lot of things today that I just didn't know before about how you work."

"I'm glad we could show you around. I hope things are a little clearer now," said Krease, getting out of his chair and coming around the front of the desk. He extended his hand to Tom, then to Karol.

"Yes, I-I think it helped a little, Sergeant Krease. I'm just so damn angry," Karol said, her voice trembling.

"Look," said Joe holding the door, "if there's anything more we can do. . . ."

She stopped and looked at him, her mouth tight. "Just get the son of a bitch off the street, please!"

26

"More wine, Stephen?" asked Carla, reaching for the burgundy.

"Hah! Trying to get this poor, defenseless priest drunk so you can have your way with him?"

"What makes you think I'd need to get you drunk? Here, let's clear the table first, then we can finish the wine in front of the fireplace. Besides, I want to talk first, then I'll have my way with you, drunk or sober!"

The table cleared, the handsome young priest put another log on the fire, while she got two large floor pillows and arranged them in front of the hearth. They sat silently for a long moment, sipping the wine, and staring at the fire. Finally, she spoke. "Stephen, I'm worried about Matthew." He turned to look at her. She continued staring at the fire.

"Oh? What do you mean 'worried'?"

"Well, I don't know. He seems to be so," she hesitated, looking for the word, "preoccupied, I guess. I mean, he's awfully moody. He's becoming more and more difficult lately."

"What kid at twelve isn't difficult? It's the age."

"No, this is different. He was always such a good student, too. But now he just doesn't seem to care about school anymore."

"You talked with his teachers?" he asked, turning back to the fire.

"They've noticed it too. Stephen," Carla turned to look at him, "Stephen, did anything happen at camp last summer?"

Father Stephen Bethleham felt his pulse jump.

"I mean, did you notice that he had any problems or anything?"

"No, not really. None that I noticed." He kept his eyes on the fire.

"The reason I ask is that this all started right after he got back. I know how close you are, but now it seems when I mention your name, he starts that moodiness. Did the two of you have words or something while he was at camp?"

The priest laughed nervously. "Actually, I did have to jump on several of the boys one night, Matthew included. They were fooling around, making a lot of noise when the others were trying to sleep. I suppose I really did give 'em hell. But as a group — I didn't single out any one individual. They all seemed fine the next morning, Matthew, too." He paused to take a drink of wine. "I don't know. Maybe I scared him."

"Stephen, I don't think you could ever scare Matt or any other child. You have a way with kids, and I know how Matt feels about you." Stephen did not respond.

"I just don't know what to think," Carla spoke again. "Since his father died, Matt's had an awful lot of responsibility for someone so young. You know, trying to be the man of the house; there're so many things he doesn't know. It's just so damned hard. . . ." Her voice trailed off. It was several minutes before either spoke.

"It's probably just a stage he's going through, Carla," said Stephen finally. "It happens to a lot of children at that age. They start to assert their independence, want their own private space. I think you ought to continue to watch him closely, like you're doing, but I really don't see any cause for alarm." He reached for the tongs to adjust a burning log.

"There's something else, too, Stephen. You know those awful child murders, the two girls and the two boys?" She stopped and sipped her wine. "Every time the story is on television and they talk about how Mark and Timmy were sexually abused and how the killer might be someone like a priest, Matt goes to his room. He won't even let me comfort him, says he just wants to be alone. . . . " Her voice broke and she began softly crying.

Stephen held her close, kissing her face lightly.

27

By now, the Special Homicide Task Force had grown larger than most of the police agencies it represented. It had stabilized at about two hundred fifty police officers within several days following the King murder. Jim Rhodes, the director of Criminal Justice for Oakland County, picked up the phone in his office and dialed Jerry Tobin. "Jerry—Jim Rhodes. Look, I've been pretty much on top of this whole thing, the size and scope of the investigation. I'm aware of the budget problems you're up against. Look, there might be a way around it. Ever hear about an outfit called the Law Enforcement Assistance Administration? We might be able to get some federal money to keep this thing alive for a while, couple months anyway. I think it's worth a shot."

A few hours later, Rhodes greeted the Birmingham Police Chief and invited him into a small conference room just off Rhodes's office. Rhodes cradled a huge, black three-ring binder and a thick legal file.

"Don't let all this crap scare you, Jerry," chuckled Rhodes. "I can cut through a lot of it," he added confidently. "Besides, I can pretty well tell you we'll get a lot of help from Blanchard and Broomfield.* They'd be crazy not to give us a boost on this and neither one of 'em is crazy. Anyway, it isn't as bad as it looks," he decided, opening the envelope to extract a stack of grant application documents. Tobin frowned, but did not reply. "All right," he finally said, taking out his pen, "What do you need from me? What're our options under this program?"

"Well," replied Rhodes, placing the grant applications on the table while he opened the binder and ran his finger down the index tabs, "first of all, we're going to need a cost projection analysis."

"I can come up with the numbers pretty quick," Jerry said. "By the way, how much are we eligible for?"

---

*U.S. Congressmen James J. Blanchard, a Democrat from Pleasant Ridge (near Ferndale) and Republican William S. Broomfield, from Bloomfield Township. Blanchard would later become governor of the state.

"That's where they pass the buck back to us. They want us to come up with what we think it'll take, then they'll tell us if we can have it."

Tobin rubbed his chin with his hand. "Manpower's the big ticket item. The overtime is what's killing everybody."

Rhodes leaned back into his armchair. "The feds prohibit using any grant funds for overtime pay. But I know some people in the State Office of Criminal Justice and we ought to be able to work something out to funnel some of the money through them."

"Over and above the manpower," Tobin said, "we're going to need everything from desks and typewriters, to heat and light, to toilet paper."

"Christ, yes," exclaimed the county official, smiling. "Better get plenty of that!" Changing the subject, Rhodes asked, "How long do you want federal funding? How close are you to the guy?"

"Jesus, Jim, I don't know," Tobin sighed, slouching down in the chair. "I've seen these things end," he snapped his fingers, "just like that. And I've seen 'em drag on for years." He took a long breath. "I want to be able to keep this thing going for five or six months, anyway, and just hope it doesn't take anywhere near that. I can give you a really rough guess of what it'll take, Jim, without any paperwork." He reached inside his coat for a pen. Rhodes ripped a page from the legal pad in front of him and offered it to the Police Chief. Jerry poised his pen over the paper, staring at the wall and chewing his lip. He scratched a number on it, then preceded it with a dollar sign. He slid it back to Rhodes and leaned back, watching the man. Rhodes's eyes widened as he picked up the paper.

"Jesus, Tobin, you don't screw around, do you!"

Rhodes worked closely with liaison people from Blanchard's and Broomfield's offices, both locally and in Washington. The two congressmen had the grant application hand-delivered to LEAA's congressional liaison, which in turn shunted it on up the bureaucratic ladder to Assistant LEAA Director Bob Grim. Said Blanchard, "I summarized the situation and stressed the urgency involved. We described what the grant is asking, and pointed out that crimes like this have happened elsewhere in the country, and are likely to occur somewhere again." Blanchard also stressed the interjurisdictional aspect of the child-killer investigation: "While at the present time, the cooperative effort on a voluntary basis has been quite spectacular, it would be an extremely difficult burden for all of the cities involved to continue the effort over an extended period of weeks and months." One other thing the astute young Congressman did was to develop the notion that the Task Force could be used as a model for similar investigations around the country, especially Oakland County's use of a computer as the linchpin of the investigation. The Oakland County Task Force could serve as a model in criminal investigation.

Rhodes also connected quickly with a friend, head of the State Office of Criminal Justice, Noel C. Bufe. Bufe immediately hopped the first flight out to Washington, where he worked with Blanchard's and Broomfield's people so as to present the best possible case in the request for federal money. It was Bufe who got around the proscription on the use of federal dollars for overtime by convincing the government to funnel at least half of the grant through his state office, which had no such prohibition.

The grant application asked for $557,494, most of which was for manpower. The balance of $61,962 was for project evaluation, travel, supplies, and operating costs. Rhodes had included three options in the original grant request, three different ways in which the money might be allocated, but recommended having each of the jurisdictions involved assign detectives who had already worked some of the murders to the Task Force. The LEAA money would be used to reimburse officers used to fill in for the Task Force detectives in their home departments, while the Task Force detectives would be paid at the rate of time-and-a-half. Rhodes pointed out that this method was by far the most effective and least expensive and was that preferred by private business and industry. Rhodes put it this way: "We want officers assigned to the Task Force fresh every day on straight time. It would take more money to recruit, hire, and train people to either work for the Task Force or work in their home departments, than it will to pay overtime rates for six months." Rhodes said the other options were included to give both parties some room for negotiating. Being no stranger to the ways of greasing bureaucratic skids, Rhodes was quick to add that the Oakland County Child Killer Task Force would serve as a pilot project for future and similar investigations.

State Police Sergeant Phil Hogan simply showed up one day, shortly after the King funeral, at the Valley Woods School. Robbie had known Phil since the late sixties, when he'd quit the State Police in a dispute over his getting the shifts he needed to permit him to go back to school. After he had learned what he wanted to learn, he got himself rehired and went back to Lansing to begin working with computers in the Uniform Crime Reporting section. He became the department's goodwill ambassador of high-tech, going out to the various local police agencies and extolling the virtues of computers in law enforcement. Phil could make them do everything but comb his hair.

Hogan brought trooper George Willoughby with him to Valley Woods. The first thing they did was to talk Hewlett Packard in Farmington Hills into letting them use their computer, tying into it by phone lines from the Valley Woods terminal. Hogan really wanted his own minicomputer, but for now, Hewlett Packard would have to do. Then he put out the call for help in sorting the data to be fed into the computer. The community fairly inundated the Task Force with volunteers.

Within forty-eight hours after moving in, Hogan was "on line," and began running thousands of tips through the Hewlett Packard computer. Over and above the fresh tips on the new forms, information on old sex crimes was fed in, in the hope of finding patterns of sex-related crimes that might bring police closer to finding the killer. Hogan hoped to set up a model that could be used in similar investigations in the future. He intended that certain detectives be schooled in computer operations, so they could retrieve information at any hour of the day or night and call up maps on a screen, pinpointing various types of reported sex crimes from any given time or area.

Since none of the victims appeared to have been taken across state lines, the F.B.I. was not officially involved from a jurisdictional standpoint in the manhunt, but it was providing support equipment, records, and advice. When Dick Bretzing, Assistant Special Agent in charge of the bureau's Detroit field office declared: "Frank Sass is the foremost authority on this type of crime known to the F.B.I.," it was quickly agreed that Sass, a former F.B.I. supervisor and retired faculty member of the F.B.I. Academy in Quantico, Virginia, be brought in as a consultant. His three-day trip to Oakland County would be financed wholly by the *Daily Tribune*.

Sass may have started off on the wrong foot the moment he stepped off the plane at Metro, reportedly remarking that he had heard things were "pretty well screwed up." Jesse Snyder, a staff reporter for the *Tribune*, described him best: "Sass is a stocky, balding man, who often stops to relight his pipe while considering a question. His speech is a curious mixture of professor emeritus and street-wise cop, punctuating scholarly reflections with salty phrases." For instance, Sass explained that while most of his F.B.I. teaching had dealt with crimes of an aberrant sexual nature, he had also taught thousands of local police officers the right way to use a nightstick.

During his stay, Sass worked with the Task Force detectives one-on-one and collectively, briefing them on every aspect of criminal sexual conduct. He had brought with him dozens of slides showing unimaginable sex-oriented mutilation that made even the most hardened street cops wince. He also spent hours pouring over the files of all seven victims, especially the last four.

Though Sass raised some eyebrows and ruffled some feathers, he did say some things that needed to be said, and his overall assessment of the Task Force was favorable. In an interview with a *Trib* reporter, he talked about what he had found.

> They [the Task Force] have done a comprehensive job so far. They have a tremendous staff and are well organized. They are looking at everything. It's difficult for laymen to grasp an officer's inability to drive down the street and pick up the suspect. It's just not that easy. Nowadays, you need proper identification based on thorough investigation, and . . . you need good evidence—legally admissible evidence—to support a probable-cause arrest warrant. With today's emphasis on the rights of the individual, police can't be wrong. You have to build a case. Even if you know who did it, you can't just throw him in jail.
>
> In a stressful situation of heinous crimes like these, the public demands a quick solution. The police out there feel this pressure, believe me. They want it over worse than anyone. But, in a democratic society, we just can't lock up everybody who has quirks that might develop into violence sometime. The elimination process of tracking a killer is an unbelievable thing. You have thousands of possible suspects from lists of people who have been convicted of sexual offenses. You look at some guy arrested 12 or 15 years ago as a peeping Tom. Is he capable of sodomy, and strangling a kid? How do you know the guy hasn't straightened out in the past 15 years? All you know is that the guy once got busted for being a peeping Tom.
>
> This Task Force has put a lot of effort into organizing their investigation, and . . . their approach is a very logical one. Good hard police work will result in a solution of these cases some day, but there is no saying how long it'll take.

Sass left town, his work with the Task Force finished.

Seven Block of Stateville Prison in Joliet, Illinois, was not Rivard's first choice of where to spend the next hour of his life, but somebody had to. If the setting was grim, the company was worse. George Cammisano, prison number SP187626, street name "Chicken George," sat on the other side of the wire mesh. At 331 pounds, he reminded Rivard of a beached whale, and the sleeveless prison-issue undershirt revealed arms the size of Rivard's thighs. He was balding on top, but the sides and back were long, the greasy hair curling down his neck, and his entire upper torso was covered with thick hair. He was ugly, and he smelled bad.

Rivard pulled up a wooden chair, turned it backwards, and sat straddling it.

"Mr. Cammisano, I guess the warden briefed you?"

Chicken George stared at the policeman from under heavy brows but did not reply.

"You know why we're here, right?"

The giant con turned away from Rivard. "Yeah, cop, I know why you're here," he grunted.

Oh boy, thought Rivard to himself, this is really gonna be beautiful. "We figured we'd talk with an expert on kiddie porn, like yourself. You know, we got this child killer running around in Michigan."

"Hey man, I don't whack no kids." He glared at Rivard. "A few pictures, yeah. . . . "

"And maybe sample the merchandise once in a while?" Rivard was disgusted by the man and knew that even the other inmates had no use for a child pornographer.

"Don't you be givin' me no shit, cop." He started to raise his bulk off the chair.

"All right, all right, sorry," lied Roger, waving a hand in the air. He got up and put one foot up on the chair.

"Look, give us some help. We just want to know how this stuff is distributed, if the guy is taking pictures of the kids before he kills 'em. I mean, if he was, where the hell would we begin trying to track the stuff?" The giant rolled his eyes and redeposited himself in the chair.

"All right, cop, you just make goddam sure you tell the warden I co-operated. I want me some good time outta this."

"Yeah, sure, whatever you and the warden work out is fine with us."

"All right. First of all, anything east of the Mississippi is gonna go through New York. But you guys are all fucked up. First of all, there's too goddam much heat on this stuff now, no way he's gonna get rid of it. Second," he continued, clasping his hands in back of his head, "from what I know about this guy from the warden, he ain't interested in takin' any pictures, or sellin' 'em, or any of that shit. He's a psycho who probably gets his nuts off by just killin' 'em."

"What about snuff movies, where they kill the victims after they do 'em?" Rivard asked.

"That's a bunch of shit, leastways over here. I seen some comin' outta Central America, but nobody I know would touch that shit. I mean, we got some morals, you know. I don't even wanna know where that shit comes from or where it goes. I mean, fuckin' a little kid is one thing, killing him is something else." He shook his head. "All right, cop. You got somethin' to write on? I'm gonna give you a list of some of the people I know who deal this stuff. You better write it down, then forget the hell who you got it from."

28

Two cops entered the office of Dr. Bruce Danto. Unlike his house, the smallish office waiting room was merely comfortable, with polished tile floors, four green leather chairs with wooden arms, a matching couch, a couple of floor lamps, and some inexpensive pictures on the wall. Magazines lay scattered across a low table in front of the couch.

"Sergeant Mike Sheldon," one of the officers said in a soft voice, as he offered his Task Force business card to the girl seated behind the sliding glass window. She smiled.

"Yes, the doctor's waiting for you. Come right in, please." She buzzed the door. The three patients in the waiting room glared impatiently as the two police officers walked into the inner office. She led them down a short hallway and ushered them into Danto's private office. The doctor popped up from his chair and came from behind his desk, clutching a large brown sealed envelope. "You from the Task Force? No offense, but let me see some I.D. Always pays to check. Ah, good," he exclaimed after squinting first at one wallet, then the other. "Now let's get down to business. It's all right here." He thrust the envelope at Sheldon. "Everything's right in here. Nobody's touched it except me and the mailman. Nobody else's prints, you know. Maybe we'll get lucky."

"Get lucky, sir?" interrupted Officer Crowley.

"Yes, maybe his fingerprints are still on it. As I say, the only other prints on it would be mine and the mailman's."

"Would you mind telling us what you're talking about, sir? What's in the envelope here?" asked Sheldon, puzzled.

"You mean Joe didn't tell you about it?"

"No. You see, Doctor, we were in the car and dispatch just told us to stop by before we came in — priority message from Sergeant Krease to pick something up from you."

"Oh, well of course you don't want to say too much on the two-ways, but this is what we've been waiting for, in this envelope. That's a letter from the child-killer's roommate. He wants to meet with me!"

Krease carefully removed the white envelope from the larger brown one and held it in front of him at arm's length, studying it. It was a regular letter-sized envelope, addressed to Dr. Bruce Danto at his office in the Fisher Building. It was postmarked Detroit, April 4, 1977. Today was the fifth, a little after 5:30 P.M. What made the envelope unusual was the message typed under the address, across the bottom: "MOST VERY IMPORTANT MOST URGENT MOST URGENT PLEASE." Krease even more carefully extracted the two folded pieces of stationery from the envelope. He leaned back, propped his feet on the desk, and began reading.

Dr. Danto
    I am dsperite and nearly gone crazy and havnt got no place left to turn. I am going to comit suicide if you cant help me. Please dont give up the killer to the police. You must help me as there is no one else I cant turn to. This is for real I know who the killer is, I live with him I am his slave. He whips me and beats me all the time. And he will kill me if he finds out that I have writen this letter. I have been with him in his car when we go out looking for boys but I swear I have never never never been with him when he picks up the ones he killsed But I amin it in it so deep I am just as juilty to the law as he is I stayed with them here here right here in our apartment during the day while he is working. That makes me just as guilty. And no one can hear them as they gaged all the time. You know he brings them in stuffed inclothes hamper no one here knows the differences. You keep saying Oakland county not true. He has delivery rout in Oakland and Birmingham places but we live in detroit. You want to know people in this building? Primps and hookers and fags, you name it. Like on Gremlin he had it sure Grimlin until last boy but no one stops him in Detroit. He junk it out in Ohio to never be found ever. I tell you what makes him do it it Vietnam, we there together, Frank and me, oh Frank not his real name I call him that here. Nam screw up your mind doc, it gotta be fuckin Nam. You ever be over there? Itwould screw up your mindtoo. Tell you something else he killed lots of little kids then with medals for it. Burned them to death bombed them with napalm it's real becautiful there doc. He wants the rich people like people in Birmingham to suffer like all of us suffered to get nothing back for what we did for our country. Hes not a monster like you think he really loves children especially that little girl for 3 weeks not doing it becuase hates childrens but doing it because hates everybody else out there and this be his way to get even and get back at everybody.

But I cannot do it any more he says he wonts but I just know he is going to kill some more. I swear I had no idea no idea he going to kill that first little boy the one with blond colred hair   I shouldn8t ever never helped but trapped too late helped him stay uncaught, I am just as guilty as he is. I cant go on like this   I fell I feel like to die.

I will turn him in if you will se swearnto help me   I dont want any of reward   I am so afraid if I turn him in I be killed or do forever to jail for what so something I didn8t want to or didn't start. If you be real doctor you must help me. If you promise and what really promise that you not punish me like you call it immuty I meeting with you this Sunday night, I swear, I swear I tell you all of it everything I have to tell someone have to tell someone. Please please please not print this in paper he Frank kill me. I am his slave and he owns me like whatever he wants almost killed me once. I be only one alive know it him. Noboyd else know. I so scared all the time policeman come to door never happen. He say we never be caught but I am scared to die. I be guilty too. I not ge be call you araid police trace all your calls back to here. But if you will onluy please please help me help me and promise me not to go to jail in writing I tell you all of it everything everything and it all be over. I never never want it to be like this with little children dead. If you will help me please please. There be no toher hope. You tell me it be all right with code in sunday papers, this sunday, news freepress. You do like other letter you write on front page of papers this sunday, it be to say, Weather beuau say Trees to Bloom in 3 Weeks—you understand what I to say to you, it be code I know you get my letter and you understand   You make it to say Trees Bloom in 3 Weeks, I know you get my letter and understdna. It mean I can trust you, I set up meeting with you, no more little childrens die. Please help me please. I feel so bad like garbage not deserve to live any more. Maybe I kill self first must get out of this some way. Please help me.

I singnd Allen

"That guy has really painted us into a corner, hasn't he? Now what do we do?" groused Roger, pushing his copy of the letter away from him. The top command of the Task Force was seated around the long table in the briefing room. It was the day after Krease had received the letter from Danto.

"Well, let me just say this," Robertson said. "This guy 'Allen' could be a major break, or he could be a kook. Hell, I don't know and I don't think any of you guys know, either. He sounds promising, though. Maybe it's because it's about the only thing we've got."

"I mean, *Danto*, Lieutenant! Does this mean we gotta let him start poking around here because this Allen is writing him letters?" Roger asked.

"No," Krease said, "but by the same token I don't see how we can avoid at least working with him in some fashion. If anybody ever found out about this letter business, and we weren't following it, there'd be hell to pay. Besides, I'm with the Lieutenant. It looks promising, and you're right," he looked at Robbie, "it's the best thing we got so far."

"I suppose that means we gotta at least cover Danto on this one," added Waldron. He leaned back. "So how the hell are we going to do it?"

Nobody spoke for a long moment. Then Krease said, "I think the first thing to do is throw a couple of taps on his phone. This guy Allen might try to get in touch with him before he sees that code in the paper. You know, 'the trees will be blooming in three weeks.' I think we ought to bug his office and his house. Heck," Joe smiled, "he'll probably love it."

"You're not talkin' about a consensual. . . ." asked Roger incredulously.

"Sure, why not? Calm down, Rog. That doesn't mean we're going to give him a badge and a gun. But like Wayne says, we've got to cover Bruce on this. We can't just hang him out to dry."

"Joe's right," agreed Robertson. "We've got to work with him on this. It's too important for us not to give him some support. He's got us right by the short hairs, you know."

"All right," Krease decided. "I think we ought to get Bruce in here, give him a tour of the place, within limits, that is, then sit him down and have him share some thoughts about the letter before he blabs it all over TV and the papers. Then, we can tell him we'd like to put some recorders on his phones and that we'll talk with the papers about putting that code in the Sunday editions. There's one way of lookin' at it, Roger," continued Krease, turning to Rivard, "if we take him under our wing, we'll at least be able to control him."

"Maybe," Roger grunted.

Danto's eyes sparkled as he was ushered through Valley Woods, talking in hushed tones. The three men sat down in the Command office.

"Dr. Danto," Krease began, "about the letter. . . ."

"I knew this guy would come out, I just knew it. Just like the Ohio case. Did you know about that?" Without waiting for an answer, Danto told them about the case in Ohio where the murderer had given himself up at Danto's request. "I think we've really hit pay dirt, gentlemen. This guy is no kook, this Allen. I really think that this is valid, that he's genuinely interested in cooperating. It's not your typical kook letter, kooks always deal in generalities. This guy is talking specifics." Danto leaned forward, elbows resting on his knees, speaking softly. "Allen might try to contact me by telephone even before we put the code in the paper. I think we should put a tap on my phones, just in case."

Robbie and Krease looked at each other momentarily. Robertson said, "Doctor, that's a fine idea. Just record everything that comes into your office and house. We'll make a cop out of you yet."

"Well, I do have some police training, Lieutenant. I'm not exactly a greenhorn."

"No, you sure aren't," agreed Krease, smiling. "That'll make things a lot easier all the way around. We'll get right on it. Will somebody be home all day?"

"Sure, the maid's always there. And about the message code in the paper, the weather forecast. . . . "

"The 'trees blooming in three weeks' thing," interrupted Joe, who figured he'd better get control of the conversation. "We'll get ahold of the editorial people down there and see if they'll put the thing in the Sunday edition."

"I can do that," exclaimed the psychiatrist.

"I think we'd better handle that part of it, sir. It might give it more credibility. No offense, Doctor, but you know how the press is — it would probably be better if the request is official, right from the State Police." It was probably his imagination, thought Joe, but he could swear that Danto looked quite hurt. He was almost sorry he'd said it.

"I'll get it, Dee," Robbie said as the phone rang. "Robertson, here. Yeah, how are you, Jim? What's up? Oh. Well, nothing official. I mean, he's given us some help on the profile, but. . . . He what?" Robbie exclaimed, stretching the phone cord into the dining room, where he took a seat at the table. "Aw, for Christ's sake . . . What the hell's the matter with him . . . that's all we need." He got up, walked back into the kitchen, hung the phone up and immediately dialed a number. "Hi, Jerry, Bob. Listen, just heard from a friend on the Oakland County Gun Board. Danto wants to get a boot gun. Yeah," he laughed. "Beats the hell out of me. I don't give a damn what the reason is, there's no way. Now, you know him better than I do, so maybe you want to tell him, might make it easier. Otherwise, I'll sure do it." He laughed again. "Christ, that's all we need, Danto running around town with half the power of God in his boot!"

Danto was sitting cross-legged again on his living room couch, propped upright in his nest of pillows. He was reading a trade journal. The telephone rang next to him on the couch.

"This is Dr. Danto. Yes, Dr. Danto. Who is this, please?" The psychiatrist glanced at his watch. It was exactly two o'clock in the afternoon, Sunday, April 10. "I can't understand what you're saying. Please, talk more clearly, more slowly. Yes, that's better. . . . Excuse me, are you Allen? Did you write me a letter recently?" Danto waited for an answer that the caller did not give. "Are you there? Okay. . . . Immunity? I don't know about that, I don't have that kind of power." Another long pause. "Pictures? You . . . oh, okay . . . yes, I'm sorry. Okay." Danto listened. He had now put both feet on the floor and was leaning forward. "Pony Cart? I-I've never seen . . . Oh, Pony Cart Lounge . . . Oh, I'm sorry . . . yes, of course, . . . okay. Yes, nine o'clock would be fine. Of course." Danto by now was on his feet. "Yes, I'll be alone. Good. Wait, please!" The caller had hung up.

Danto stood for a moment, looking at the phone he held in front of him. He hung it up, then walked slowly to the glass wall that overlooked the expanse of backyard. He stared for several minutes, hands clasped behind his back, at a flock of starlings and several bluejays picking at the thawed ground around the bird-feeder. He turned, walked back to where the phone sat on the couch, then changed his mind. He would make the call on the private line in the study, so he could leave the tape running. Perhaps the man would call again.

The editors of the *Detroit News* did not exactly leap at the chance to dummy up a weather forecast for their Sunday edition. Something about the integrity of journalism, not to mention all the calls and letters they would get from people wanting to know what the nonsense was about trees blooming in three weeks. So it was with a large smile on his face that Krease opened the Sunday paper at the breakfast table, while digging into a waffle, and read on the front page in the box at the left:

WARM EASTER SPELL EXPECTED TO LINGER
The warm weather of this Easter weekend should continue for several days, the Weather Service says.
Highs in the 70's are expected — at least through Tuesday — although there will be some rain.
If the warming trend persists, trees should be blooming in three weeks.

"Play the goddam thing again. Sure sounds like a bunch of horseshit to me," growled Rivard, glaring at Danto. Krease had put Roger in charge of the Danto caper. He knew Roger had a real problem with the psychiatrist, but then it sometimes seemed Roger had a real problem with just about everybody and everything. Nonetheless, Roger was a good cop and could keep Danto on a short leash if anyone could. They were at the Detroit Artillery Armory on Eight Mile Road in Oak Park, headquarters of the State Police Intelligence Section. It was 7:30 P.M., Monday, April 11.

Dick Mundy of the State Police ran the tape back and restarted it. Everybody around the table leaned forward to catch every word and nuance of the recording:

> I want (unintelligible) immunity. I want it by tomorrow night I mean tomorrow 9:00 (unintelligible). You be at Seven Mile and Woodward you know where Pony Cart Bar, you listen to me this only time I'm calling you (unintelligible). You want hang up, you hang up (unintelligible) but this is what I'm telling you (pause). You be Pony Cart bar tomorrow night at 9:00 with letter from governor of Michigan giving me total immunity in return I give you polaroid pictures proving he kill them (pause). That's all I'm going to say (pause). You be there (pause). This is a bar (pause). Jesus (unintelligible). Seven Mile near Woodward (pause). Be there (unintelligible). Pony Cart Bar (pause). You be there, no police (pause). I know everybody in there (long pause). You no bring police you be there by yourself (pause). You be there 9:00 tomorrow (pause). No it's a bar you stu (unintelligible). You be there 9:00 tomorrow (pause.) You no bring police I prove he kill them. That's all I say.

Then a dial tone. Mundy shut the recorder off. Nobody spoke for a few moments. Danto shifted uneasily in his chair. Rivard leaned back in his chair, hands clasped behind his head. "All right," he said to Danto, "you want to meet this guy?" The psychiatrist fidgeted in his seat.

"Y-Yes, I think we, er, I think I should, don't you?"

"We can't make you do it, you know."

"I know, and yes, I want to do it. How's it going to go down? We don't have much time, you know."

"Okay. Here's what you're gonna do." He got up from his chair and put one foot on the seat, leaning toward Danto over the table. "It's real simple, Bruce. We're gonna wire you up, and you're gonna go in there and sit and wait. You'll just order a drink and sit and wait for this guy. Try not to strike up any conversations with anybody, either. We don't want to have to sort through a lot of garbage on the tape."

"What if somebody comes over and starts talking to me?"

"Tell them you're waiting for someone. I don't know, just get rid of them the best way you can without blowing your cover." Rivard went on a little impatiently, "Jerry Tobias here is going to go in with you." Tobias nodded.

"You mean we walk in together?"

"Jerry's gonna walk in before you and sit himself down at another table and watch the whole room, including you."

"Oh," said Danto apologetically. "Yeah, sure."

"Another thing," said Rivard, "you know anything about this Pony Cart Bar? What kind of clientele hangs out there?"

"No. No, not really. Just regular people, I guess."

"Well, not exactly," Roger stated flatly. "Most of the customers are gay. All right, Doctor, let's do it. Get your shirt off! Let's get you all wired and taped."

29

Danto wheeled his Mercedes around the back of the Pony Cart Lounge and into the parking lot. His headlights picked up two of the cover officers sitting in a car on the opposite curb, just beyond the parking lot entrance. They stared into Danto's headlights as he turned, like zombies. Danto hadn't noticed the other two cover teams, but then he wasn't supposed to, if they were doing their jobs properly. He parked, got out, and walked to the back door of the building, his heart racing.

The psychiatrist had expected the worst but was pleasantly surprised at the decor and the patrons. The atmosphere was rather soft and intimate. The patrons — there were perhaps a dozen — were all males casually dressed, and looked like young professionals. He wondered if Allen was already there, watching him as he walked, rather unsteadily, over to the bar. He felt himself enter a controlled state of panic. How would the man know him? That was discussed only briefly at the Armory, and it was simply assumed that Danto's picture had been plastered in enough newspapers and seen on enough television sets, that he would be readily recognizable.

He took a barstool close to the service area. There were two men a couple of stools down, caressing each other and laughing softly. Another lone male was seated around the corner of the bar. Judging from the glass and change on the table, he was waiting for his boyfriend to return from the restroom or perhaps the dance floor.

The bartender stepped over from the cash register, smiled, placed a napkin in front of Danto, and said, "Yes, sir, what can I get you?"

"Um, a beer, I guess. Yes, Miller, if you have it. That'll be fine."

"Tab, sir?"

"What?"

"I say, would you like me to run a tab?"

"Oh, sure, a tab. Yes, a tab'll be fine."

"Meeting somebody?" the bartender inquired as he took a couple steps and reached under the bar for the beer. He was tall and blond, fine-boned with long, slender fingers.

"No. Well, I don't know, maybe. I mean, why do you ask?" replied the psychiatrist as the bartender set a glass in front of him and poured. He could almost hear Rivard cursing him at the other end of the wire. What was it the cop had said, don't be striking up any conversations with anybody? Well, I've got no choice!

"Oh, I don't know," answered the bartender, leaning over both hands on the bar. "Attractive man like yourself, well dressed, just thought you must have a friend. Really love the outfit," he added. He pushed himself away and began wiping glasses. Danto felt himself flush. He was wearing a blue wool sportscoat, heavy white turtleneck, grey flannels, grey socks, and black penny loafers. Simple, but elegant, he thought to himself. He let the conversation stop there, took a sip of beer, and turned to take in the rest of the place.

From his seat, Danto could see into the dance area, which was separated from the lounge by a floor-to-ceiling glass partition. Two couples — four men — were swaying and dipping to Johnnie Ray's "Little White Cloud That Cried." Danto watched them kiss, fascinated. He had talked with and counseled dozens of gay men and women in his professional life, but he had never seen them interact on the street. He found it hard not to stare. He wondered if the others in the bar thought he was gay. Of course they did, he concluded. He turned back to face the bar in time to notice that Tobias had come in and was sitting at one of the tables at the far end of the bar close to the rear door. He looked at him for a long moment, hoping for a sign of recognition. None came. Tobias had a university syllabus, a textbook, and some papers spread out on the table. He appeared to be correcting tests, for God's sake. He was nursing a beer. Danto wondered if Jerry was wired. Nothing had been said about it at the briefing. He must be. Danto shifted in his seat. The skin under the tape that held the tiny transmitter and battery-pack to his chest began to itch. He squirmed again while sipping his own beer and discreetly tried to scratch. The bartender came over again.

"What's your name?" he asked, polishing a cocktail glass.

"Ah, well, Bruce."

"Well, Bruce, I'm David." The bartender set the glass and towel down and offered a soft hand to Danto. Danto grasped it tentatively over the bar. He caught Tobias looking his way from the corner of his eye. "Haven't seen you here before, Bruce. First time?"

"I . . . well, yes. I've never been here before."

"You from around here, I mean, you work around here?" David smiled. Danto took another swallow of beer. He knew the barkeep's interest in him went beyond the normal bartender's chat. He figured he'd be able to play on that. Maybe he could find out something about the man he was waiting for.

"Well, yes, as a matter of fact, I'm a doctor. My office is downtown, but I live out here, that is, I live in Bloomfield." He could see the young man's eyes brighten with this information.

"Oh, really! We don't get many doctors in here. You say you're waiting for someone?"

"Well, yes, as a matter of fact."

"Has your friend got a name? Maybe I know him." David looked genuinely disappointed.

"Yes, yes, maybe you do. His name is Allen. I don't know his last name," Danto said apologetically, looking down at his beer.

The bartender chuckled. "Nobody's got a last name in here, Bruce. Let's see." He thought while rubbing his chin. "Allen . . . Allen." He shook his head." Know anything else about him, like what he looks like?"

"No, not really. He might be, well, I got a letter from him, and I talked with him on the phone once."

"Blind date, eh?"

"No, nothing like that," Danto tried to explain. "You see. . . . "

"Sure, I see. I understand," the barkeep interrupted flippantly.

"No, I'm not sure you do, David." Danto laughed nervously. "This isn't a blind date or anything of the sort. You see, I'm not. . . . "

"Oh, no offense, Doctor." Now it was the barkeep's turn to sound apologetic. "Shouldn't have pried."

"No, you're not prying. I'm the one that asked you if you knew a man by the name of Allen. It's just that I'm supposed to meet him here. It's important—a business matter. This is where he wanted to meet me."

David laughed. "Well, whatever. I don't know this Allen. At least the name doesn't ring a bell. How about another beer, on the house?"

Danto was sorry he'd started the whole thing. He glanced at his watch. "Yeah, sure."

A man walked off the dance floor and came to stand behind Danto momentarily. He was dressed neatly—brown slacks, brown loafers, white shirt, brown tie, and a brown leather flight-jacket—and slightly built, maybe about five feet ten inches. He had neatly trimmed brown hair, blow-dried. He did not speak but just stood behind Danto for perhaps thirty seconds. He started to step forward toward the doctor but then changed his mind and walked into the men's room. He emerged several minutes later and looked toward Danto again. Danto did not see him. The man walked slowly toward where Tobias was seated, correcting papers. He stood looking down at Jerry, hands in his jacket pockets.

"You would like to drink with me?" the man said haltingly to Tobias, who looked up slowly. "I buy. . . . "

"No thanks, really. I'm fine," Jerry said, raising his nearly full glass.

"Oh, I like to buy . . . you . . . you," he stammered. "I like talk. . . . "

"Well, I don't," interrupted Tobias. "Look, thanks for the offer, but I'm just trying to get some paperwork done, and I really don't have the time to talk. Okay? Maybe next time." The man looked down at the floor, turned slowly, and walked out the back door.

Danto had noticed none of it.

"God damn it! What the fuck are those two doing?" Rivard screamed at Mundy from inside the van parked a half block up Woodward from the bar. "You believe this shit? A guy who could be our man comes right up to Tobias and wants to buy him a drink—and he says no! And what the fuck is Danto doing sitting at the bar telling some faggot bartender his whole life story! I want both of them the hell outta there! Now! I don't believe this shit! I can't deal with this!" Rivard picked up the mike. "Benson! One of you guys go in there and get those two. Tell 'em I wanna see 'em both back at the Armory!"

Krease opened the large envelope and took out the contents. Four typewritten pages on F.B.I. Lab letterhead, from Washington, D.C., to the Special Agent in charge of the F.B.I.'s Detroit field office. It was dated May 27, 1977.

RE: TIMOTHY KING - DECEASED
      MISSING PERSON; POLICE COOPERATION
FBI FILE NO. 79-32528
LAB NO. CR-14654 TF
     D-770519007 IL
EXAMINATION REQUESTED BY: DETROIT
REFERENCE: COMMUNICATION DATED 4/18/77,
          BUCALL 5/5/77
EXAMINATION REQUESTED: CRYPTANALYSIS — DOCUMENT
SPECIMENS RECEIVED 4/21/77
    Q1 One tape cassette labeled "Telephone Call to Dr. Danto Re: Tim King Homicide"

Q2   One letter beginning "Dr. Danto I am dsperite and nearly gone crazy . . . "

REMARKS: Examination of the tape and letter indicates that it is likely that the caller as recorded on Q1 is the same individual as the letter writer, who identifies himself as Allen.

Krease flipped over the administrative page to page 2 and began reading the letter:

Not only is the subject's manner of speaking compatible with the syntax contained in the letter, but also his highly distraught emotional state, as manifested in both, is very similar.

This individual appears to be a male between the ages of 25 and 30, of Latin descent, probably Spanish. From the contents of the letter, it appears that he is the female counterpart of a homosexual relationship with the suspect.

Due to the complete lack of any background noise, it is believed that the call was made from an apartment house rather than a phone booth. This apartment house, being very well constructed, is most likely located in an older area of town, on a street less likely to have truck traffic. There are noises at the end of the tape which appear to be those of the caller fumbling with the telephone, an indication that the caller is using a cradle-type phone rather than one which hangs on the wall.

Because this individual claims to know everyone in the bar, it can be assumed that he goes there often and possibly lives within walking distance of it, since homosexual bars are rather plentiful, and he would logically frequent the one nearest his residence. Moreover, the possibility exists that these roommates have only one vehicle between them, and that the author of the letter, "Allen" does not even own a driver's license, since in the letter, he never makes reference to his own driving but only to his roommate's driving, his roommate's Gremlin, and his roommate's delivery route.

It is noted that there are no strike-overs in the letter, nor is there any attempt to erase the repeated words. There are instances in which the writer tends to reverse letters in words which are clearly not misspellings but rather typographical errors, (e.g., understdna, noboyd), again, with no attempt to correct the errors. This individual appears to be extremely nervous while typing this letter and possibly afraid that his roommate will return home unexpectedly.

The way in which he describes the apartment building in which he lives gives the impression that he is not prosperous. Also, he may be unemployed, because he writes, "I stayed with them the children here here right here in our apartment during the day while he is working." The possibility exists that this individual, having served combat duty in Vietnam, incurred injuries for which he is now collecting Disability Compensation, which provides him the additional financial support he would need to remain at home unemployed.

It is also noted in the letter that "Allen's" roommate has a delivery route of some sort, and that he puts the children in a clothes hamper, which suggests the possibility of a laundry route of some kind (linens, diapers, shirts, etc.). Moreover, it is noted that his delivery route takes him into the wealthier neighborhoods of Birmingham and Oakland, which could afford to make use of such laundry services. "Allen" writes of his roommate, "He wants the rich people like people in Birmingham to suffer like all of us suffered to get nothing back for what we did for our country." He expresses that his roommate kills these children as his means of seeking vengeance from these rich people. His roommate's delivery route would certainly make him easily accessible to the children of these wealthy families. Moreover, being daily exposed to the carefree, comfortable lives of these people could work to continually plague his mind and distort his thought processes.

In accordance with referenced telephone call on May 5, 1977, it is noted that all of the victims were thoroughly cleaned with "Phisohex," a product which was taken off the market several years ago. Since this procedure would necessarily require a fairly large amount of this product, the possibility exists that the individual involved in these killings is employed by a company (pharmaceutical, laundry, etc.) that would have used this product in large quantities, and rather than throw it away, gave it out freely to its employees, when it was declared unmarketable.

Krease took off his glasses and rubbed his eyes. He wondered about hospital employees — doctors, orderlies, even male nurses. People like that would certainly have access to Phisohex even if it were no longer on the market. He put the letter down and stared at the ceiling, trying to put it all together. Why the hell was the killer cleaning these kids up? Was it some kind of weird ritual, did it have cult overtones? He put his glasses back on and continued reading.

Also, referenced telephone conversation indicated that two of the murders occurred on a Wednesday and two occurred on a Sunday. Because it seems possible that the individual committing these murders might utilize the time beforehand to indulge in some particular activity which would then incite him to the commission of these crimes, it seems plausible that such an individual might be employed in a job in which he had time off on Wednesdays and Sundays.

Examination of the typewriting on the Q2 photocopy reveals that it most closely resembles a standard maintained in the Laboratory for Underwood pica style of type, spaced 10 letters to the inch. Q2 was also searched through the appropriate sections of the Anonymous Letter File without making an identification.

The above is for investigative information only. No report is being submitted. Returned herewith are specimens received, Q1 and Q2.

Krease put the letter on his desk, got up, and walked into the tip room. He stood at the door and called to Varajon, who was on the phone, "Mike, see you a minute?"

Varajon cupped his hand over the mouthpiece. "Sure, Joe, just a minute." Krease turned and walked back to his office. He was rereading the F.B.I. report when Mike walked in and pulled up a chair. "What's up, Joe?"

"This Pony Cart Lounge thing, Mike. There are too many unanswered questions."

"Yeah, I hear Rivard really gave Danto and Jerry hell for screwing up. Why'd Jerry refuse that guy anyway? He doesn't seem to want to talk about it much."

"Oh, I don't know. Probably just figured he didn't want to interact with anybody in the bar, figured it was all Danto's show, I guess. Look, Mike," Joe went on, changing the subject, "we've got some follow-up to do on this thing." He reached inside a desk drawer and pulled out a cassette. "I want to try something. I talked with a guy name of Brawner, Commander Revel Brawner. He's in charge of the Eleventh Precinct, which includes the Pony Cart. It's a long shot," he continued, handing the tape to Varajon, "but maybe we'll get lucky. Let's run it over to him. He'll get ahold of the guy who owns the bar and let him have a listen. Maybe the owner will recognize the voice, if the guy is a regular customer. I think it's worth a shot."

Mike Logan, the manager of the Pony Cart, listened to the tape several times in Brawner's office. Varajon and Sergeant James Cowie were there. Logan couldn't recognize the voice, but suggested that his night manager, Danny Rashid, was more familiar with the customers and might be of more help. Rashid was asked to come over to the Eleventh Precinct later that day.

"Yeah . . . yeah, could be," muttered Rashid. "Lemme hear that last part again." Varajon rewound the tape and played it back. "Yeah. You know, there is this guy, Lonnie's his name, I think, he comes into the bar mostly on Saturday, Sunday, and Monday nights. Could be his voice. It's the way he talks, too."

"What time's he usually stop in?" asked Brawner.

"Oh, around eleven, I guess. Always stays till closing."

"Listen, Mr. Rashid, this is very important. Can you describe him for us?" Varajon asked, taking out a notebook and pen.

"Sure. I'd say he's about thirty-five or forty, maybe five-eight or nine, medium build. He's a white guy but dark complexion, you know, maybe Arab or something. Black curly hair, heavy eyebrows, and a mustache."

"How's he wear his hair?" asked Mike.

He thought for a moment, staring at the ceiling. "Pretty full all over but always neat, combed, never a hair outta place, you know. Straight teeth, his hands are real soft-like."

"Jesus," exclaimed Varajon, "that's a helluva description. You really notice your customers!"

"Yeah," Danny laughed, a little embarrassed. "Part of my job, you know, to notice things. You want to know how he dresses?"

"Yes!"

"Okay. The guy always wears brown — dark brown suit, yellow shirt, dark brown tie, gold tie-bar and watch. When he's not wearing the suit, he's got maybe a lighter brown color sport-jacket, with the dark brown pants, of course, rust-colored shirt and brown tie."

"Anything else?"

"Yeah, a couple of things. I don't know if you want to know 'em or not."

"Try me," Varajon replied, poising his pen again.

"Well, he always gives the doorman a hard time when he comes in. Nothing physical, just a lot of shit about how he knows everybody in the place. He always parks it at the end of the bar near the rear door. Never sits past the service rail. Always orders a Budweiser, takes a couple sips, and then orders a Johnny Walker Red. He'll go through three or four set-ups. Smokes Winstons or Marlboros, always leaves them on the bar. Uses book matches to light up. One thing's kinda unusual about him, though," added Rashid, his voice trailing off.

"Oh, what's that?" asked Varajon.

"Well, a customer who comes in like that and spends a couple hours at the bar usually leaves his money on the bar. Just habit with most people, I guess. That way they don't have to keep reaching in their pockets."

"And this Lonnie doesn't?"

"He always reaches into his rear pocket and brings out his wallet. He doesn't bother tipping, either, but he sure dresses like he could afford to."

"Does he talk a lot at the bar while he's sitting there throwing the drinks down?"

Rashid looked at Logan, his boss, who nodded almost imperceptibly. "Well, I'm always pretty busy, you know, making sure all the customers are happy, but, yeah," he paused, "I guess you could say he talks a little. I mean, I don't talk with him that much."

"Know anything about his sex life?" Brawner knew what Varajon was getting at.

"Well," Rashid looked again at Logan, who gave another subtle nod to show it was okay for Rashid to tell the police everything he knew. "Well, I know the guy likes young boys."

"How is it that you know?" Brawner interrupted.

"It's my job to know as much about the people who come in to see us as I can," replied Rashid, a little rattled. "Anyway," he said, turning toward Varajon again, "I know he likes the real young stuff, but I never saw him leave with anybody. I mean, he's always talking about the chickens to the bartenders."

"What's he say about them?" asked Varajon.

"Well," he looked down at his hands, "like how the really young ones got all that" he hesitated, "all that sweet juice."

"I get the idea," said Varajon, not wishing to go into any more detail. "Anything else about his sex life?"

"Not much. Guy says he was married once. I mean, to a woman. Got some kids, says he was divorced a couple years ago."

"Ever mention where he works?"

"Nope, not to me, anyway."

"How about the military? Ever say he's been in the service?"

"Yeah, I did overhear him telling David — that's one of our bartenders — that he was in the navy in 'Nam."

"All right, Mr. Rashid," said Varajon, reaching inside his coat pocket. "I want to show you a police composite. I want you to take a good look at it and take your time. Tell us if you think you've seen him before. Do you think this might be the Lonnie you've been telling us about?"

Rashid looked at the composite and hesitated. "Nah," he said, finally. "That don't look like Lonnie."

Following the interview with Logan and Rashid, Krease ordered a check of all Pony Cart Lounge employees. Some interesting, if not substantive things, surfaced. To begin with, Mike Logan's real name turned out to be Frank Michael Logan. The fact that "Allen" called his roommate

"Frank," heated up a few detectives. However, it was hardly enough to bust the man and charge him with the slayings of four children. His street name was Mike, aka "Mike the Bike," as he was a cyclist. As a matter of fact, a rundown on Logan by the State Police Intelligence Unit and the Detroit Police Organized Crime Section failed to turn up so much as an unpaid parking ticket on Logan. However, if Logan was squeaky clean, his night manager was somewhat less so. The same checks on Rashid revealed that he had at one time unlawfully driven away an automobile, for which he paid the state thirty-two months.

A flushing of the Woodward Corridor by a dozen teams of detectives, particularly around the Pony Cart, turned up one snitch who claimed to have been in the bar the night Mike, whom he described as the owner, was sitting with a bartender, whose name was either Mike or Larry, and a giant of a man who answered to the name of George. The informant described George as at least six-seven and of Greek or Italian extraction. The informant told the detectives he had heard Mike exclaim that he killed the children.

"Yeah, I couldn't fuckin' believe it! They're just sittin' there at the bar, you know, the three of them, and Mike's real drunk, and he's talkin' real loud. Then the big dude says somethin' I couldn't hear, and Mike says 'Shit, it's easy to kill. I'd just walk up behind them and knock 'em out with ether and a cloth over their mouth and throw 'em in the truck.'"

Not surprisingly, Logan denied ever having said anything even remotely like that. "I don't know what the hell your informant is talking about," said Logan to the investigators. "I'm not hiding the fact that I'm a homosexual, and sure, I'll go to bed with any guy between the age of eighteen and eighty. But kids, no. No thrill there. I like for the guy to know how to do me." Logan was questioned by different investigators on several different occasions. He gave officers permission to search his home (they did and came away with samples of his carpeting and hair) and volunteered to take a polygraph test.

The gay community was for the most part extremely cooperative in the investigation. They were as anxious to get the killer off the streets as the rest of the population, perhaps more so, since the public perception of the child killer as a homosexual could only make their lives more difficult.

Another interesting bit of information surfaced during the Pony Cart Lounge investigation. In an effort to find the owner of the property, detectives checked with the Assumed Names Section of the City Clerk's Office and found that a woman by the name of Joanna McCall owned the Pony Cart's liquor license. Logan's relationship to her was uncertain. McCall's employer — she worked full-time in an auto parts company — said that she was divorced but lived with Logan in East Detroit. The employer added that he believed McCall had either adopted Logan or allowed him to live with her when he was very young. According to the employer, Mc-Call had bankrolled Logan in several different ventures, the most recent of which was the Pony Cart Lounge.

30

"Newsroom, Nancy McCauley. May I help you?" the attractive Channel 2 reporter said, answering her desk phone. She had just finished her morning coffee and was going over background for her first assignment of the day. "Yes, this is Nancy," she repeated, grabbing her pen and quickly turning over a piece of yesterday's wire copy. "Oh, yes, of course," she paused. "Look, can you tell me your name? Oh, well, all right. Can you give me the information now, over the phone?" Another pause. "Yes, I underst. . . . " A longer pause this time. "Sure. Okay, yes, I know right wh . . . about three . . . all right, that's fine. You can't tell me who you are? Yes, of course. Wait, how will I be able to recognize you? Oh, all right, then, I'll see. . . . " The caller hung up.

"Hi, Nance — hey, you okay?" It was Jimmy, the intern, brushing by her desk. He stopped. "Hey Nance, something the matter?"

"Huh? Oh, hi, Jimmy." She looked up startled. "No, I'm fine," she laughed softly, and placed the phone back in its cradle.

"Oh. You look kinda strange."

"Yeah, I just got a pretty strange phone call. Say, Mike still in the meeting?"

"I guess," the intern replied.

"Yeah, okay. I've got to see him. . . . " her voice trailed off as she walked to VonEnde's office where the morning editorial meeting was going on with the day editors and producers. She knocked on the glass of the open door as she walked in. "Hi guys. Say, Mike, excuse me for a minute, but I just got a phone call, and I think we should talk about it. . . . "

"Yeah, sure, Nancy. Have a seat." Mike motioned to a chair. "What's up?"

"Well," she began, taking the chair and joining the four men seated in a semi-circle in front of the News Director's desk, "I just got a phone call from some man who says he's got information about the child killer."

"Oh?" said VonEnde, "well, you've got our attention, Nancy." He smiled and leaned back in his chair. "Talk to me."

"He just called. Wouldn't give me his name, but says he knows that Allen guy that wrote Danto the letter. Says he's got some other information about the case too, but he'll only give it to me if I meet with him, says he can't go into it on the phone." Nancy leaned forward in the chair and looked down at the few notes she'd been able to jot down. Then, after a long pause during which no one spoke, she said, "Mike, I told him I would. Three o'clock, corner of Seven Mile and Woodward."

"John," VonEnde turned to an editor, "what about crew?"

"No problem, Mike. We ought to be able to scare up somebody — everybody's on board and the day doesn't look busy."

"Good. Now Nancy, how do you feel about this? I mean, what's your reading of this guy. Wacko maybe?"

"Hard to say, Mike. Probably, but. . . . "

"But maybe not," VonEnde finished the thought. "Did your caller sound like he's getting an early start on the cocktail hour?"

"No. He sounded pretty sober to me, didn't slur any words, seemed to know just what he wanted to tell me. Sounded like he's all business. I just don't think we should pass it up."

"Neither do I," agreed her boss. "How do the rest of you feel?" he looked around the room. "Discussion?"

The four staffers nodded their agreement. It was Tom, a producer, who spoke. "I don't think we should pass it up, either, but how are you going to handle it logistically with the crew and all? You can probably kiss him goodbye if he sees anything that even hints of a camera or crew."

"No question about that," replied Nancy. "I'll just have them hang back."

"Yeah, and how are you supposed to know who this guy is? Did he tell you what he looks like, or what he'll be wearing?"

"No, he didn't. I asked him how I was supposed to recognize him and all he said was 'I'll know you. I see you on television all the time.'"

"All right," interjected VonEnde. "I only have one reservation, Nancy. I don't want you meeting this guy alone even if it is the middle of the afternoon on a busy street corner."

"Aw, Mike!"

"Yeah, I know." VonEnde waved his hand aimlessly and leaned forward on the desk. "Look. You don't know what kind of thing you're walking into. The guy could be a real looney and pull out a knife and start slashing. I don't know, but it's not worth it. Somebody's gotta go in with you. Look, here's what you do. Talk to your people at the Task Force. If this guy's who he says he is, a friend of Allen's, the cops better know about it anyway. Normally, I wouldn't get involved with them, but this isn't a normal case. They've been really straight with us, and we should be up front with them. So let's tell them about it and see if they won't kick loose one of their undercover guys to go in with you. You can tell your informant he's a boyfriend, or a new reporter, I don't care how you cover your tracks. You'll think of something—if the guy shows up at all."

"But if he sees I'm with somebody, maybe he won't show up."

"Well then, I guess we waste an hour or two. It's the only way it's going to happen, Nancy," VonEnde concluded. "Now you better talk with Robertson over there and set this thing up, then get with your crew." VonEnde glanced at his watch and got up, a signal that the meeting was over.

Bud Johnson was one of the finest TV cameramen in the business. He was a real pro who'd earned his spurs on the streets of the nation's fifth largest city for over two decades. Riots, mobs, fires, murders, and countless covert assignments had honed his instincts and nerves to a fine edge. Nancy felt good with Bud.

"You've got the mini-corder in your bag?" he asked as he pulled up to the curb a half block north of Seven Mile on Woodward.

"Yeah," she felt around for it in her purse. "Right here."

"Good. We're going to wire you anyway, but flip the mini on as a back-up, okay?"

"Sure," she smiled. A little nervously, Bud thought. Then, looking at her watch, she said, "Guess I better head over to the restaurant."

"Yeah, about that time."

"You guys staying over here?"

"Yeah, this is pretty good. I can get a pretty good shot of the whole corner from here."

She started to get out of the unmarked news wagon. He grabbed her arm. "Good luck. And Nancy," his voice rose a little, "that guy makes one wrong move, just start hollering! I figure I can still do the hundred in ten flat, okay?"

Robertson had made arrangements to have one of the Task Force detectives accompany Nancy. He would meet her in the restaurant just a half block up from the street corner thirty minutes before the meeting was to take place and stay with her. Robertson had also sent a back-up team to cover both of them. If indeed, the mysterious informant was a friend of the child-killer's roommate, they'd scoop him up in a hurry.

Meanwhile, in a hotel meeting room down in Atlanta, Georgia, a convention of southern police chiefs was being treated to a speech about Oakland County.

"Believe it or not, there is an intersection in our county that is policed by four jurisdictions, as well as served by the State Police and the Sheriff's Department. Yet," the speaker continued, "if an officer from each jurisdiction met at that location, they could not communicate unless they got out of their cars and talked face-to-face. They are all on different radio frequencies. This is not coordination. This is inane. Yet each police agency jealously guards its bailiwick from encroachment by other police agencies as a king would his kingdom. Efforts to coordinate law enforcement are met with suspicion and disfavor by many of the local chiefs and their political superiors." Spreen paused. It was hot and humid in Atlanta, and in spite of the air-conditioning the air in the hotel's meeting room was close. Spreen dabbed at his forehead and the back of his neck with a napkin he'd wet just before getting up to speak. He took a big swallow of iced tea, and continued.

"Mark's body was found next to a dumpster in the parking lot of a shopping mall in the City of Southfield. Although the State Police maintain two relatively nearby crime labs, and the Oakland County Sheriff's Department also has an excellent crime lab available, none were called to process the scene. By the time the investigator from the Oakland County Medical Examiner's office had arrived, the body had been moved from its original position. The body was then transported to the Southfield Police Department, rather than directly to the Oakland County Morgue. The clothes were taken off the body and when it finally arrived at the morgue, it was devoid of all clothes. No one really knows what might have been found at the scene had proper crime-scene procedures been followed and a crime lab been present." If it occurred to Spreen that his remarks would be taken out of context and misconstrued back home, he didn't care.

"The dissemination of information to the press was another problem. In an attempt to coordinate this function, I understand the State Police asked the Oakland County Prosecutor's Office to act as spokesman. The politically ambitious prosecutor seized this opportunity and assumed the role of coordinating the investigation. . . ."

Later on in the speech, Spreen challenged Patterson's call for the fingerprint expert from Toronto, saying the Sheriff's Department had "an equally experienced expert." Of the rewards being offered for the child killer, Spreen used an unfortunate simile. "People in the immediate area," he said, "as well as throughout the United States, began to use the case as a lottery, with the prize being seventy thousand dollars, and the pawn being a friend or neighbor who they thought might be weird. Parents turned in sons, brothers turned in brothers, and church members turned in their pastors."

Fortified by the iced tea, Spreen continued to hold the Chiefs' interest. "Although admirable efforts were made at supervision, coordination was near impossible. It was a case of too much, too late. There were occasions when one team of investigators was virtually following the trails of other investigators. During the early stage of the King homicide, numerous bits of information were lost forever due to the inadequate reporting procedures and unfamiliarity of the cases. In addition, at this early stage, some departments were virtually using the Task Force as a training experience for their personnel. Chiefs were committing rookie detectives and patrol officers to investigate the homicides, and were rotating their personnel periodically to allow everyone to participate in the investigation. The mere fact that some of the investigators were inexperienced resulted in the improper elimination of some suspects. Recently, the Task Force was forced to review all of the tips that were submitted during the five-day period that Timothy King was missing and had to re-investigate almost half of them."

"What is the answer?" he asked his audience rhetorically. "Ideally, one county police agency may be the answer. One can hardly argue against the economics of the principle. Under one agency, you can enjoy one set of procedures, one command, and expertise that can hardly be gained by very small departments. Duplication of effort is all but eliminated. While a single county police department may be the answer, politically in many areas it is an impossibility, especially in Oakland County. Mayors, city managers, township supervisors, and police chiefs are reluctant to relinquish their power." Spreen stopped for a minute and used the dramatic pause to wipe his brow again and take another slug of iced tea.

"Let's take a look at the case at hand," he began again. "What if the Sheriff's Major Crime Unit, consisting of Sheriff's Investigators teamed with the best investigators from local agencies within the county, had been trained and ready to be summoned to the crime scene? The investigation would have been under one command. With the expertise and talent available within the county, I sincerely doubt that experienced homicide detectives would have mishandled evidence. Lab technicians, trained in evidentiary rules, would have handled the crime scene. Reports would be professionally written. Perhaps with the responsibility on the shoulders of one man, that man would properly coordinate press releases and the media," another dramatic pause, "the media would not be privileged to confidential police information that could impede the investigation. With an experienced Major Crimes Squad, would it be necessary to call upon the services of three hundred investigators? Don't you think that thirty investigators, who frequently work together, would have been adequate?"

At the Valley Woods School in Birmingham, Michigan, Spreen's speech was less well received. As one investigator put it, "Those of us who had some doubts about Johannes have now made up our minds." At the very least, Spreen's talk to the Southern Police Institute Alumni Association was badly timed. Given during the height of the investigation, it was perceived as a frontal assault by the investigators back home, who felt betrayed. After all, they were working day and night, seven days a week, and one of the most influential men in law enforcement had seemingly raked them over the coals.

Of medium build with long, straight hair, well-groomed and nicely dressed in an inexpensive suit, the cop didn't look much like a cop. His presence didn't make a statement, like most cops. Maybe that's why Nancy was relatively at ease with him. He also didn't have much to say and let Nancy do most of the talking over coffee as they waited. They left the restaurant at precisely three minutes to three for the short walk down the block to the corner of Seven and Woodward. They had decided back at the restaurant that the cop, whose name was Tom, would be a new Channel 2 reporter fresh from another city, who was spending a couple of days on the street with Nancy just to learn the city. They stood on the corner and talked for perhaps five minutes. Nancy was checking her watch, when he came up behind Tom.

"Hi Nancy, it is you, isn't it? I'm glad you came!" The stranger was well-groomed and muscular, bulky like he pumped iron, and his hair was red and short. He was wearing slacks and sportcoat with a sweater underneath. Not a bad-looking fellow, thought Nancy, who also thought she detected a hint of a lisp in the man's speech. He was carrying a small brown-paper bag, which he clutched in his left hand.

She contrived a smile. "Hi."

"Yeah, I watch you all the time on the news," the stranger exclaimed gleefully. Then he turned to Tom, who had taken a step back. "Who's he? He with you?"

"Well, yes. This is Tom. He just started with us, and he's going along with me for a week or so, just to get the feel of things."

"I don't know . . ." He glared at Tom suspiciously.

Nancy figured she'd better get control of the meeting quickly. "You said this morning you were a friend of Allen's."

The man turned from Tom and spoke to Nancy directly. He'd lost his initial momentum and was not smiling. "You wanna see what I got in the bag, here?"

"No, not really, I guess," she laughed nervously. Jesus, she thought, this isn't turning out the way I expected. This guy is really squirrelly!

Tom took a step toward the man. "Yeah, I'd like to see what you've got in the bag." As Tom took the step, Nancy noticed his right hand snake smoothly around to his lower back. He kept it there and sort of grimaced, as if he were scratching. She knew the hand was up under the flap of his coat, resting on his gun.

The stranger focused hard on the undercover cop, as he raised the bag with both hands, opened it delicately, peered into it and said, without looking up, "Are you sure you want to see what I got in here, Tom?"

Tom nodded. "Yeah, I like surprises," he replied, eyes glued to the movement of the man's hand.

"Well, I sure got a nice one for you in here," said the stranger, grinning. He dipped into the sack with his right hand, appeared to fiddle with its contents momentarily, then slowly began withdrawing it. Tom's grip tightened around the gun butt. He unsnapped the holster strap with a slight movement of his finger. Nancy's throat was dry. She tried to swallow and felt herself take two steps back, her eyes also on the stranger's hand.

The stranger, giggling softly to himself, pulled his hand from the brown-paper sack, revealing a small figurine, a swan. Tom stepped back, his shoulders relaxing. He resnapped the holster strap, and Nancy breathed a sigh of relief. Neither could speak.

"Isn't it pretty?" the stranger asked soberly, holding it in front of her. "My mommy gave it to me, yes, she did, yes, she did." He turned it slowly, seemingly mesmerized. Suddenly, he jammed it back into the sack and shook it wildly. "And you're not going to get it, and you're not going to get it," he taunted in a sing-song voice. Nancy, having collected her thoughts, was just beginning to respond when the strange man abruptly turned on his heel and bolted down the street at a dead run.

He was never seen or heard from again.

31

The Task Force had produced valuable results. A certain number of child molesters had been identified and arrested, and one of them, a high-level manager in an auto-related industry, resigned his executive position with a worldwide boys' organization as a result. In another incident, a large-scale, out-of-state child pornography ring was broken up as the result of a tip and the subsequent Task Force investigation. But in the search for the child killer, as the days turned into weeks, and the weeks turned into months, what had been confidence in the beginning gradually became merely hope.

The Task Force had employed considerable ingenuity in exploring every possible means of ferreting out the killer. The employment records of workers at the five ski resorts in Oakland County were checked, since seasonal employees might have the freedom of movement the child killer seemed to have. Consultation with an anthropologist, a doctor, and two scholars from the Wayne State University School of Mortuary Science failed to link the condition of the bodies with the burial rituals of any particular religious, cultural, or ethnic group. Because of the reference in Allen's letter to a delivery route, the Task Force, with the aid of the Teamsters' Union, checked out countless drivers of delivery vehicles.

A well-known author of mystery stories surveyed the abduction sites and noted that each was in close proximity to a hobby shop. Since hobby shops attract children it was thought that they might have attracted the killer as well. But a questionnaire sent to every hobby shop in the area yielded nothing.

Occasionally, frustrations came from an unexpected quarter. The Task Force asked police departments not directly involved in the investigation for assistance in checking out low-priority tips involving their jurisdictions. Frequently tips came back with no action having been taken at all. Tobias developed a form to help track down every one of Michigan's eight thousand blue Gremlins and sent it to departments all over the state.

Some forms came back months later, and many never came back at all. Eventually, after only three thousand Gremlins had been checked out, the project had to be abandoned.

"Joe, how do you feel about trying a psychic?" Robertson asked Krease in the Valley Woods office. It was early afternoon, August 8, 1977.

"If you're asking do I believe in them, no, I don't."

"Not asking if you believe, Joe, just asking how you feel about trying one?" Robbie repeated, a little impatiently. He didn't believe in psychics, either.

"I don't know. It's liable to turn this thing into a dog-and-pony show. But then," he continued, walking over to the window to stare out into the parking lot. "Hey, here she is again!" He was squinting at the car parked in the corner of the lot farthest from the building entrance. "Yep, here he comes too."

Robertson got out of his chair and joined the Sergeant at the window. "Sure enough." He looked at his watch. "12:30 right on the button."

The woman, tall and blond, wearing a yellow see-through sundress and white, high-heeled sandals, got out as the man pulled alongside, locked her car, and quickly scooted into his. They kissed. He slowly turned the car and headed out the drive. They would be back in exactly two hours.

Robbie chuckled as the two policemen went back to their desks. The "Lovers," as they became affectionately known to the entire Task Force, met twice a week in the Valley Woods parking lot. Nobody knew who they were, but almost everybody in the Task Force had a pretty good notion of what was going on.

Joe laughed again. "Oughta put a tail on 'em one day, just to see where they go."

"Yeah, might be kinda interesting. Wonder if they know this building is full of cops?" Robbie mused.

"Anyway, the psychic. On the other hand," Joe continued, "a lot of people are clamoring for us to at least try one. Jesus, everytime the *National Enquirer* comes out with something about a psychic, the damn switchboard goes nuts."

"And you know, Joe, we have to keep the public on our side, especially at this point. A psychic sure can't do any worse than us."

If the Task Force was going to use the services of a psychic, they would go about it properly and quietly, getting as much information about parapsychology as they could before making the commitment. It was agreed that they'd give it a try. Through Tobias, Robertson got ahold of the *Encyclopedia of Human Behavior*. It told him that "only a small percentage of American psychologists consider ESP (Extrasensory Perception) an established fact. On the other hand, few psychologists rule it out as an impossibility; the rest maintain it is simply unproven at present. Interestingly, the attitude of psychologists toward ESP has become somewhat more positive over the years." So far, so good.

Next was a long-distance phone call to Dr. Russell Targ, of the Stanford Research Institute in Palo Alto, California. Targ suggested a call to the American Society for Psychological Research in New York City, to a Mr. Karlis Ogis, Director. Targ felt that Ogis might be able to suggest some individuals who lived nearer the Task Force than anybody he might recommend from the West Coast. Ogis gave Robertson the names of four people who had worked, with varying degrees of success, with ESP. Included was a Philip Jordan of Candor, New York. After a thorough review and background check it was agreed by Task Force Command that they would follow up on Jordan. In addition to his apparent success with ESP experiments, Jordan also taught the subject at the Tompkins-Cortland Community College, and had some police training. A call to the Tioga County Sheriff verified Jordan's status as a part-time special deputy, and the fact that in May he had graduated from an accredited police academy. The sheriff said that while he wasn't ready to exactly endorse Jordan's psychic powers, it's pretty hard to dispute him when you see him work. The Sheriff did say that Jordan had found a lost child and the body of a missing person. The lawman also said that Jordan was "100 percent trustworthy" and he figured, based on what Robertson had told him, that the Task Force certainly had nothing to lose by giving Jordan a chance.

Robertson's next call was to Jordan himself. Yes, of course, he would be very interested in working with the Task Force, and there'd be no fee involved. All Jordan wanted was his transportation, room, and meals taken care of. One other thing. Jordan asked that he be allowed to bring a friend, Tioga County Deputy Sheriff David Redsicker. Jordan said Redsicker had helped him with other cases by doing a lot of the legwork, drawing composites, and handling general interrogation.

A week later, Jordan and friend were picked up at Metropolitan Airport outside Detroit. Jordan wasted little time in dazzling those who greeted him at Metro. On the way over (presumably) he had written on a piece of paper that he would be picked up in a blue vehicle and that the first name of the woman in the pick-up party would be Mary. So far, the psychic was batting a thousand.

After settling Jordan and Redsicker at the posh Kingsley Inn in Bloomfield Hills, Tobias brought the visitors to the Valley Woods School, where they were briefed. Jordan wanted three things. First, he wanted pictures of the victims. Then, he wanted pictures of the crime scenes. Finally, he wanted to be given clothing or perhaps some other personal items belonging to the victims, and he wanted to be given these items while he was actually at the crime scenes. The Task Force wanted Jordan to characterize the killer; it wanted him to draw a picture of the suspect; and it wanted him to pinpoint on the map, where he lived or stayed.

Jordan was quick to comment on the King photo. Staring down at the picture on the table, head bowed, massaging both temples with his fingers, he said "I-I feel . . . a grassy play area . . . yes, a park, perhaps . . . large, shaped like a triangle . . . yes, three sides." He stopped abruptly and looked up at Tobias. "Jerry, I keep feeling, no, seeing a park with this kid. I'm not sure what it means, exactly."

"There is a park, Poppleton Park, just north of town. We set up a command post there right after Timmy was abducted." Tobias chuckled, somewhat amazed. Jerry was too science-oriented to be totally taken in by things-that-go-bump-in-the-night, but, like the Tioga County Sheriff, he found it pretty hard to dispute some of the things this guy did. He was sure nothing had been said to Jordan about Poppleton Park and the King case beforehand. Could he have read something about it? The story was highly publicized locally and nationally. But Jordan himself had said during the ride from the airport to the Kingsley that he knew virtually nothing about the investigation and, furthermore, didn't want to know anything about it. After all, the psychic had noted, he had his own credibility to think about.

Some other things concerned Jordan during the session with the pictures. He "felt" the strong smell of freshly baked bread. Maybe a bakery, he told Tobias. Then, there was the number 704. Somehow that number was important. Could it be part of a license plate number? Maybe an address? Three digits of a phone number? And the name "Bruce Levin." That was important, too, noted Jordan. (Danto's first name was Bruce, then, there was Bruce Lane, where Kristine's body was dropped. Levin was also a well-known name in local politics.) This was all pretty weird, thought Tobias as he drove the psychic to the Timothy King drop site.

The Task Force had given Jordan Timmy's hockey jacket, which he kept across his lap on the way over, fingering it sometimes. He had told Jerry before they got into the car that he didn't want to have any conversation from the moment they left until the moment they returned from the crime scene. Jerry was to let him out at the exact spot along the ditch where Timmy's body was dropped, then pull back up the road a couple of car lengths, and wait for him. It wouldn't take long, perhaps ten minutes. He would leave the jacket in the car, but would take a clipboard and pen with him as he worked the scene to jot some of his primary thoughts and feelings down. He would fill in on the way back.

Jerry pulled slowly down Gill Road, stopped at the exact spot along the ditch where Timmy's body had lain some five months ago, and the psychic got out. Jerry pulled back about thirty feet and parked, letting the engine idle. He watched Jordan pace the site, staying pretty much within a fifteen foot radius of where the body had lain. He watched him stoop several times, resting the clipboard on his knee to make notes.

Jordan finished in about fifteen minutes. He walked slowly back up Gill Road to where Jerry sat. The psychic turned once to look back at the site he'd just finished working, then wordlessly got into the car. He immediately began fingering the jacket again as he continued jotting more thoughts down on the clipboard. Tobias turned the car and headed back to Valley Woods.

Jordan's debriefing was completed in less than two hours. The session was recorded, then transcribed for distribution to Command. The psychic's thoughts were interesting, but far from revolutionary. Of the list of fifty items, or "thoughts," many were general in nature, some, though specific, could be made to fit the scenario if one tried hard enough, and some were downright wild and appeared to be little more than guesses. A few were common-sense thoughts, such as Jordan's "feeling" that King went willingly with his abductor. There were many similar "thoughts" expressed by the man from New York. The transcription prepared by Tobias for distribution to Command included the following list:

Transcript Summary B — Comments from the Timmy King drop site. (Subject utilized the King boy's jacket here.)
1. Jordan feels that a white van may be involved here.
2. It is a step van with sliding door.
3. There is a large tank of water associated with this. The killer and King had to pass this tank [there is a water tower near Poppleton Park — author's note].
4. There is a pine tree farm associated with this, a nursery.
5. The killer and Timothy came by a tree farm and water tank.
6. The killer stopped by a water tank for some purpose.
7. Jordan sees a number 722 or 272. These numbers could be arranged differently.
8. The white van may be associated with the killer's employment rather than the abduction [perhaps the delivery route Allen referred to in his letter to Danto — author's note].
9. Jordan feels that a sedan may have been used in the crime.

10. Tim was not as tormented as the others. It doesn't seem as though he was tormented for any length of time.
11. He [Tim] did not go through some of the things the others did.
12. The killer wanted to get rid of Tim as quickly as possible.
13. There was a fear with him, a fear of disposing of him.
14. He [Jordan] feels that a dark blue vehicle (sedan) was used.
15. Killer came from the north (Eight Mile Road) onto Gill Road.
16. Tim was in the back end of the car (trunk).
17. Killer came from the west to Gill Road and left in that direction (toward the expressway).
18. Killer was frightened by something.
19. The tree farm was significant.
20. He [Jordan] smells the odor of grapes (may be significant).
21. He [Jordan] is concerned with a sewage-treatment plant or water-treatment facility.
22. He [Jordan] is drawn to the park again (Poppleton).
23. Tim was wrapped in a rug at some time.
24. Kensington is significant. Jordan is drawn to this area [there is a metropolitan park called Kensington about forty miles west of Birmingham . . . also numerous streets in the metropolitan area are named Kensington — author's note].
25. The rug is maroon or pink, a more fleshy color.
26. The car is a bigger car, it is not an economy car.
27. It is blue in color.
28. There were two vehicles. One is used to pick up the victim, while the other is used to transport the body.
29. He [Jordan] is also drawn to Lathrup Village.
30. The water tower is on a stand.
31. He [Jordan] sees the boy walking towards the tank (tower) with a skateboard and gum [the skateboard was all over the newspapers and television — author's note].
32. Tim went willingly with his abductor.
33. Tim approached the abductor's vehicle from the passenger side.
34. He [Jordan] feels that the abduction of the King youth took place in the center of the parking lot.
35. The abductor went out the south side and turned right toward Woodward.
36. He [the abductor] then turned right again and went to the park (Poppleton).
37. The park is significant.
38. He [Jordan] feels that the abductor may have previously observed the child.
39. He [Jordan] sees a dark green car (a metal-flake green).
40. It is a large car (Pontiac or Oldsmobile size).
41. Tim did approach the car from the passenger's side, and the window was down; he spoke to the abductor through the window.

42. Jordan feels that the abductor asked Tim for directions or told him that
    he was sent to take him somewhere.
43. Tim went voluntarily.
44. The abductor was in the drugstore.
45. He was using the second phone to the left.
46. The abductor may have purchased beer.
47. The abductor was dark with black hair.
48. Jordan has two people in mind.
49. The abductor may have been talking to this other person on the phone.
50. Jordan had written the word "moffet" this morning. It may have been
    "buffet" for Monahan's Buffet (a local eatery).

After visiting the King crime scene, Jordan was taken to the Mihelich
drop site. The following are some of his observations as they appeared
in the investigation file:

The psychic "felt" there was an Irish Setter barking somewhere close-by; the
name Sherry was significant—the killer may have been calling the victim
Sherry; the girl's body was in the front seat, and the person unloading her
was crying; the smell of baby powder.

Then, the psychic wished to visit the area around the Seven-Eleven
store where the abduction was presumed to have taken place.

[He] received indications that Kristine did not make it to the Seven-Eleven
store; that the abductor sat and watched her cross the street from a parking
lot; that she may have been tied for a short period of time; that she was
passive and submissive when taken captive, there was no harsh treatment;
that the killer felt regret when he killed her; that if he had sexual contact
with the child, it would have been oral.

The psychic also felt that:

Her captor killed her because he was doing away with something in his past;
that he really preferred male victims, but he was trying to prove he is normal, that is, heterosexual, and that is why he took a female victim.

The following day, Jordan and Redsicker were driven to the spot
along busy I-75 where Jill Robinson's body had been found. His observations again were interesting, even startling, but not particularly useful.

He again "felt" a blue car, with two men in it arguing, one of them (not the
killer) had dark hair, and was the subject he heard on the Danto tape (the

phone call from Allen); he felt that Jill was cooperative at first, and the killer (or the passenger, he wasn't sure which) had intended to release her, but then she became uncooperative and wanted to go home, and this caused the violent act (shotgun); he also "saw" the two men arguing, and this too could have prompted the violent act.

Jordan then went on to mix a little basic psychology with his ESP:

He suggested that the man committing the violent act seems to be very concerned at having a child of his own and feels he is giving love to the child. But, when the child rejects his love, the child is eliminated. He also thinks that the killer has, at some time, applied for a foster child, or an adopted child, and been rejected. And, since the killer has no children of his own, he takes other people's children, and he kills them when they ultimately reject him.

From the outset, Jordan appeared to have a clearer "feeling" about the Mark Stebbins murder than the others. He told investigators at Task Force headquarters that "Mark was picked up in a work vehicle. The killer is a delivery man, possibly associated with a linen company" (Jordan had not seen Allen's letter). "I think," he paused in his stream of consciousness, "I think that Woodward Avenue is significant as the abduction site, and that the suspect lives in that general area, close by, maybe six or seven minutes away by car. I think the boy was tied to a bed, and yes, I see Mark and at least one, maybe two people with him in the room. I think he was watching television, a color TV, something on a Tuesday night. . . . "

"What kind of room?" asked one officer at the de-briefing. "Describe the room for us."

"Nicely done, furnished, affluence, maybe an apartment with several rooms . . . living room, large windows, sliding glass doors . . . gold carpeting, wall-to-wall . . . light blue porcelain in the bathroom . . . I don't know, I'm — I'm . . . it's going away, fading." He stopped, looked at the ceiling and closed his eyes. After a longer pause, he continued. "I'm seeing a modern sort of place, half-moon-shaped chairs for watching television . . . large windows high off the ground . . . hallway running through the middle of the apartment. It's a. . . ." He stopped again. "It's a high building, more than just two or three stories.* Some art, no, more like craft-type wall hangings. I don't know, it's gone again. I need some coffee."

"Sure." Tobias got up and walked to the coffee pot. "Cream, sugar?"

---

*There were several apartment buildings in the general area with more than two or three stories, although most were limited to that.

"Black's fine, Jerry, thanks." Tobias filled the cup and returned to the table, setting the coffee down in front of the psychic.

"What about the call and the letter, Phil? Have you digested them enough to give us some thoughts?" Tobias put a foot up on the chair and leaned on his elbow.

Jordan hesitated. "Sure. They're both pretty important—I think they're real, in good faith, not a hoax or a crank." He sipped the coffee and made a face. "I feel that I'm getting Spanish, or Mexican on the guy, something like that. No doubt he's a homosexual. Has a close relationship with another guy, but," another pause, "the relationship may end soon. Maybe another month or six weeks. Then you might have another one."

"Another what?" asked Kalbfleisch.

"Well, another abduction and murder, I suppose. . . ." The psychic's voice trailed off. The detectives looked at each other. Jordan continued, "I keep getting the bakery smell, strong again, from the letter and the call. I think the guy might even work in a bakery. That could be the delivery route."

"But at the King drop site you got the smell of grapes, didn't you?" Kalbfleisch reminded him, after refreshing his own memory from some earlier notes.

"Yeah, I know. I'm getting both grapes and bread, baked goods of some sort. I did get the bakery smell pretty strong when I looked at King's picture, too," he said, somewhat defensively. "This isn't an exact science, you know. It's just what I feel, and I don't claim to be 100 percent accurate."

"Sure, Phil," Tobias cut in, "we understand all that."

"Anyway," Jordan continued, sitting up straighter in the chair, "I think both the killer and the other guy are pretty religious. I see a picture of Jesus on the wall in the killer's room." He stopped talking, staring down at his coffee. For a minute or so no one spoke. Then he said, "Another month."

"Another month, what?" asked Kalbfleisch curiously.

"Well, maybe by mid-October, you are going to catch him."

"Beautiful," grumbled Rivard, his first word since sitting down for the debriefing over an hour and a half before. "How many kids is he gonna kill between now and then?"

"God damn it!" exclaimed Krease, as he slammed the phone back onto its cradle.

"Problems?" inquired Kalbfleisch, who'd just come in from the street. It was evening, the day of Jordan's briefing.

"Yeah, he wants to talk with the parents."

"Who's that, Jordan?"

Krease grunted. "I'm gonna have to go over there and straighten him out. Jesus! Some psychic shows up on the Kings' front doorstep sniffing the air and baying at the moon, and we can all pack it in! Want to go along for the ride?"

"Where, the Kingsley?"

"Yeah, he's over there in his room now. That was O'Brien on the phone. It was his turn to watch him today."

Kalbfleisch looked at his watch. "Why not? This ought to be good."

Krease was already halfway down the hall.

Jordan took the first flight out the next morning and was not heard from again.

32

At a meeting over coffee and donuts in the Squad Room at Valley Woods School, Robertson was saying, "Joe and I want some input, so let's share some thoughts." He leaned back against the wall at the front of the room. "Maybe we're headed off in the wrong direction on this thing. I'm talking mainly about our killer's profile. I mean, what do we really know about him? Think about it for a minute."

He was speaking to Krease, Rivard, Tobias, Kalbfleisch, Strauss, Green, Itami, Doan, and Mort Nichols of the F.B.I. The investigators looked at each other but said nothing. Each had entertained the same notion at various points during the long investigation.

"I guess what we're saying," Krease said, "is maybe we ought to freshen up the profile, or at least make sure that the guy compares now with what we thought he was at the beginning. Bring in some new ideas. We'll still be working with educated guesses, but we're no further ahead now than we were six months ago, so maybe we're way off track on his psychological makeup."

"What do you have in mind, Sarge?" asked Itami.

"The Lieutenant and I have been thinking about bringing three of the best psychologists in the country in here, real experts on pedophilia. We'll sit 'em down and talk about abnormal sexual behavior. Lay it all out for them, then work with the best they have to offer."

"All due respect, Joe, Lieutenant, but what the hell good's that gonna do?" inquired Rivard, panicky at the word "psychologist." "I mean, haven't we had our fill of that kind of shit?"

"Aw, c'mon, Rog," flared Tobias, "there's a helluva difference between a psychic and a psychologist. Jesus!" he spat disgustedly.

"Yeah, well. . . ."

"Yeah, well nothing! You don't know what the fuck. . . ."

"All right! Stop your goddam picking at each other, will you?" The frustration was obvious in Joe's voice.

"So just what exactly are these guys going to do?" inquired Strauss, hoping to get the discussion back on course.

"Well, we'll give them what we have and let them tell us how they feel about the guy, just like we did in the beginning," Krease explained, thankful for the question. Good old Jack, Joe thought. Always knows just when to step in.

"I'd be for it, Joe," said Nichols. "Like you say, freshen it up a bit. Sometimes it's good to start back at square one. Give it a new spin and see what happens." Mort was a pretty good guy, Krease decided.

"Thanks, Mort. How about the rest of you?" There was some general discussion among the investigators, none of whom could think of any negatives.

Robertson and Krease spent the next couple of hours with Tobias, finding out where to begin looking for three experts on pedophilia. Jerry suggested a phone call to the American Psychological Association, in Washington, D.C. Robertson called and talked to a Dr. Gary Vandenbos, explaining that the Task Force needed a very specific profile of the child killer, and that it wanted three of the top people in the country to draw it. Could he steer them in the right direction? Yes, he would try. Dr. Vandenbos would canvass the nation's specialists and try to come up with two or three names.

Meanwhile, Krease contacted Lieutenant Darrell Pope, head of the Sex Motivated Crimes Unit, Michigan State Police, in Lansing. Pope suggested Dr. Ralph Rabinovitch, at the Hawthorn Center in Northville, Michigan, as a noted authority. After a little homework, Robertson and Krease decided that Dr. Rabinovitch would be one of the three psychologists they would use.

Vandenbos called back several weeks later. He had located someone he felt would be able to assist the Task Force. He was recommending a Dr. Nicholas Groth, presently with the Massachusetts Center for Treatment of Sexually Dangerous Persons, a noted authority, highly regarded by his peers and the law-enforcement community. They contacted Groth, who agreed to come to Michigan and work with the Task Force for expenses and a one-hundred-dollar-a-day honorarium. The third member of the team would be Dr. Harley Stock, of the State Center for Forensic Psychiatry.

At the meeting with Groth, Stock, and Rabinovitch were Pope, Gary Backus, and Jim Hauncher from the State Police Crime Lab, Charlotte Day of the State Police Crime Lab in Madison Heights, Nichols of the F.B.I., and Task Force members Kalbfleisch, Green, Itami, Doan, and

Strauss. It went well, that is, there were no fistfights. There were some very minor disagreements, primarily between the three psychologists. For instance, Stock and Groth had divergent opinions as to the killer's street personality. Stock felt the subject could very well be passive and quiet, while Groth saw him as being more outgoing. However, there was general agreement on many key items. While the killer was intelligent, he was probably not formally educated to any great degree. The child slayer probably had a low white-collar, or maybe even a blue-collar job and was definitely not in a position of authority. He very possibly had a criminal history and indeed may have been arrested at one time or another for a destructive type of crime.

Groth, Stock, and Rabinovitch decided that while the killer certainly needed professional help, he wouldn't seek it on his own. They also suggested that the age and appearance of the youngsters might very well be more important than their sex, and that the obvious abnormal sexual behavior by the killer might well be insignificant. They felt strongly that the slayer of the four Oakland County children was not a sex killer, as such. As Rabinovitch put it, "I have some serious reservations as to whether he gets any sexual gratification from the killings." All agreed that the killer probably had roots in the area, and that the Task Force was most likely looking in the right places for him. The reason he hadn't killed again (it had been nearly six months since Timmy was murdered) was probably that the man was already in jail for some other crime or had been institutionalized.

Those were the general areas of agreement—really nothing that hadn't been thought of before, but nonetheless valuable insofar as it served to confirm earlier psychological profiles, with some exceptions. Each doctor was asked to submit a written report. Groth's made for especially interesting reading:

> The task of developing a dependable psychological profile of the offender that might prove helpful in processing suspects is a difficult one due to the paucity of information available in regard to the crimes. It is hard to be specific or definite when the data at hand are so sparse and general. The difficulty is in differentiating the psychological components in the offenses from the situational ones. Where do situational facts account for the offender's activity, and where are psychological determinants crucial? What is significant as opposed to what is merely coincidental? This report will offer my views as to the possible psychological significance or meaning(s) of the available data.
>
> 1. Victim Choice

It seems puzzling that the offender would seek out local community children as his victims when street kids or hitchhikers would be easier marks. It may be that the winter cold discourages hitchhiking, or it may be that street kids will accept a sexual encounter for money and that is not the specific type of interaction the offender is seeking, or perhaps the disappearance of street kids is simply not noted or reported. It may be, however, that for some psychological reason, the offender wants "nice" children, that is, innocent and trusting.

The fact that he chooses both boys *and* girls also appears unique. This may suggest that age is a stronger determinant than sex in regard to victim choice, that is, he is looking for a child rather than an adult as opposed to a male rather than a female. Since all his victims are pre-adolescent and have not matured sexually, he may be avoiding confrontation with adult sexuality, which he may be conflicted over, and see as unclean or threatening in some way. The cleansing of some of the bodies may also in part serve this motive. He wants a victim who is sexually safe, clean, pure and sexually inexperienced.

The four victims do physically resemble each other — all were attractive youngsters — and this may suggest that he selects a specific type of victim rather than this being a random event. He may see them as symbolic of something he wants or resents. He may see them as projections of himself.

The depositing of the bodies in highly visible locations may simply be expediency, or it may have some psychological significance. It could serve to call attention to his crimes, and in that way give him a feeling of recognition. Or, it may be prompted by a wish to see the deceased victim receive proper funeral and burial.

2. Sexual Behavior

The data are ambiguous in regard to sexual molestation. The girls appear untouched, whereas the anus is dilated in both boys. If the victims have been sexually molested, it may be that they are forced to perform and/or submit to oral sex, and the boys, in addition, are sodomized. But these acts take place sometime prior to their deaths so that evidence (sperm) is absorbed into the body, or eliminated. It could also be that the offender wears a condom when sodomizing the boys, or penetrates them digitally or with some foreign object. It could also be that the offender is sexually dysfunctional and does not ejaculate. Or, it could be that his sexual interests focus more on looking, touching, and ritualistic bondage than on penetrating. For example, he may simply masturbate himself while watching the child tied naked to the bed.

If he is sodomizing the boys and did not molest the girls, this could mean that he is sexually more comfortable with males, and females are psychologically more threatening. The fact that he does take female victims as well as male victims could then suggest that he is striving to resolve the conflicts he is experiencing in regard to women by using a child: someone safer and easier to control, and who cannot easily refuse or reject him; someone who is sexually inexperienced, that is, a virgin whom he feels he can more easily impress or master, and with whom he feels more of a man.

I feel the offender is engaged in adult sexual encounters which are conflictual for him. He had reverted to children as these pressures and stresses in his adult relationships have increased. I do not think we are dealing with a person who throughout his life has preferred and been persistently involved with children sexually, or in an exclusive way. Nor do I think this person has well-defined sexual interests in adult males. He may be sexually involved and active with another man, but I would speculate that (1) he fells uncomfortable and unsatisfied with this type of relationship, and does not think of himself as really being "gay," and (2) any such involvement is more a result of the non-sexual advantages he obtains from the relationships (such as material rewards or a sense of personal power and control) than from sexual needs. My hunch is that he does not have the skills and resources to negotiate adult relationships with any degree of success over time. He is narcissistically oriented, that is, self-centered, and adult relationships ultimately prove frustrating and unstable. Perhaps the only thing he has to offer is his body—he may be physically attractive, but does not have the personality skills to establish mutually rewarding and lasting relationships with women. A gay man may be more willing to tolerate the offender's immaturity and self-centeredness, in exchange for sexual access to him, especially if the gay man himself is older. The offender may have turned to the use of alcohol or drugs in order to function in the relationship. Although a mutual and pathological dependency exists on the part of both men, I think the offender grew increasingly disenchanted with his part of the bargain, so to speak. An adult relationship with another man is not gratifying some essential needs, and he is not successful in establishing a relationship with a woman, so he turns to children as a solution.

3. Role of Aggression

The most confusing aspect of the crimes is the death of the victims. We are dealing with a child killer. The difficulty is knowing whether the killing is sexually motivated, that is, done to provide some type of gratification to the offender, or if it is the result of something not going according to plan. He could be killing in panic, or he may kill the children to reduce the chances of getting caught by simply eliminating the witness. The murders appear intentional, rather than inadvertent. But are they premeditated? It may be that the offender's original intention (with Mark Stebbins) was not to kill his victim, but only to engage in some sort of sexual fantasy encounter with him, and something went wrong. Mark's reaction was not what the offender anticipated, and he had to strike Mark over the head to subdue him. He now realized the seriousness of his actions (abduction and assault) and to prevent disclosure, felt he had to murder the boy. He turns to a second victim, a girl, but Jill Robinson is a rebellious and difficult child—not the loving, affectionate response he anticipated—and in anger and fear he murders her. There's too much at risk to let the victims live and yet the sexual compulsion is too great to abandon. From this perspective then, the deaths are more situationally determined than psychologically determined.

However, we cannot completely rule out the possibility that we are dealing with a sadist, that is, someone who derives pleasure from the infliction of suffering on the child. The method of killing the victim (smothering) typically produces struggling and writhing on the part of the victim, which, in the offender's mind, simulates orgasm and excites him. Bind marks on the boys' wrists and ankles may suggest that bondage played some part in the offense, but these might simply have been the result of restraints to prevent the victim from escaping, or the result of the elastic in the cuffs of the victim's jacket. The use of an instrument with which to "rape" the boys anally would also be consistent with sadistic assault. Also, there appears to be a ritualistic quality to the disposal of the victim's body: washed, dressed, left in a cradled position in a highly visible location. Again, is this psychologically significant, or simply an expeditious way of getting rid of the body with all traces of evidence eliminated? There are a number of things which are *not* consistent with sadistic assault: (1) the extent of time the victims were held captive. Usually the sadist strikes, kidnaps the victims, completes the ritual assault and flees. He doesn't keep the victim for almost 3 weeks, as was the case with Kristine; (2) the victim will usually be tortured, injured, even mutilated in some way—typically sexual areas of the body (breasts, buttocks, genitals) become the targets of abuse (bites, cigarette burns, punctures, etc.) and nothing of this nature was evident in these cases; (3) the children did not appear to be abused or neglected. In fact, they were protected from the elements and well nourished. The fact that they were apparently eating well would indicate they were not in extreme fear, distress, or terror for their lives.

In every case of sexual assault, three components are involved: anger, power, and sexuality. From the facts in this case, it would appear that power or control is the dominant component. There is little evidence of anger toward the victims, with the exception of Jill Robinson whose head is partially blown off by the shotgun blast. Otherwise, the victims are not battered or abused. Although sadism cannot be ruled out, there is little evidence indicating that aggression is eroticized by this killer. We are not dealing with a child batterer or a child "collector." It appears that the intent of the offender is to have control over the victims, to have them in his power. The abduction and holding of his victims over an extended period of time are consistent with this. Each victim is held for a progressively longer period of time, except for the last (but I think the killer's plans for Timothy King were interrupted by the intensive search launched by the police at this point). This would suggest two major issues in regard to the offenses: (1) the offender is attempting to compensate for not feeling in control of his life by controlling the victims — this may serve to make him feel strong, powerful, and in charge. They must do what he says and in this fashion, he defends against his underlying feelings of helplessness, weakness, and vulnerability; and (2) the offenses seem to be an attempt to live out some unresolved issue in the offender's life, quite possibly some traumatic event (loss, rejection, etc.) that happened to him at the same age as his victims, and may be associated with the winter season. There is sparse information regarding what happens with the victims during their captivity. If they are well treated, it would suggest the offender is longing for affection and validation. His keeping Kristine for the longest period of time would tend to support this interpretation, since she reportedly was an affectionate, obedient youngster. The fact that he could murder her after getting to know her over the space of almost three weeks indicates his desperation, his pathology, or both. If the victims were mistreated physically or psychologically, it would suggest the offender is punishing them for some guilt, or trying to symbolically destroy something about himself which they represent to him. In either case, the victims constitute some symbolic representation of himself. The offenses strike me as the acting out of some fantasy-scenario. Each encounter fails to resolve the underlying problem, and fails to fulfill the fantasy expectations. It doesn't work out as the offender anticipated, so he goes in search of another victim. The progression in the amount of time the victims are held captive might be understood to mean that he becomes more comfortable, and feels increasing control with each successive crime and that in each successive offense, he more closely approximates the enactment of his fantasy.

4. Spontaneous Termination

Why does he stop? Perhaps the most logical reason is that he has been stopped, that is, he is in prison, in a mental hospital, or dead. It would be easier to explain why he stopped, if we knew why he started. What precipitated these offenses? The particular set of events, factors, and pressures that combined to activate the lethal potential of this individual may have changed in some significant way so that the pathology has again become dormant. Or, it may be that the work of the Task Force is directly responsible for deterring him. He may realize there is little chance of striking again without discovery, or he may have had a close brush with the law through Task Force operations, and this has scared him. Or it may be that he has realized that his offenses did not in reality satisfy or fulfill his expectations, and the risk isn't worth taking anymore. Maybe someone close to him has exerted some control over him in this regard. I myself tend to doubt spontaneous

resolutions of such serious pathology, and am more inclined to believe something stopped him rather that he stopped himself. But the ultimate answer
may be a combination of these and other factors.

While entertaining, Groth's report and insights were less than enlightening from an investigative point of view. What it did, however, was
to lend support and credibility to theories already a matter of record, that
is, theories developed early in the case by Krease, Tobias, and, to some
extent, Danto. There was really only one way to find out if any of this
was valid, if they indeed had been on the right track all these months —
catch the child killer.

The volume of mail flowing into the Task Force from literally all
across the country and around the world was overwhelming. Everybody
had his or her own ideas of just who the Task Force ought to be looking
for, and where they ought to be looking. Thousands of armchair detectives had thousands of theories on why he was doing it, including why
he started and why he would, or would not, stop. Some of the mail came
from the most unlikely places:

Dear Mr. Tobin,
　　This letter is going to be hard to write so please bear with me.
　　I am an inmate in the Southern Ohio Correctional Facility in Lucas-
ville, Ohio, and I have been here 2 years.
　　I am writing to you because I know myself who killed the little Timmy
King and also the Stebbins boy in your area. I know where the person is
and all about him.
　　Also, sir, I know how and why and when and where it took place.
　　Sir, I am not writing a prank letter or anything, and I will state that
I don't get along with the authorities here and I am not liked at all.
　　I am called a punk by the authorities here at the prison. So my profile
is very, very poor.
　　But I am writing this to tell you that I am being completely honest
with you.
　　If by chance you believe me in what I'm saying, I can give you some
help. But before I would talk with you, if you would come to see me you
would have to bring a attorney with you to represent me, and also the prosecutor. I say this is because if what I know, charges may be filed against me,
and I would want immunity from any prosecution.
　　I'm not looking for anything at all except not to be arrested myself.

I go before the Parole Board here in two months, and I am 95 per cent sure I will make parole because my term was only 2 to 5 years, and I doing flop time now, and the charge was a bad check.

Now, if you don't believe me, because of what maybe the authorities from the Institution may tell you if you would question them, then, please as a favor to me forget this letter.

I have no reason to want to lie to you or make up a story. You would save cost and time if you believe someone else's story about me. But if not, I can help.

But this is your decision to make. As I stated I would talk to you, a Prosecutor, if I was represented by a attorney. I have no money to get one myself so that's the reason for the attorney request.

But other than you three people I will not talk to anyone else. The three of us would have to be alone with no one else present.

But again I express the fact I am not lieing [sic] or have reason to. So this would be your decision to make. If you would like to talk to me and make the trip, please write me a note and state when you will visit.

But in all due respect, I would like you to acknowledge this letter, and tell me if you received it and if you believe me or not.

So I will close for now and anxiously await your reply. Please.

Sincerely,
Maxwell Kincaid

On State Police letterhead, Robertson replied:

Dear Mr. Kincaid:

Your letter to Chief Jerry Tobin was forwarded to me from his office as I am the coordinator of the Special Task Force investigating the homicides in South Oakland County.

I have read your letter, but I am reluctant to send an investigator, prosecutor, and attorney to visit you on the face of your letter. If you are sincere in your comments that you are not seeking any personal gain from this action, I see no reason why you can't tell me what you are going to talk about, either in a letter to me, or give me a telephone number so I can call you if you have access to a telephone.

After receiving your reply, if we should decide to visit you, please indicate what an appropriate time would be, and, obviously we would at that point, be required to notify your local authorities of our plan to visit.

Sincerely,
F/Lt. Robert H. Robertson
Assistant District Commander
Second District Headquarters

Kincaid was never heard from again.

During the many months of the Child Killer probe, investigators learned of the existence of several groups and organizations that condoned, and in most cases, actively promoted sexual activity involving terribly young children. One such group out of Beverly Hills, California, called itself "The Rene Guyon Society," so named after Dr. Rene Guyon, who had been, according to the Society's correspondence, a judge on Thailand's Supreme Court for thirty years. In an effort to gain as much insight as possible into the adult/child sexual relationship, Robertson wrote to the Society requesting that they send all available information and literature. For this ploy, he used the name "Dr. Robert Firestone."

The "Dr." lent credibility, and along with the address of 32605 Bellvine Trail, North Pod, Birmingham, Michigan, was meant to show that the writer was a man of letters, not a crank and most certainly not a cop. After making an original inquiry and receiving some literature, Robbie wrote this follow-up:

Mr. Jim Darling
Rene Guyon Society
256 S. Robertson Blvd.
Beverly Hills, California 90211

Dear Mr. Darling:
Thank you for your response to my inquiry. I found the literature most enlightening and would appreciate receiving more material on sexual freedom of children.

I am a Doctor of Philosophy and teach in the local Community College. For several years now I have had secret desires to do something about the unreasonable child sexual laws in our state. Because of my position I feel that I am a stranger in this endeavor and I would appreciate any support of other persons having the same feelings in the Detroit area. If you know of any such persons, you may have them correspond with me or send me their name and address and I will contact them. Although I am not sure just what I could do, at least I would feel more comfortable discussing my secret desires.

Please find enclosed $5.00 and hopefully I will be able to send you at least $5.00 every other month to help support your courageous stand in our society.

Sincerely,
Dr. Robert Firestone

Darling replied in a cover letter:

> It is normal for an adult to want to gratify a child's sex needs. It is abnormal to suppress individually and by laws the sexual interplay between children and adults. That is why you people in Birmingham have the child killer at large.
>
> We are working to get the newly passed anti–child porn laws cancelled.

But Dr. Firestone's request to be put in touch with other persons sharing his "feelings" was refused: "We have a strict policy against penpal activity or introducing people to each other because we want to discourage breaking the law." Along with Darling's letter was a ten-page "Treatise," typed on plain white stationery. The Society's basic premise was to "combat a whole host of problems that are crushing our social order from within" and ultimately had their nascence in the Western World's taboos against adults having sex with children.

> Our immediate and practical goal is the amendment of the statutory rape law. We believe that parents or guardians should be allowed to give consent for sexual activities of their minors. We feel that the law prohibiting sex between a young person and a person more than 10 years older should be abolished.
>
> We also urge the Legislature to pass a resolution stating that it is the intent of the Legislature that children should have sex by the age of eight years.

The Guyon Society wasn't the only organization crusading for the liberalization of child sex laws. Dr. Robert Firestone also attempted to correspond with "The Childhood Sensuality Circle" in El Cajon, California, and a group calling itself "Hermes," which operated from an address in North Chicago. Correspondence to both of these organizations was returned and marked "Not Deliverable. Unable To Forward."

"Joe, have you thought about what we're going to do if we get another one?" asked Robbie as he looked at the luncheon menu.

"Huh? Another what?" Robbie put the menu down as the waitress came over to take their orders. They waited until she was gone again.

"Another abduction. You know, winter isn't that far off, and we're going to have to have something ready to go. Another couple of days and the federal grant expires. Of course, the local chiefs will do as much as they can, a couple hundred bucks a month and a few men, but Joe, we're going to have to move out of Valley Woods pretty soon." Robbie paused. "What I'm trying to say is that the ballgame's damn near over."

"Yeah," replied Krease, absently staring down at the napkin he was doodling on with his pen. "Yeah I know. I been thinking about it." Krease put his pen away and took a sip of water. "Where did we blow it, Lieutenant? God damn it! We turned over every rock in the county, checked more than eight thousand Gremlins, checked twelve thousand tips, cleared a couple dozen people on the bug. Where the hell did we blow it?"

"Joe, I don't think we ought to be conducting any postmortems yet. That son of a bitch takes one more kid, and we own him, no question about it! My money says he knows it, too. But with winter coming on, and say there is something to this talk about him striking when it's cold, we have to be ready to pounce on him right now." Robbie thumped his knife handle on the table. "And we want to be able to push a button and have things fall right into place, especially if everybody's scattered all over hell and gone." He stopped as the waitress returned with their food. When she left, he said, "Now, we have to work out some kind of manual with all the stuff in it that everybody needs to know who might be called in to work another case. I mean all the rules and regulations, everything from dress code to tip procedures, so if we have to reactivate on a moment's notice, all we'll have to do is hand 'em a manual and they'll know all about what's expected of them and what they can expect of us."

"I see what you mean," muttered Joe as he bit into his charburger.

"I think we did a helluva job, Joe, considering that none of us had ever done anything like this before, but I can see where we made a lot of mistakes just in putting the investigation together. Christ, we had people wandering in and out of that place, we didn't even know who they were half the time. I think everybody connected with the operation ought to have special Task Force ID. Maybe a one-day training session for any new people we take in so they know how we do business."

"Yeah, I can see where we need something like that. It would make it a lot easier."

Neither man spoke for a time. Lunch finished, Krease signaled the waitress for more coffee. "Lieutenant," he began, "I have a feeling. Everything all set at District?"

"For what?"

"You know. Where we'll take the guy when we nail him."

"Oh, sure, welcome mat's out."

It had been decided earlier in the investigation that the very nature of the crime dictated that security for the killer be given top priority. It was determined that the only safe place to incarcerate the child killer was Second District Headquarters in Northville. After all, it was a State Police case, and District was well fortified. There was a heliport in back, high fences, lots of troops, and even a kitchen and sleeping quarters. If the Oakland County child killer could be protected from an outraged citizenry anywhere, it was there.

Krease had a feeling they might need it soon.

33

Father Bethleham had been waiting for the knock on the door for several months. He knew it had to come sooner or later, so it was almost with a sense of relief that he sighed, got up from his desk, and walked to the front door. He opened it.

"Evening, Sir. Father Stephen Bethleham?" asked one of the two middle-aged men standing on the small front porch of the Rectory. The man who'd spoken was holding an open black wallet, showing police ID and a badge.

"Yes," replied the priest. "Yes, I'm Father Bethleham. Please come in. I-I think," his voice caught, "I think I know why you're here. I'd just like to get some things, okay?" He held the door as the two Farmington detectives stepped past him inside. He closed the door. "I'll just be a minute, I just want to get some things."

"Please, Father, a moment while we explain the reason we're here."

"No, that's okay. I know."

"Well, sir, we have to. We have to tell you why we're here," said the second officer. He started to put his hand on the priest's shoulder in a reassuring manner, then quickly withdrew it, thinking the gesture might be misinterpreted.

"If you must, then I understand," the priest said softly. "Please," he gestured to the divan, "come sit down. May I get you something to drink, some wine, perhaps?"

"No, no sir, thanks anyway. We'd just like to make this as quick as possible. It'll be easier for everybody," said the plainclothesman who'd shown the badge. He took a deep breath. "Father, there've been some serious allegations made against you, and I'm afraid we're going to have to take you with us."

Bethleham swallowed hard, "You mean you're here to arrest me? That's it, isn't it?" He looked almost childlike.

"Yes, Father, we're going to have to place you under arrest until we can clear this matter up. There's been a complaint linking you, well," the detective stopped. He reached into his inside coat pocket and pulled out a folded document. He opened it. "We have a warrant."

"Yes, I know, the youngsters."

"Please, sir, don't say anything right now," said the other police officer. He reached into his breast pocket and pulled out a wallet-sized card. "We have to advise you of your rights." The sergeant looked down at the small card he held cupped in his right hand. "Father Bethleham, you have the right to remain silent. Anything you say can and will be used against you in a court of law. You have the right to talk to a lawyer before answering any questions, and you have the right to have a lawyer present with you while you are answering any questions." He paused, watching the priest, who stood there solemnly, head bowed, arms dangling limply at his sides. "If you cannot afford to hire a lawyer, one will be appointed to represent you before any questioning, if you wish. You have the right to decide at any time before or during questioning to use your right to remain silent and your right to talk with a lawyer while you are being questioned." The cop looked up. The priest smiled understandingly, but said nothing. "Now, sir, do you understand each of these rights I have explained to you?"

"Yes, yes, of course, officer," Bethleham answered softly. "Yes, I'm quite aware of *Miranda*. *Miranda* versus *Arizona*, 1966. Excellent precedent." The two policemen looked at each other.

"I have a law degree, too," the priest explained. "I practiced in Nevada for a year and a half before I decided the Church was more important."

"Yes, sir," the detective nodded. "I'm sure you did. Do you want to talk to a lawyer before answering any questions?"

"Yes, I think so. I guess there's still enough lawyer in me to not want to represent myself." He managed a nervous smile. "Yes, I'd like to talk with someone, please."

"Of course," agreed the officer. "Now, if you'd be good enough. . . . "

The only difference between Bethleham's arraignment and a three-ring circus was that nobody was selling peanuts. Reporters packed the little district courtroom and stampeded for the telephones when it was over. Dick Carson, his lawyer, pleaded his client mute to assure any and all rights down the line. A not-guilty plea abrogates certain defense options. Carson knew his client was guilty of child molesting as charged in the warrant, but the People still had to prove it. Carson would probably try to cut a deal somewhere along the way. He needed all the help he could get.

The attorney played ball with the reporters, telling them as much as he dared without compromising the investigation or his case.

The Archdiocese maintained a low profile, refusing to comment on "the ongoing investigation." In the early days of the Task Force, the Archdiocese had determined, unilaterally, that any Task Force activity regarding priests had to be funneled through Deputy Detroit Police Chief Jerry Hale. It was also supposed to be a two-way street, that is, information was supposed to flow from the Task Force to the Archdiocese, and from the Archdiocese to the Task Force. However, it turned out to be a one-way street, and it wasn't long before Krease and Bishop Gumbleton got into it over an article the *Free Press* ran. Gumbleton was sure all the leaks about alleged rampant indiscretions within the priesthood came from Krease. Krease was just as sure they didn't, and the matter quickly escalated into a dispute that left bad feelings on both sides.

While the Church's response to the priest's arrest was to maintain low visibility, privately the Archdiocese was beside itself. Bethleham's arrest would put the Church in the worst possible light by reviving perennial speculation about the storied homosexuality within the priesthood. To make things worse, the media hype turned the priest into the child killer overnight. All they really had to do was print the facts. The priest's striking resemblance to the composite, both physically and psychologically, gave the readers and listeners all they needed to put two and two together to come up with five. The community was ready to break out the champagne. The child killer had been caught at last, hadn't he?

The priest had been tipped quite early in the investigation, within days of Timmy King's funeral. Bethleham was by no means the only priest to find his way into Hogan's computer—there were perhaps a dozen others, along with a score of clergymen of various and sundry faiths. The Task Force learned from routine checks on the clergy that just because a man wore the cloth didn't mean he wasn't into some pretty kinky activities.

Bethleham's arrest raised the community's blood pressure, but did little to raise Krease's. Krease was not excitable, and there had been scores of prime suspects that had been tipped over the months, then cleared after an investigation. As far as Joe was concerned, Bethleham was just another possibility that had to be checked out.

"Gimme your best shot, Joe. What're we looking at here?"
"Well, I don't know, Lieutenant. We've had our guys checking him

for the past couple of days. I've just been telling the media we're going to look at him just like we do anybody else. That's just the way I feel, I guess. Farmington dicks got a lot of crap."

"You mean some other stuff besides the warrant?"

"Well, yeah. I think they got him dead to rights on the warrant, you know, the eleven- and thirteen-year-old. Maybe some other incidents, too. Street is saying they're talking deal even now, but I don't know. They're keeping him wrapped pretty tight."

"You talked with him yet?"

"Just Carson, his lawyer."

"And?" Robbie asked, leaning against the edge of his desk.

"Well, he's going to work with us. Says they'll give us all the cooperation they can."

"What the hell's that supposed to mean?"

"Aw, he wants another couple days with Bethleham, just to talk some more with him and calm him down. Says he also wants to have some more dialogue with the Archdiocese, too."

"Screw them."

"Yeah, that's the way I feel, too. Anyway, then we can have him after that. I suppose we could have him here in an hour if we made enough noise. I guess I just don't see the rush."

"You talked polygraph with his lawyer yet?"

Krease began fishing around his desk top looking for Carson's business card. "Glad you reminded me. I'm supposed to call him at ten. He said late yesterday he'd talk to him about the poly and let us know this morning."

The priest, dressed in a red-and-black lumberjack shirt and tennis shoes, looked surprisingly fresh as he was hustled from the car and through the back door at District by four plainclothes State Policemen. Once inside, his handcuffs were quickly removed. He stood for a moment massaging his wrists, and was then directed down a long corridor, two cops in front and two behind. No one spoke until they entered a rather large room with several desks in it, unoccupied save one. Carson got up as they entered.

"Listen, will you guys give me some private time with my client before we get started? Just a couple minutes."

"Yeah, sure, counselor. We'll go see if Chet's all set up. About ten minutes, okay?"

"Fine, Charlie." He turned to Steve as the four cops left the room. "You okay?" he asked. "Here, sit down." He motioned to a desk chair, as he leaned against the edge of the desk opposite.

"Yes, fine. I got a pretty good night's sleep last night, for a change. I'll just be glad to get this part of it over with."

"Yeah, me too. Now, you know I can't go in there with you, but I'll be right here. Romatowski is the best, so don't worry. He's not going to ask you anything about anything except the Oakland County cases, nothing about the charges on the warrant. You nervous?"

"Yes, a little, I guess," replied the priest, folding his hands on the desk top.

"Good, that's normal, and it's all built into the program. I'd worry if you weren't a little nervous. Hell, I get nervous when they hook me up to an EKG," he laughed. "Just be damned straight with him."

"I guess I'm just worried that he may throw some kind of trick question."

"No, that isn't the way they play the game. No trick questions. As a matter of fact, he'll probably tell you what questions he'll ask on the test beforehand, that's the way it usually works."

"How long will it take?"

"Well, the test itself doesn't take long, maybe fifteen or twenty minutes. But he'll talk with you first. You know, find out a little bit about you, then go over the questions. Then you'll take a little break before he hooks you up. It's no big deal," lied Carson.

"Easy for you to say," chuckled Bethleham.

"Well, you know what I mean," smiled his lawyer. "We both know you didn't have anything to do with killing those kids, don't we?"

The Task Force worked on the assumption that the polygraph cannot be beaten when in the hands of an examiner who knows how to prepare the subject, formulate the questions, and interpret the results. One of the reasons Romatowski was so good at what he did was that he liked people, and people generally liked him. He had a way of making them feel comfortable on first meeting. He was nonthreatening, and his voice was heavy, steady, and calming. He looked directly into the priest's eyes, as he introduced himself with a firm handshake.

"Father, I'm Detective Sergeant Chet Romatowski. Have a seat. Let's get to know you, okay?"

The room was small, not much bigger than a large walk-in closet.

The floor was carpeted, the walls covered with a textured fabric of neutral color. Set into the wall was a mirror about two and one-half feet high and eighteen inches wide. Steve wondered if it was a two-way mirror that somebody could see through from the other side while you were adjusting your tie. Probably. There were two wooden armchairs on either side of a grey metal table. The polygraph sitting in one corner of the room resembled an EKG machine, with wires dangling over the sides. He didn't like the looks of it. He sat down opposite the polygraph expert.

"So how are you, Father?" Romatowski smiled as he leaned back in the chair.

"Fine, I guess, under the circumstances," replied the priest nervously.

Romatowski leaned forward on the table. "I'm sure everything's going to work out for you. Why don't you start by telling me a little bit about yourself, then I'll explain what we're going to do and how we're going to do it."

They talked for about fifty minutes, during which Romatowski learned the man was very well educated and in good health. A person's general health was a determining factor in whether he or she should even be hooked up to the machine, since certain types of medication could render the polygraph results invalid. The polygraph registered the subject's cardiovascular reactions to questions, and medication could alter cardiovascular responses. The extent of the subject's education determined exactly how the specific questions would be drawn up. The subject had to have a clear understanding of the questions to answer them truthfully. As Romatowski himself always said, "We don't test anybody we don't think we'll get good results from." By "good results" he didn't mean catching the person in a lie, but getting valid responses, one way or the other.

Romatowski and the priest also discussed the child-killer case, not in great detail, but enough to convince Chet that Bethleham knew he was being asked to take the polygraph to eliminate him as a suspect. That was always the approach. They never asked you to take a lie-detector test to prove that you were guilty; after all, the polygraph couldn't prove guilt or innocence. That could only be done in a court of law. The polygraph could only determine whether you were giving truthful responses to specific questions. Romatowski also told Bethleham the questions he would ask during the examination. There were about a dozen, and some were totally unrelated to the case.

"Okay, Father, let's take five and then we'll wire you up." Romatowski excused himself and left the room. Steve was alone. He got up and rubbed his eyes. The two detectives on the other side of the mirror watched him run his fingers through his hair, sit back down, and finger a small rosary he produced from his shirt pocket.

The priest felt trapped. He was part of the machine now, attached by a blood-pressure cuff on his upper arm, the upper and lower pneumographs around his chest and abdomen, and the electrodes at his fingertips. He could feel his heart race. He'd fail it for sure, he thought, as Chet bent over the graph and turned the machine on. It made a soothing whir. The graph glided past him on the table top. He watched the needle jump.

"Calm down, Father," said Romatowski in a soft, reassuring voice. "Nothing to it." His eyes never left the graph the machine was disgorging. The needle leveled off. "Okay, is your name Stephen Patrick Bethleham?"

"Yes."

"Okay, good. Are you a Roman Catholic priest?"

"Yes, of course!"

"Please, just yes or no, Father."

"Yes."

"Did you cause the abduction and death of Timothy King?" The voice was calm and steady. Bethleham closed his eyes and answered, "No."

"Do you have a law degree?"

"Yes."

"Do you know who caused the abduction and death of Timothy King or any of the other three children?"

"No." Bethleham swallowed hard. Romatowski looked up from the graph and into the priest's eyes.

"Is today Monday?" He looked back down at the paper and marked it with a red pencil.

"No."

"Do you know who caused the abduction and death of Timothy King or any of the other three children?" Same question again. Bethleham's mind raced. What was wrong with his last answer?

"No."

"Okay, fine." He marked the graph with the red pencil again. "Do you live at 138 Grand River?"

"Yes."

"Were you present when any of the four children were abducted or killed?"

"No."

"Did you volunteer to take this test?"

"Yes."

Romatowski paused for a long moment, picking up the graph paper with both hands and scanning it. His head moved from side to side.

"Did you plan with anyone else to abduct and kill the four children?"

"No, . . . no."

The machine kept pushing the graph out. Romatowski made another mark, then reached to the left and turned the polygraph off.

Romatowski tore off the long sheet of graph paper from the machine. He placed one end on the table, letting the other hang to the floor. He scanned it from side to side, making several more marks with the red pencil. Still without saying anything, Chet got up from his chair, walked around the table, and began unhooking the leads. He draped them over the machine and rolled it back to the corner. He came over, sat down again, and resumed studying the graph.

Bethleham couldn't stand it. "Well, did I do all right?" He was rubbing the circulation back into his arm where the blood-pressure cuff had been. It was a long moment before the other answered.

"Well," Chet's eyes swung back and forth over the graph again, "you had nothing to do with the Oakland County child killings."

The priest sighed. "It's over."

"Not really, Father." Romatowski got up and opened the door. "We're all done with you, but I'm afraid Farmington hasn't even started yet. And the rest is between you and God."

The Federal Grant expired on October 11, 1977, but was extended until the money was gone, but no later than December 31 of that year. During the latter part of October, Valley Woods was endowed by a local philanthropist and turned into a girl's school. The Task Force could stay, but it had to give up some space and pay rent.

34

There is a theory in law enforcement that no one ever commits a crime without at least one other person knowing about it. According to the "somebody knows theory," all you have to do is look long and hard enough and talk to enough people. Sooner or later you are bound to flush somebody who has that vital scrap of information to set things moving. But the months of the Task Force's second year dragged by, and the person who knew, if there was one, kept his own counsel.

In December 1977 the Federal Grant, already extended, expired. With salaries and employee expenses paid by the investigators' various home departments, and operating expenses picked up by the police community of South Oakland County, the Task Force continued to operate. From July to December of 1978, nineteen communities contributed monthly to keep it going. On December 12, 1978, three days before the Task Force closed its doors at the Valley Woods school, Robertson sat down in his office and composed the toughest letter he'd ever had to write.

Dear Mr. and Mrs. King:

As you already know, the Oakland County Task Force will move its existing quarters on December 15, 1978. All files and information will be moved to the Michigan State Police District Headquarters office in Northville.

Everyone at the Task Force shares my thoughts on how sorry we are that we have not as yet brought Timmy's abductor to justice. But I want you to know that we will always continue to consider the file open until we have exhausted all avenues or until we do apprehend the person responsible.

The Task Force members will meet every two weeks for several months to make work assignments to the individual officers, to discuss new information, and to keep the unit in a ready state.

Obviously, we don't feel the personal loss you do, but Timmy has been a great part of all of our lives during the last twenty months.

I would like to thank everyone in your home for doing their best to help us do our job. So many times we bothered the family for an answer and you were always very gracious to us.

Once again, from all of us at the Oakland County Task Force, good luck, and may God be with you.

Sincerely,
Lt. Robert H. Robertson

It was cold and grey as Krease and Robertson headed for their cars in the Valley Woods parking lot for the last time. Next month would be the second anniversary of the formation of the Task Force, and it was hard to know what to say. In spite of the biting wind, neither man seemed quite ready to leave. They paused by the cars.

"How does it feel?" asked Robertson.

"Rotten. I keep thinking about the kids' families and the trust they've had in us."

"I know what you mean. It's hard not to think of the mistakes we've made. But remember, Joe, we had to build from the ground up. You've been running the largest murder investigation this country has ever seen, and you've done a fine job. If you hadn't, police departments from all over the country wouldn't be calling for advice."

"But the other police departments are finding the people they're looking for," Krease said bitterly. "We haven't."

"Well, what did we have to work with? Not a single witness to any of the crimes, a total lack of physical evidence — not a fingerprint, not a thread. And who ever heard of a serial child killer who goes after both sexes? You can't compare this case with any others, and you know it!"

"Yeah, I know it. But it doesn't help."

A girl in a red jacket burst from the school's side door and ran toward a group of her classmates who were already running and whooping in the newly fallen snow. With her fair complexion and shoulder-length brown hair, she looked, thought Krease, a lot like Mark, Jill, Kristine, and Timmy. He wondered if somewhere, driving slowly through the residential neighborhoods of Oakland County, there was someone else who would think so too.

Robertson, who had also watched her, started to say something more, but changed his mind. Instead he shook hands and got into his car, gunning the engine as he backed out, then raising a hand in salute as he pulled onto the road. Krease turned back to the playground and stood for a moment, resting his arms on the top of his car and watching the girls laughing and sliding in the snow.

Tommy McIntyre has been a broadcast newsman for more than thirty years. He is an investigative reporter and news commentator for WWJ radio and has specialized in news stories about organized crime, the courts, and public corruption. He extensively covered the Oakland County child killings and the exhaustive search for the children's murderer. He previously worked for Michigan radio and television stations in Lansing, Battle Creek, Dearborn, Pontiac, and Southfield.

The manuscript was edited by Walter Michener. The cover was designed by Joanne Elkin Kinney. The book is printed on 50-lb. Glatfelter text paper. The typeface for the text is Palatino, designed by Hermann Zapf.

Manufactured in the United States of America.